THE NEGROES IN
NEGROLAND

The Negroes in Negroland

A COMPILATION

Hinton Rowan Helper

Abdul Alhazred

Forbidden Books

Contents

The Negroes in Negroland		1
Forward		4
Introduction		7
1	Cannibalism in Negroland	13
2	Human Butcheries and Human Sacrifices in Negroland	19
3	Human Skulls as Sacred Relics and Ornaments in Negroland	27
4	Blood-Thirstiness and Barbarity of the Negroes in Negroland	32
5	Slavery and the Slave-Trade in Negroland	42
6	Heathenish Superstition and Witchcraft in Negroland	52
7	Fetichism, Priestcraft, and Idolatry in Negroland	68
8	Rain-Doctors and Other Doctors in Negroland	85
9	Nakedness, Shamelessness, and Prostitution in Negroland	91
10	Drunkenness and Debauchery in Negroland	97

11	Night Carousals, and Noisy and Nonsensical Actions in Negroland	100
12	Inhospitality to Strangers, Begging, Extortion, and Robbery in Negroland	103
13	Wrangling, Lawlessness, Penury, and Misery in Negroland	112
14	Theft as a Fine Art Among the Africans	119
15	Lying as an Accomplishment Among the Africans	123
16	Duplicity and Venality of the Negroes in Negroland	125
17	Revolting Voracity and Gluttony of the Negroes in Negroland	128
18	Dislike of their Own Color by the Negroes in Negroland	131
19	Courtship, Marriage, and Concubinage	136
20	Mumbo Jumbo in Negroland	151
21	Funeral and Burial Rites in Negroland	153
22	Indolence and Improvidence of the Negroes	158
23	Timidity and Cowardice of the Negroes	163
24	African Anecdotes	169
25	Utter Failure and Inutility of All Missionary Enterprises in Negroland	174
26	Miscellaneous Peculiarities, Habits, Manners, and Customs of the Negroes in Negroland	182

27	Huts, Hovels, and Holes (But No Houses) in Negroland	199
28	Gradual Decrease and Probable Extinction of the Negro Race	207
29	Natural, Repulsive, and Irreconcilable Points of Difference, Physical, Mental, and Moral, Between the Whites and the Blacks	211
30	American Writers on the Negro	225
31	Mulattoes; The Offspring of Crimes Against Nature	278
32	Albinos; White Negroes and Other Creatures of Supernatural Whiteness	286
33	Increasing Pre-Eminence and Predominance of the White Races	291
Appendix 1: Radicalism in the South: Its Black and Blighting Sway		303
Appendix 2: Identicalness of the Sentiment and Scope of "The Impending Crisis of the South," and "Nojoque." A Letter from Mr. Helper.		324

The Negroes in Negroland

THE NEGROES IN AMERICA; AND NEGROES GENERALLY. ALSO, THE SEVERAL RACES OF WHITE MEN, CONSIDERED AS THE INVOLUNTARY AND PREDESTINED SUPPLANTERS OF THE BLACK RACES.
A COMPILATION,

BY HINTON ROWAN HELPER, A RATIONAL REPUBLICAN,

Author of "*The Impending Crisis of the South*," "*Nojoque*," and other writings in behalf of a Free and White America.

"A compassion for that which is not and cannot be useful or lovely, is degrading and futile."
RALPH WALDO EMERSON.
"Among the negroes, no science has been developed, and few questions are ever discussed, except those which have an intimate connection with the wants of the stomach."
DAVID LIVINGSTONE.
"It has been proved by measurements, by microscopes, by analyses, that the typical negro is some- thing between a child, a dotard, and a beast. I cannot struggle against these sacred facts of science."
WINWOOD READE.

"Our country might well have shrunk from assuming the guardianship of the negro."
GEORGE BANCROFT.

"It is the strictly white races that are bearing onward the flambeau of civilization, as displayed in the Germanic families alone."
JOSIAH CLARK NOTT

The early history of Guinea is necessarily more obscure than that of the Sudan. It lay beyond the limits of knowledge of the Arab authors who wrote about the Sudan between the eighth and the fifteenth centuries. From the fifteenth century onwards, European writings become of increasing value; but it was not until the nineteenth century that European observers began to penetrate inland...

The historian must therefore rely heavily upon orally-maintained traditions whose historicity cannot always be clearly established...

-*A Short History of Africa,* by Roland Oliver and J. D. Fage

The Negroes in Negroland was originally published in New York by
G. W. Carleton in 1868.
The book is in the public domain. No changes have been made.
Editing and cover design by Abdul Alhazred.
Forbidden Books, 2024: Banned Books for a Postliberal Age

Forward

Noticing in the 19ᵗʰ Century

Hinton Rowan Helper was an enigmatic man: a character with so many surprising beliefs and associations that modern men can scarcely imagine what to do with him other than block him from their minds by calling him a racist. Helper was a Southerner, a radical abolitionist, a supporter of Lincoln, an avowed white nationalist, and a chronicler of racial differences. Like Ralph Waldo Emerson, Helper's frank and progressive belief was that the white races were destined to supplant the inferior nations of Africa, and contended, like Lincoln and Grant, that racial separatism and racial self-determination was absolutely necessary for both white and black Americans. It is only because most Americans casually gloss the surprising racial opinions of men like Lincoln that they continue to feel lost in this period of their own history.

Helper was considered an extremist by the Southern leadership of his own day. Lee and Jefferson Davis were both of the opinion that, while black Americans were naturally subordinate to white and relatively irresponsible as a group, blacks could be educated, could take on more civil and social responsibilities, and were providentially joined with Southern civilization. Davis, as a large slaveowner, experimented with slave-led jury trials on his plantation, and contended for the intellectual property rights of one of his slaves who had invented an engine. Davis had also taken a remarkable interest in the capacity of his slaves to be educated. Lee gradually emancipated the slaves from his wife's Arlington estate and privately expressed his preference for gradual emancipation generally. In a famous letter to his wife in 1856, Lee wrote that black Americans "were immeasurably better off here than in Africa," and noted his belief in the moral evil of the institution of slavery itself. In contrast, Helper believed the relative moral, religious, and physical improvements of the black man in America were nothing compared to the degradation of American society by their presence. In the years after the War, when newly emancipated and perfectly ignorant blacks were thrust into positions of authority in order to humiliate and punish Southerners, Helper raised an alarm by a flurry of publishing, constantly insisting that the loss of social norms was a crucial defeat for American civilization generally, and that white Americans worthy of their heritage must own it.

Helper's radical stance against the organic and common relationships between white and black Southerners alienated him from his native state and his own people. Aside from mountaineers who lived in poorer lands unfitted for slavery, the vast majority of white Southerners were very accustomed to blacks and were used to eating, worshipping, and working with them in the hierarchical relation of slavery. Even so, the South was still the home of the largest free black population before the War. Helper was not comfortable with this arrangement, and was, ironically, even more upset with the post-war order.

Helper was the unusual Southerner who vocally supported Lincoln in the name of white nationalism. Lincoln himself did not discourage this, but openly championed a white nationalism of the western territories, noting that he believed they should be reserved "for white people" exclusively. Lincoln openly and freely denied any intention to interfere with slavery in his inaugural address, and denied, in his debates with Douglass, any intention to make voters or jurors out of Negroes. Several northern and western states had adopted provisions championed by Helper forbidding the entry and settlement of free blacks into the confines of their states, including Ohio, Oregon, and Lincoln's home state of Illinois. Lincoln was always quick to reward Southerners who dared to support the Republican platform, and sent Helper to Argentina as the American consul for most of the War.

Helper thought American leaders were willfully blind to important political and social differences white and black Americans had inherited apart from what they chose or were nurtured to be. He believed these differences were durable and important. Although he frequently spouted emotional bursts of rhetoric to his enlightened critics, Helper decided to rely on the testimony of others in his edited volume, *The Negroes in Negroland*. As his successors well know, the true liberal believes in a sacred dream as certainly as a Marxist believes in the Manifesto, and no experience or sight will induce him to believe his lying eyes. Experience is the great touchstone of realism, but Helper became a scholarly compiler for this effort. He gathered together the greatest authoritative observers of Africa of his age and organized their writings by category. Beginning his book with observations of cannibalism and human sacrifice in Africa, Helper was obviously drawn to the lurid, but these were also prominent concerns of Bernal Diaz and the early records of the Spanish Conquistadors. The starkness of difference between European civilization and African barbarism demands stark contrast.

Helper said frankly what Lincoln's Northern supporters privately believed about slavery. Helper harshly elucidated the foundational opinions and assumptions of the colonization camp: the most popular and mainstream American position on the abolition of slavery. Helper was unpopular in his native Southland because of his illiberal advocacy and focus on the well-being of the white population, which put him squarely at odds with the paternalist, slaveholding elites of the South, who were, ironically, much more optimistic and hopeful about the cultural assimilation of subordinate population.

There was a time when Africans had no European influences at all. None today exist without this influence, and the world described in these observations is dead.

The reader is invited to believe what he wishes.

  Abdul Azhelred
  Black History Month, 2024

Introduction

INTRODUCTION.

THE compiler of this volume deems it proper to protest here, at the very outset of his undertaking, against the un- just and ill-boding practice of indiscriminately stigmatizing as a traitor almost every man, whether in the North or in the South, in the East or in the West, who, in the exercise of his constitutional rights and honest convictions, raises his voice in opposition to the revolutionary and destructive measures of the party now dominant in our National Legislature. With deep solemnity and truth, he declares that he was always earnest and emphatic, and even enthusiastic,→ and not less so now than heretofore, in deploring and condemning the act of secession, and, at the same time, in justifying and defending the principles upon which the Government of the United States, when opposed by force of arms, maintained itself, and re-established its authority from the Potomac to the Rio Grande. Why, then, why does a man who never, by word nor by deed, gave the least aid or comfort to the rebellion, but, on the contrary, did all he could to weaken and suppress it, why does a man of these antecedents, a plain, unpretentious citizen, who, until he became a Republican, was always a Whig of the school of Clay and Webster; who, from first to last, heartily endorsed and supported the administration of Abraham Lincoln, and who has no ambition beyond the exact knowledge and performance of his duty; - why does a man of this sort find it impossible to yield his suffrage or commendation to the party now in power, - — - a party which, with Pharisaical boasting, lays claim to the distinctive and exclusive patriotism of having saved the country from disruption? The reason is broad, plain, and even more than sufficient. The party has, since the termination of the war, viciously and unpardonably abandoned the old landmarks of just and sacred fealty to race; and it is now advocating what means the prostitution in bulk of a great and good white integer to a small and bad black fraction. The policy of the Radical (not the Republican) party, if carried out to its logical ends, will inevitably result in the forced political, religious, civil, and social equality of the white and black races; and the direful sequence of that result, so flagrantly unnatural and wrong in itself, can only be reasonably looked for in the ultimate degradation, division, and destruction of the Republic. It is in the sincere hope of lessening at least some of the dangers of the shocking and wide-spread calamities thus alluded to, that this compilation is offered to an intelligent and discriminating public.

There are now in the United States of America thirty millions of white people, who are (or ought to be) bound together by the ties of a kindred origin, by the affinities of a sameness of noble purpose, by the links of a common nationality, and by the cords of an inseparable destiny. We have here also, unfortunately for us all, four millions of black people, whose ancestors, like themselves, were never known (except in very rare instances, which form the exceptions to a general rule) to aspire to any other condition than that of base and beastlike slavery. These black people are, by nature, of an exceedingly low and grovelling disposition. They have no trait of character that is lovely or admirable. They are not high-minded, enterprising, nor prudent. In no age, in no part of the world, have they, of themselves, ever projected or advanced any public or private interest, nor given expression to any thought or sentiment that could worthily elicit the praise, or even the favorable mention, of the better portion of mankind. Seeing, then, that the negro does, indeed, belong to a lower and inferior order of beings, why, in the name of Heaven, why should we forever degrade and disgrace both ourselves and our posterity by entering, of our own volition, into more intimate relations with him? May God, in his restraining mercy, for- bid that we should ever do this most foul and wicked thing!

Acting under the influence of that vile spirit of deception and chicanery which is always familiar with every false pretence, the members of a Radical Congress, the editors of a venal press, and other peddlers of perverted knowledge, are now loudly proclaiming that nowhere in our country, hence- forth, must there be any distinction, any discrimination, on account of color; thereby covertly inculcating the gross error of inferring or supposing that color is the only differ- and that a very trivial difference - between the whites and the blacks! Now, once for all, in conscientious deference to truth, let it be distinctly made known and acknowledged, that, in addition to the black and baneful color of the negro, there are numerous other defects, physical, mental, and moral, which clearly mark him, when compared with the white man, as a very different and inferior creature. While, therefore, with an involuntary repugnance which we cannot control, and with a wholesome antipathy which it would be both unnatural and

unavailing in us to attempt to destroy, we behold the crime-stained blackness of the negro, let us, also, at the same time, take cognizance of—
His low and compressed Forehead;
His hard, thick Skull;
His small, backward-thrown Brain;
His short, crisp Hair;
His flat Nose;
His thick Lips;
His projecting, snout-like Mouth; -
His strange, Eunuch-toned Voice;
The scantiness of Beard on his Face;
The Toughness and Unsensitiveness of his Skin;
The Thinness and Shrunkenness of his Thighs;
His curved Knees; His calfless Legs;
His low, short Ankles;
His long, flat Heels;
His glut-shaped Feet;
The general Angularity and Oddity of his Frame;
The Malodorous Exhalations from his Person;
His Puerility of Mind;
His Inertia and Sleepy-headedness;
His proverbial Dishonesty;
His predisposition to fabricate Falsehoods;
and His Apathetic Indifference to all Propositions and Enterprises of Solid Merit.

Many other differences might be mentioned; but the score and more of obvious and undeniable ones here enumerated ought to suffice for the utter confusion and shame of all those disingenuous politicians and others, who, knowing better, and who are thus guilty of the crime of defeating the legitimate ends of their own knowledge, would, for mere selfish and partisan purposes, convey the delusive impression that there is no other difference than that of color.

Now, far more than at any time hitherto, the white people of the United States, influenced by circumstances which are well understood, seem to be particularly interested to know precisely what manner of man the negro is. This is an auspicious fact. It augurs favorably for the whole country. What the people require now is light, information, knowledge. Let them have this, and the great principles of Virtue, Truth, Right, and Honor will be maintained. Only let the masses of our people earnestly and fairly prosecute their inquiries and investigations in reference to the negro, and they will, erelong, by the irresistible force of involuntary conviction, come to pronounce an enlightened and just judgment upon all of the more important questions which now affect the relations of the two heterogeneous races among us. In the very nature and fitness of things, it cannot be otherwise than that the verdict which, at no distant day, may thus be looked for from the public, will be a conclusive finding and a finality against the negro, a verdict which, of rightful necessity, must be sweepingly abrogative of all the hasty and unsound decisions which have been so recently and so rashly pronounced by the corrupt arbiters to whom the Radical party owes its inexpressibly ignoble and pernicious existence. -

To many worthy persons, who desire to deal intelligently and honestly with the political questions which are now agitating the public mind, a thorough knowledge of the nature of the negro has become almost indispensable; and, to all persons of this sort, it is humbly hoped and believed that this compilation may prove highly serviceable. Attention is particularly invited to the testimonies, herein quoted, of such observant and veracious African travellers as Mungo Park, Denham, Clapperton, Lander, Livingstone, Barth, Lichtenstein, Du Chaillu, Caillie, Valdez, Bruce, Baker, Speke, Dun- can, Wilson, Moffat, Reade, Richardson, Burton, and Barrow. Following the interesting and instructive statements of these disinterested white men, mostly Europeans, who have seen the negro in Negroland, are also portrayed the opinions of numerous American writers, whose views of the negro, and of the races of men generally, are equally essential to a proper understanding of all the points in controversy. Of these American writers, those from the North are here more particularly referred to; and it is trusted that the reader will ponder well the words of such truly able and representative men as John Adams, Daniel Webster, Horace Mann, Theodore Parker, Samuel George Morton, William Henry Seward, and others of scarcely less distinction. Among the ablest and best of the Southern men, from whose writings on the negro, and on other kindred subjects, extracts are here given, will be noticed the names of Thomas Jefferson, Henry Clay, Thomas Hart Benton, Abraham Lincoln, Montgomery Blair, and Josiah Clark Nott. No language of the compiler can do justice to the perfect portraiture which we have of the negro from the pen of the philosophic and profound Jefferson. Let his sterling words of wisdom be most thoroughly and attentively perused. It will be particularly observed that everything herein quoted from him was written many years subsequently to the time when he drafted the Declaration of Independence. The fact should also be constantly borne in mind that, while in the Declaration of Independence Mr. Jefferson, in all rational probability, had no reference whatever to any race except that to which he himself belonged, in the extracts herein given, he discusses the negro by emphatic and frequent designation, and in the most direct and positive manner. By reference to the Index, the reader will perceive the names of many other eminent and unimpeachable writers, both North- ern and Southern, and also European, - to all of whom the compiler, at least, would here offer his most hearty acknowledgments for much new and valuable information. —

There are many points of general dissatisfaction and dispute, which should not, on any account, be overlooked in the discussion of the subjects here presented. One of these is, that white people, whose reason and honor have not been vitiated, object to close relationship with negroes, not wishing to live with them in the same house; not wishing to fellow- ship with them in the same society, assembly, or congregation; not wishing to ride with them in the same omnibus, car, or carriage; and not wishing to mess with them at the same table, whether at a hotel, in a restaurant, on a steamer, or elsewhere. Now, any and every white person who does not think and act in strict accordance with the just and pure promptings here indicated, is, in reality, a most unworthy and despicable representative of his race. Even the lower animals, the creatures of mere instinct, the beasts, the birds, and the fishes, many distinct species of which are apparently quite similar, set us daily and hourly examples of the eminent propriety of each kind forming and maintaining separate communities of their own; and so we always find them, in herds, in flocks, and in shoals. How can the negro be a fit person to occupy, in any capacity, our houses or our hotels, our theatres or our churches, our schools or our colleges, our steamers or our vehicles, or any other place or places of uncommon comfort and convenience, which owe their creation, their proper uses, and their perpetuity, to the whites alone, places and improvements about which the negro, of himself, is, and always has been, absolutely ignorant and indifferent? Neither in his own country nor elsewhere has the negro ever built a house or a theatre; he has never erected a church nor a college; he has never constructed a steamer nor a railroad, nor a railroad-car,—nor, except when under the special direction and control of superior intelligence, has he ever invented or manufactured even the minutest append- age of any one of the distinctive elements or realities of human progress. Yet, let this not, by any means, be understood as an argument, nor even as a hint, in behalf of slavery. It is to the great and lasting honor of the Republic that slavery in the United States is abolished forever. In losing her slaves, the South lost nothing that was worth the keeping. Had slavery only been abolished by law many years ago, our whole country would be infinitely better off to-day.

Never will it be possible for the compiler to erase from his memory the feelings of weighty sadness and disgust which overcame him, a few months since, when, while sojourning in the city of Washington, he walked, one day, into the Capitol, and, leisurely passing into the galleries of the two houses of Congress, beheld there, uncouthly lounging and dozing upon the seats, a horde of vile, ignorant, and foul-scented negroes. He was perplexed, shocked, humiliated, and indignant, and could not sit down. With merited emotions of bitterness and contempt for those narrow-minded white men, through whose detestable folly and selfishness so great an outrage against public propriety and decency had been perpetrated, he turned away;—indeed, it was not in his power to contemplate with calmness that motley and monstrous manifestation of national incongruity, ugliness, and disgrace. Then it was that, for the first time in his life, he wished him- self a Hercules, in order that he might be able to clean, thoroughly and at once, those Augean stables of the black ordure and Radical filth which, therein and elsewhere, had already accumulated to an almost insufferable excess. was the powerful and long-lingering momentum of the im- pressions received on that occasion, more than any other circumstance, that gave definite form and resolution to the purpose (although the idea had been previously entertained) of preparing this compilation. The object of the compiler will have been well attained if the work aids materially in more fully convincing his countrymen, North, South, East and West, that negro equality, negro supremacy, and negro domination, as now tyrannically enforced at the point of the bayonet, are cruel and atrocious innovations, which ought to be speedily terminated.

H. R. H.

ASHEVILLE, North Carolina, June 2, 1868.

1

Cannibalism in Negroland

"It is plain, from all history, that two abominable practices, the one the eating of men, the other of sacrificing them to the devil, — prevailed all over Africa. The India trade, as we have seen in very early ages, first established the buying and selling of slaves; since that time, the eating of men, or sacrificing them, has so greatly decreased on the eastern side of the peninsula, that now we scarcely hear of an instance of either of these that can be properly vouched. On the western part, towards the Atlantic Ocean, where the sale of slaves began a considerable time later, after the discovery of America and the West Indies, both of these horrid practices are general."
—*Bruce's Africa*, Vol. I., page 393.

"The common food of the natives of Ansiko is men's flesh, insomuch that their markets are provided with that, as ours in Europe with beef or mutton: all prisoners of war, unless they can sell them alive with greater advantage, otherwise, as we said, they fatten them for slaughter, and at last sell them to the butchers. To this savage barbarity they are so naturalized, that some slaves, whether as weary of their lives, or to show their love to their masters, will proffer themselves freely to be killed and eaten. But that which is most inhuman, and beyond the ferocity of beasts, is, that the father scruples not to eat his son, nor the son his father, nor one brother the other, but take them by force, devouring their flesh, the blood yet reeking hot between their teeth."

— *Ogilby's Africa*, page 518.

"Whosoever dies, be the disease never so contagious, yet they eat the flesh immediately, as a festival dish."

— *Ogilby's Africa*, page 518.

"Bello, the Governor of Sackatoo, said that whenever a person complained of sickness amongst the Yamyams, even though only a slight headache, they are killed instantly, for fear they should be lost by death, as they will not eat a person that has died by sickness; that the person falling sick is requested by some other family, and repaid when they had a sick relation; that universally when they went to war, the dead and wounded were always eaten; that the hearts were claimed by the head men; and that, on asking them why they eat human flesh, they said it was better than any other, and that the heart and breasts of a woman were the best part of the body."

— *Denham and Clapperton's Africa*, Vol. IV., page 262.

"Many of Ibrahim's party had been frequent witnesses to acts of cannibalism, during their residence among the Makkarikas. They described these cannibals as remarkably good people, but possessing a peculiar taste for dogs and human flesh. They accompanied the trading party in their razzias, and invariably ate the bodies of the slain. The traders complained that they were bad associates, as they insisted upon killing and eating the children which the party wished to secure as slaves; their custom was to catch a child by its ankles, and to dash its head against the ground; thus killed, they opened the abdomen, extracted the stomach and intestines; and tying the two ankles to the neck, they carried the body by slinging over the shoulder, and thus returned to camp, where they divided it by quartering, and boiling it in a large pot. One of the slave girls attempted to escape, and her proprietor immediately fired at her with his musket, and she fell wounded; the ball had struck her in the side. The girl was remarkably fat, and from the wound a large lump of yellow fat exuded. No sooner had she fallen than the Makkarikas rushed upon her in a crowd, and, seizing the fat, they tore it from the wound in handfuls, the girl being still alive, while the crowd were quarrelling for the disgusting prize. Others killed her with a lance, and at once divided her by cutting off the head, and split- ting the body with their lances, used as knives, cutting longitudinally from between the legs along the spine to the neck."

—*Baker's Great Basin of the Nile*, page 201.

"The butchers' shops of the Anziques are filled with human flesh, instead of that of oxen or of sheep. For they eat the enemies whom they take in battle. They fatten, slay, and devour their slaves also, unless they think they shall get a good price for them. There are indeed many cannibals, · .. - but none such as these, since the others only eat their enemies; but these eat their own blood relations."

— *African Explorations by Eduardo Lopez,* quoted by Huxley, in Man's Place in Nature, page 55.

"On the occasion of the appointment of a chief to the supreme command, a bullock is sacrificed by the Samba Golambole, as also a white sheep, and a white or fawn-colored pigeon, together with various other victims. But the principal sacrifice is that of one slave from each of the nations under the dominion of the para- mount chief, the heads of whom are carried in triumph and exhibited to the populace, accompanied by drums and other instruments. The bodies are added to those of the other animals, and all cooked together, and distributed as a savory dish to the chief and the other nobles."

—*Valdez's Africa*, Vol. II., page 331.

"The next morning we moved off for the Fan village, and now I had the opportunity to satisfy myself as to a matter I had cherished some doubt on before, namely, the cannibal practices of these people. I was satisfied but too soon. As we entered the town I perceived some bloody remains which looked to me to be human; but I passed on, still incredulous. Presently we passed a woman who solved all doubt. She bore with her a piece of the thigh of a human body, just as we should go to market and carry thence a roast or a steak."

— *Du Chaillu's Equatorial Africa,* page 103.

"Until to-day I never could believe two stories, — both well authenticated, but seeming quite impossible to any one un- acquainted with this people, — which are told of them on the Ga- boon. A party of Fans, who came down to the sea-shore once to see the sea, actually stole a freshly-buried body from the cemetery, and cooked it and ate it among them; and another party took another body, conveyed it into the woods, cut it up, and smoked the flesh, which they carried away with them. The circumstances made a great fuss among the Mpongwe, and even the missionaries heard of it, but I never credited the stories till now, though the facts were well authenticated by witnesses. In fact, the Fans seem regular ghouls, only they practise their horrid custom unblushingly and in open day, and have no shame about it. These stories seem so incredible, and even the fact that these people actually buy and eat the corpses of their neighbors — resting as it does upon my statement alone - has excited so much evident disbelief among friends in the country, to whom I have mentioned this custom, that I am very glad to be able to avail myself of the concurrent testimony of a friend, the Rev. Mr. Walker, of the Gaboon mission, who authorizes me to say that he vouches for the entire truth of the two stories above related.".

— *Du Chaillu's Equatorial Africa*, page 120.

"While I was talking to the king to-day, some Fans brought in a dead body, which they had bought in a neighboring town, and which was now to be divided. I could see that the man had died of some disease. I confess I could not bear to stay for the cut- ting up of the body, but retreated when all was ready. It made me sick all over. I remained till the infernal scene was about to begin, and then retreated. Afterward I could hear them from my house growing noisy over the division. This is a form of can- nibalism-eating those who have died of sickness-of which I had never heard in any people; so that I determined to inquire if it were indeed a general custom, or merely an exceptional freak. They spoke without embarrassment about the whole matter, and I was informed that they constantly buy the dead of the Osheba tribe, who, in return, buy theirs."

— *Du Chaillu's Equatorial Africa*, page 120.

"After visiting the house assigned me, I was taken through the town, where I saw more dreadful signs of cannibalism in piles of human bones, mixed up with offal, thrown at the sides of several houses."

— *Du Chaillu's Equatorial Africa*, page 105.

"On going out next morning I saw a pile of ribs, leg and arm bones, and skulls piled up at the back of my house, which looked horrid enough to me. In fact, symptoms of cannibalism stare me in the face wherever I go.".

—*Du Chaillu's Equatorial Africa*, page 106.

2

Human Butcheries and Human Sacrifices in Negroland

"THE main object contemplated in the national anniversary of Dahomey is, that the king may water the graves of his ancestors with the blood of human victims. These are numerous, consisting of prisoners taken in war, of condemned criminals, and of many seized by lawless violence. The captives are brought out in succession, with their arms pinioned, and a feticheer, laying his hand upon the devoted head, utters a few magic words, while another from behind, with a large scimitar, severs it from the body, when shouts of applause ascend from the surrounding multitude. At any time when the king has a message to convey to one of his deceased relations, he delivers it to one of his subjects, then strikes off his head, that he may carry it to the other world; and, if anything further occurs to him after he has performed this ceremony, he delivers it to another messenger, whom he despatches in the same manner. Another great object of this period chiefs and nobles. No choice on this occasion is allowed to the purchaser. In return for his twenty thousand cowries, a wife is handed out, and, even be she old and ugly, he must rest con- tented; nay, some, it is said, have in mockery been presented with their own mothers. The king usually keeps his wives up to the number of three thousand, who serve him in various capacities, being partly trained to act as a body-guard, regularly regimented, and equipped with drums, flags, bows and arrows, while a few carry muskets. They all reside in the palace, which consists merely of an immense assemblage of cane and mud tents, enclosed by a high wall. The skulls and jawbones of enemies slain in battle form the favorite ornament of the palaces and temples. The king's apartment is paved, and the walls and roof stuck over with these horrid trophies; and, if a further supply appears desirable, he announces to his general that his house wants thatch, when a war for that purpose is immediately under- taken."

— *Murray's African Discoveries,* page 199.

"At Coomassie the customs, or human sacrifices, are practised on a scale still more tremendous than at Dahomey. The king had lately sacrificed on the grave of his mother three thousand victims, two thousand of whom were Fantee prisoners; and at the death of the late sovereign, the sacrifice was continued weekly for three months, consisting each time of two hundred slaves. The absurd belief here entertained, that the rank of the deceased in the future world is decided by the train which he carries along with him, makes filial piety interested in promoting by this means the exaltation of a departed parent. On these occasions, the gaboceers and princes, in order to court royal favor, often rush out, seize the first person they meet, and drag him in for sacrifice. While the customs

last, therefore, it is with trembling steps that any one crosses his threshold; and, when compelled to do so, he rushes along with the utmost speed, dreading every instant the murderous grasp which would consign him to death."
—*Murray's African Discoveries,* page 204.

"The practice of offering human sacrifices to appease evil spirits is common; but in no place more frequent, or on a larger scale than in the kingdoms of Ashantee and Dahomi, and in the Bormy River. Large numbers of victims, chiefly prisoners of war, are statedly sacrificed to the manes of the royal ancestors in both of the first-mentioned places, and under circumstances of shocking and almost unparalleled cruelty. At the time of the death of a king, a large number of his principal wives and favorite slaves are put to death, not so much, however, as sacrifices to appease his wrath, as to be his companions and attendants in another world, a practice, which, though cruel and revolting in itself, nevertheless keeps up a lively impression of a future state of existence."
- *Wilson's Africa,* page 219.

"We find throughout all the country north of 20°, which I consider to be real negro, the custom of slaughtering victims to ac- company the departed soul of a chief, and human sacrifices are occasionally offered, and certain parts of the bodies are used as charms."
- *Livingstone's Africa,* page 631.

"When a chief dies, a number of servants are slaughtered with him to form his company in the other world."
— *Livingstone's Africa,* page 342.

"When an Ashantee of any distinction dies, several of the deceased's slaves are sacrificed. This horrible custom originates in some shadowy ideas of a future state of existence; in which they imagine that those who have departed hence stand in need of food, clothing, and other things, as in the present world; and that, as a vast number of concubines and slaves are the chief marks of superiority among them here, so it must also be in a future state. Accordingly, as I walked out early in the morning, I saw the mangled corpse of a poor female slave, who had been beheaded during the night, lying in the public street. It was partially covered with a common mat, and, as this covering is unusual, I concluded that it was thrown over, in order to hide it from my view. In the course of the day I saw groups of the natives dancing round this victim of superstitious cruelty, with numerous frantic gestures, and who seemed to be in the very zenith of their happiness. That only one person was immolated, I believe, resulted entirely from my presence in the town."

—*Freeman's Africa,* page 24.

"Amidst great ostentatious display, I saw what was calculated to harrow up the strongest and most painful feelings, the royal executioners, bearing the blood-stained stools on which hundreds, and perhaps thousands, of human victims have been sacrificed by decapitation, and also the large death-drum, which is beaten at the moment when the fatal knife severs the head from the body, the very sound of which conveys a thrill of horror. This rude instrument, connected with which are most dreadful associations, was literally covered with dried clots of blood, and decorated with the jawbones and skulls of human victims."

— *Freeman's Africa,* page 47.

"To-day another human victim was sacrificed, on account of the death of a person of rank. As I was going out of the town, in the cool of the evening, I saw the poor creature lying on the ground. The head was severed from the body, and lying at a short distance from it; several large turkey-buzzards were feasting on the wounds, and rolling the head in the dust. He appeared to be about eighteen years of age; a strong, healthy youth, who might, in all probability, have lived forty, fifty, or even sixty years longer."
— *Freeman's Africa*, page 28.

"Throughout the day I heard the horrid sound of the death-drum, and was told in the evening that about twenty-five human victims had been sacrificed, some in the town, and some in the surrounding villages, the heads of those killed in the villages being brought into the town in baskets. I learned that several more human victims had been immolated during the day, but could not ascertain the exact number. The most accurate account I could obtain was, that fifteen more had suffered; making a total of forty, in two days. These poor victims were allowed to lie naked and exposed in the streets, until they began to decompose; and such is the callous state of mind in which the people live, that many were walking about among the putrefying bodies, smoking their pipes, with amazing indifference."
— *Freeman's Africa*, pages 53 and 54.

"The executioner, at one blow on the back of the neck, divided the head from the body of the first culprit, with the exception of a small portion of the skin, which was separated by passing the knife underneath. Unfortunately, the second man was dreadfully mangled, for the poor fellow, at the moment the blow was struck, having raised his head, the knife struck in a slanting direction and only made a large wound; the next blow caught him on the back of the head, when the brain protruded. The poor fellow struggled violently. The third stroke caught him across the shoulders, inflicting a dreadful gash. The next caught him on the neck, which was twice repeated. The officer steadying the criminal now lost his hold on account of the blood which rushed from the blood-vessels on all who were near. The executioner, now quite palsied, took hold of the head, and, after twisting it several times round, separated it from the still convulsed and struggling trunk. During the latter part of this disgusting execution the head presented an awful spectacle, the distortion of the features, and the eyeballs completely upturned, giving it a horrid appearance. The next man, poor fellow, with his eyes partially shut and head drooping forward near to the ground, remained all this time in suspense; casting a partial glance on the head which was now close to him, and the trunk dragged close past him, the blood still rushing from it like a fountain. The fourth culprit was not so fortunate, his head not being separated till after three strokes. The body afterwards rolled over several times, when the blood spurted over my face and clothes. The most disgusting part of this abominable and barbarous execution was that of an old, ill- looking wretch, who, like the numerous vultures, stood with a small calabash in his hand, ready to catch the blood from each individual, which he greedily devoured before it had escaped one minute from the veins. After decapitation the body is immediately dragged off by the heels to a large pit at a considerable distance from the town and thrown therein, and is immediately devoured by wolves and vultures, which are here so ravenous that they will almost take your victuals from you."

- *Duncan's Africa*, Vol. I., pages 250 and 252.

"On our way up the river Calabar my attention was attracted by something of a very extraordinary appearance hanging over the water from the branch of a tree. My curiosity was excited by it, and I was at a loss to conjecture what it was. I did not remain long in suspense, for we soon passed sufficiently near it to enable me to discover that it was the body of one of the natives suspended by the middle, with the feet and hands just touching the water. The natives of this place are pagans, in the most depraved condition. They believe in a good spirit, who, they imagine, dwells in the water; and sacrifices such as that just mentioned are frequently made to him, with the idea of gaining his favor and protection. The object selected for this purpose is generally some unfortunate old slave, who may be worn out and incapable of further service, or unfit for the market; and he is thus left to suffer death, either from the effects of the sun, or from the fangs of some hungry alligator or shark which may chance to find the body. The circumstance of the hands and feet being just al- lowed to be immersed in the water is considered by these deluded people as necessary, and they are thereby rendered an easier prey."

- *Lander's Travels in Africa*, Vol. II., page 315. ◈

"The sixth of the month was announced as the beginning of the sacrificial rites, which were to last five days. Early in the morning, two hundred females of the Amazonian guard, naked to the waist, but richly ornamented with beads and rings at every joint of their oiled and glistening limbs, appeared in the area before the king's palace, armed with blunt cutlasses. Very soon the sovereign made his appearance, when the band of warriors began their manœuvres, keeping pace, with rude but not unmartial skill, to the native drum and flute. A short distance from the palace, within sight of the square, a fort or inclosure, about nine feet high, had been built of adobe, and surrounded by a pile of tall prickly briers. Within this barrier, secured to stakes, stood fifty captives, who were to be immolated at the opening of the festival. When the drill of the Amazons and the royal review were over, there was, for a considerable time, perfect silence in the ranks and throughout the vast multitudes of spectators. Presently, at a signal from the king, one hundred of the women departed at a run, brandishing their weapons and yelling their war-cry, till, heedless of the thorny barricade, they leaped the walls, lacerating their flesh in crossing the prickly impediment. The delay was short. Fifty of these female demons, with torn limbs and bleeding faces, quickly returned, and offered their howling victims to the king. It was now the duty of this personage to begin the sacrifice with his royal hand. Calling the female whose impetuous daring had led her foremost across the thorns, he took a glittering sword from her grasp, and in an instant the head of the first victim fell to the dust."

- *Canot's Twenty Years of an African Slaver,* page 267.

3

Human Skulls as Sacred Relics and Ornaments in Negroland

"HUMAN skulls were built in the walls of the palace, about half the skull projecting beyond the surface of the walls. After a number of introductions, similar to those on the former days, the king's mother entered the court, preceded by six women, carrying large brass pans filled with skulls, with shank-bones fixed perpen- dicularly to the outside of the pans. Another pan, covered with scarlet cloth, as also two other pots of an oval shape, were carried on the heads of females, with a skull placed on the top or over the mouth of each. After parading these different vessels round the palace-yard, they were placed on the ground, in front of several calabashes (previously placed there), containing a number of scalps."

- *Duncan's Africa*, Vol. I., page 253.

"About ten yards in front of the place where his majesty lay, three skulls were placed on the ground, forming an equilateral triangle, about three feet apart. At a little distance from the three-named skulls, a calabash was placed, containing several skulls of distinguished men taken or killed in war. The pole of each standard was mounted with the skull of a caboceer, or ruler of a town."
- *Duncan's Africa*, Vol. I., page 245. ·

"In the collection of skulls, I found a number of them ornamented with brass, and riveted together with iron. These were the heads of rival kings, who were killed by the king's women or wives. Amongst these was the richly ornamented skull of the King of Nahpoo, in the Annagoo country; his name was Adaffo. His town was taken, and he himself made prisoner, by the female regiments, commanded by the female commander, Apadomey. Many of the skulls still retained the hair. It appears that this part of the human body has always been a favorite ornament on the palace walls of Abomey, and even in the walls, entrances of gateways and doorways."
— *Duncan's Africa*, Vol. II., page 276.

"Permission to see the town was given, and we paid a visit to the Juju-house; a noisy crowd attempted to rush in after us; but a vigorous application of the long sticks of the guards drove them back. Masses of human skulls hang from the walls, and numerous rows of skulls cover the roof of a sort of altar. In front of this altar sat the Juju-man, having a footstool of human skulls. The Okrika had eaten the victims whose skulls decorate the Juju- house. An old man who accompanied us spoke with evident gusto of the different cannibal feasts he had partaken of, and mentioned the parts of the human body which he considered the sweetest."
— Consul Charles Livingstone; at the Bight of Biafra.

"When a guest is entertained of whom presents are expected, the host, in a quiet way, goes from time to time into the fetich-house and scrapes a little bone-powder from a favorite skull, and puts it into the food which is being cooked, as a present to the guest. The idea is, that, by consuming the scrapings of the skull, the blood of their ancestors enters into your body, and thus, becoming of one blood, you are naturally led to love them, and grant them what they wish. It is not a pleasant subject of reflection, but I have no doubt been operated upon on previous journeys; being now, however, aware of the custom, I refused the food, and told Mayolo I cared very little to eat of the scraped skull of his grandfather."

-Du Chaillu's Ashango-Land, page 200. 66

"On a small island, near the mouth of the Niger, the people have some strange customs. They have a large town, of about three thousand inhabitants; their huts are built within mud walls, with the streets crossing each other at right angles. At every corner there is a creature stuck up, like our scarecrows in Amer- ica, with a gourd for a head, and dressed up with clothes, shells, and beads. This thing is called Juju, and whatever is devoted to it is sacred. Thus the little animal called the Iguana a species of lizard, which elsewhere is eaten - here is allowed to increase and run all over the island. At one end of the town there is a temple dedicated to the Juju. It is higher than most of the other houses, with an arched doorway, the sides and arch of which are formed of human skulls. Inside the hut, at one end, is a sort of sacred altar, that, with an arched recess behind, is formed of children's skulls, the east side and floor being the skulls of adults. In the eye-sockets of each a square piece of board is inserted, first painted red, and then an eye painted on it. Outside the door is a post to which prisoners are tied, and beaten to death with clubs,

and then their skulls, after being dried and bleached, are used for replacing any that may have become cracked or otherwise injured. There are three priests whose business is to put prisoners to death, to take care of the temple, and attend to the dressing of the Ju- jus."
-Brittan's Every-Day Life in Africa, page 343.

"It is revenge, as much as desire to perpetuate the remembrance of victory, which makes them eager for the skulls and jawbones of their enemies, so that in a royal metropolis, walls, and floors, and thrones, and walking-sticks are everywhere lowering with the hollow eyes of the dead. These sad, bare, and whitened emblems of mortality and revenge present a curious and startling spectacle, cresting and festooning the red clay walls of Humassi, the capital of Ashantee."
— *Foote's Africa and the American Flag*, page 56.

"When a human head is desired to be preserved, the brains are extracted through the spinal connection, and the head held on the end of a stick in the smoke till it becomes quite hard and dry. I have seen some thousands preserved in this way in Dahomey."
—*Duncan's Africa*, Vol. II., page 159.

"Near the king were placed several large staffs or walking-sticks, with a skull fixed on the upper end of each, the stick passing through the skull so as to leave about seven inches of the stick above the skull for the hand when walking."
— *Duncan's Africa*, Vol. I., page 246.

"The father of Moyara was a powerful chief, but the son now sits among the ruins of the town, with four or five wives and very few people. At his hamlet a number of stakes are planted in the ground, and I counted fifty-four human skulls hung on their points. These were Matebele, who, unable to approach Sebituane on the island of Loyela, had returned sick and famishing. Moyara's father took advantage of their reduced condition, and, after put-ting them to death, mounted their heads in the Batoka fashion. The old man who perpetrated this deed now lies in the middle of his son's huts, with a lot of rotten ivory over his grave. One can-not help feeling thankful that the reign of such wretches is over. They inhabited the whole of this side of the country, and were probably the barrier to the extension of the Portuguese commerce in this direction. When looking at these skulls, I remarked to Moyara that many of them were those of mere boys. He assented readily, and pointed them out as such. I asked why his father had killed boys. To show his fierce-ness,' was the answer. 'It is fierceness to kill boys.' 'Yes; they had no business here.' When I told him that this probably would insure his own death if the Matebele came again, he replied, 'When I hear of their coming I shall hide the bones.' He was evidently proud of these trophies of his father's ferocity, and I was assured by other Batoka that few strangers ever returned from a visit to this quarter. If a man wished to curry favor with a Batoka chief, he ascertained when a stranger was about to leave, and waylaid him at a distance from the town, and when he brought his head back to the chief, it was mounted as a trophy, the different chiefs vy-ing with each other as to which should mount the greatest number of skulls in his village."

-*Livingstone's Africa*, page 569.

4

Blood-Thirstiness and Barbarity of the Negroes in Negroland

"THERE is apparently in this people a physical delight in cruelty to beast as well as to man. The sight of suffering seems to bring them an enjoyment without which the world is tame. In almost all the towns on the Oil Rivers, you see dead or dying animals fastened in some agonizing position. Poultry is most common, because cheapest; they are tied by the legs, head downwards, or lashed round the body to a stake or a tree, where they remain till they fall in fragments. If a man be unwell, he hangs a live chicken round his throat, expecting that its pain will abstract from his sufferings. Goats are lashed head downwards tightly to wooden pillars, and are allowed to die a lingering death; even the harmless tortoise cannot escape impalement. Blood seems to be the favorite ornament for a man's face, as pattern-painting with some dark color like indigo is

the proper decoration for a woman. At funerals numbers of goats and poultry are sacrificed for the benefit of the deceased, and the corpse is sprinkled with the warm blood. The headless trunks are laid upon the body, and if the fowls flap their wings, which they will do for some seconds after decapitation, it is a good omen for the dead man.".
-*Hutchinson's Western Africa*, Vol. II., page 283.

"It is not so easy to offer any probable reason for the eagerness to share in cruelty which glows in a negro's bosom. Its appalling character consists rather in the amount of bloodshed which gratifies the negro, than in the studious prolongation of pain. Superstition probably excused or justified to him some of his worst practices. Human sacrifices have been common every- where. There was no scruple at cruelty when it was convenient. The mouths of the victims were gagged by knives run through their cheeks; and captives among the southern tribes were beaten with clubs in order to prevent resistance, or to take away their strength, that they might be more easily hurried to the hill of death,' or authorized place of execution."
-*Foote's Africa and the American Flag*, page 52.

"It is hard to make them feel that the shedding of human blood is a great crime; they must be conscious that it is wrong, but, having been accustomed to bloodshed from infancy, they are remarkably callous to the enormity of the crime of destroying human life."
- *Livingstone's Africa*, page 217.

"The late Matiamvo sometimes indulged in the whim of running a muck in the town and beheading whomsoever he met, until he had quite a heap of human heads. Matiamvo explained this conduct by saying that his people were too many, and he wanted to diminish them. He had absolute power of life and death."

-*Livingstone's Africa*, page 341.

"Nothing less than the entire subjugation, or destruction of the vanquished, could quench their insatiable thirst for power. Thus when they conquered a town, the terrified inhabitants were driven in a mass to the outskirts, when the parents and all the married women were slaughtered on the spot. Such as have dared to be brave in the defence of their town, their wives, and their children, are reserved for a still more terrible death; dry grass, saturated with fat, is tied round their naked bodies and then set on fire. The youths and girls are loaded as beasts of burden with the spoils of the town, to be marched to the homes of their victors. If the town be in an isolated position, the helpless infants are left to perish either with hunger, or to be devoured by beasts of prey. On such an event, the lions scent the slain and leave their lair. The hyenas and jackals emerge from their lurking-places in broad day, and revel in the carnage, while a cloud of vultures may be seen descending on the living and the dead, and holding a carnival on human flesh."

- *Moffatt's Africa*, page 365.

"We found the criminals seated on blocks of wood, in a street near the king's residence, each accompanied by an executioner. One of the executioners was the lad who told me, on the 17th of December, that he had himself decapitated eighty persons. Two knives were forced through the cheeks of each criminal, one on each side, which deprived them of speech. This is done, it is said, to prevent them cursing the king. We did not stop to gaze on the horrid spectacle."

— *Freeman's Africa*, page 164.

"When any one of these chiefs dies, the news of his death is not made known for one or two months afterwards; and if any person who has learned the fact of his death discloses the secret, he is immediately decapitated, and his family and relatives sold into captivity. If there be no purchasers for them, they are all conducted to the banks of the river, and there decapitated by the Samba Golambole, or common executioner; the bodies are then thrown into the river, and the heads are piled up at the entrance to the capital, as a warning to all disclosers of state secrets."
-*Valdez's Africa*, Vol. II., page 331.

"The head and legs of the ox were then drawn together, and it fell bellowing to the ground. The animal was now secured firmly, and prevented from rising. The chief butcher then, with a large knife, cut open about a foot of the skin of the belly; and lying on the ground, amidst the groans of agony and helpless struggles of the unfortunate brute, he thrust his right arm up to the shoulder into the ox, gave a twist and a pull at the heart, ruptured one of the large arteries, and drew away the omentum, which was thrown on a fire, cooked and eaten, before the convulsions of the victim had ceased."
-*Alexander's Africa*, Vol. II., page 132.

"The guide, attached to the expedition on return from Ujiji, had loitered behind for some days, because his slave girl was too footsore to walk. When tired of waiting he cut off her her head, for fear lest she should become gratis another man's property.
- *Burton's Africa*, page 515.

"Tembandumba, the Amazonian and cannibal queen of Congo, commanded that all male children, all twins, and all infants whose upper teeth appeared before their lower ones, should be killed by their own mothers. From their bodies an ointment should be made in the way which she would show. The female children should be reared and instructed in war; and male prisoners, before being killed and eaten, should be used for purposes of pro- creation, so that there might be no future lack of female warriors. Having concluded her harangue, with the publication of other laws of minor importance, this young woman seized her child which was feeding at her breast, flung him into a mortar, and pounded him to a pulp. She flung this into a large earthen pot, adding roots, leaves, and oils, and made the whole into an ointment, with which she rubbed herself before them all, telling them that this would render her invulnerable, and that now she could subdue the universe. Immediately her subjects, seized with a savage enthusiasm, massacred all their male children, and immense quantities of this human ointment were made. It is clear enough that Tembandumba wished to found an empire of Amazons, such as we read of as existing among the Scythians, in the forests of South America, and in Central Africa. She not only enjoined the massacre of male children, she forbade the eating of woman's flesh. But she had to conquer an instinct in order to carry out her views; she fought against nature, and in time she was subdued.".

-*Reade's Savage Africa,* page 292.

"On our march to the market-place we passed along part of the walls of the palace, which covers an immense space. The walls as well as houses are made of red, sandy clay, and on top of the walls, at intervals of thirty feet, human skulls were placed along their whole extent. On approaching nearer the market-place we beheld, on an elevated pole, a man fixed in an upright position, with a basket on his head, apparently holding it with both hands. A little further on we saw two more men, now in a state of decomposition, hung by the feet from a thick pole, placed horizontally on two upright poles about twenty feet high. Passing close to them the smell was intolerable. The arms hung extended downwards, and at a little distance a stranger would (from their shrivelled and contracted condition) suppose them to be large sheep or goats; the skin, from exposure, had turned nearly to the color of that of a white man. I found, upon inquiry, that the bodies had been in this position about two and a half moons. All reckoning here is by the moon. The vulture was industriously endeavoring to satisfy his appetite, but the heat of the sun had dried the skin so as to render it impenetrable to his efforts. On the opposite side of the market were two more human bodies in the same position as those I have just mentioned, with the exception that the bodies had been mutilated."

— *Duncan's Africa*, Vol. I., page 219.

"I have already spoken of the system of intermarriages, by which a chief gains in power and friends. But there are other means of securing allies. For instance, two tribes are anxious for a fight, but one needs more force. This weakling sends one of its men secretly to kill a man or woman of some village living near, but having no share in the quarrel. The consequence is, not, as would seem most reasonable, that this last village take its revenge on the murderer, but, strangely enough, that the murderer's people give them to understand that this is done because another tribe has insulted them; whereupon, according to African custom, the two villages join, and together march upon the enemy. In effect, to gain a village to a certain side in a quarrel, that side murders one of its men or women, with a purpose of retaliation on somebody else."

-*Du Chaillu's Equatorial Africa*, page 74.

"Sali showed extreme folly in remaining behind, and Kamrasi, suspicious of his complicity, immediately ordered him to be seized and cut to pieces; he was accordingly tied to a stake, and tortured by having his limbs cut off piecemeal, the hands being first severed at the wrists, and the arms at the elbow-joints.".
-*Baker's Great Basin of the Nile*, page 406.

"A number of old women had been taken in the general slave hunt; these could not walk sufficiently fast to keep up with their victors during the return march; they had accordingly all been killed on the road, as being cumbersome. In every case they were killed by being beaten on the back of the neck with a club."
-*Baker's Great Basin of the Nile,* page 405.

"Amarar called his soothsayer, and required him to name a propitious moment for the sally. The oracle retired to his den, and, after suitable incantations, declared that the effort should be made as soon as the hands of Amarar were stained in the blood of his own son. It is said that the prophet intended the victim to be a youthful son of Amarar, who had joined his mother's family, and was then distant; but the impatient and superstitious savage, seeing a child of his own, two years old, at hand, when the oracle announced the decree, snatched the infant from his mother's arms, threw it into a rice mortar, and, with a pestle, mashed it to death. The sacrifice over, a sortie was ordered. The infuriate and starving savages, roused by the oracle and inflamed by the bloody scene, rushed forth tumultuously. Amarar, armed with the pestle, still warm and reeking with his infant's blood, was foremost in the onset. The besiegers gave way and fled; the town was re-provisioned; the fortifications of the enemy demolished; and the soothsayer rewarded with a slave for his barbarous prediction! At another time, Amarar was on the point of attacking a strongly fortified town, when doubts were intimated of success. Again the wizard was consulted, when the mysterious oracle declared that the chief "could not conquer till he returned once more to his mother's womb!" That night Amara committed the blackest of incests; but his party was repulsed, and the false prophet stoned to death."

- *Canot's Twenty Years of an African Slaver,* - page 333.

"It was not long after my instalment at Cape Mount, that I accidentally witnessed the ferocity of the chief. Some trifling country affair caused me to visit the king; but, upon landing at Toso, I was told he was abroad. The manner of my informant, however, satisfied me that the message was untrue; and accordingly, with the usual confidence of a white man in Africa, I searched his premises till I encountered him in the palaver-house. The large inclosure was crammed with a mob of savages, all in perfect silence around the king, who, in an infuriate manner, with a bloody knife in his hand, and a foot on the dead body of a negro, was addressing the carcass. By his side stood a pot of hissing oil, in which the heart of his enemy was frying! My sudden and, perhaps, improper entrance seemed to exasperate the infidel, who, calling me to his side, knelt on the corpse, and digging it repeatedly with his knife, exclaimed, with trembling passion, that it was his bitterest and oldest foe. For twenty years he had butchered his people, sold his subjects, violated his daughters, slain his sons, and burnt his towns; and with each charge, the savage enforced his assertion by a stab."

-*Canot's Twenty Years of an African Slaver*, page 432.

"By degrees the warriors dropped in around their chieftain. A palaver-house, immediately in front of my quarters, was the general rendezvous; and scarcely a bushman appeared without the body of some maimed and bleeding victim. The mangled but living captives were tumbled on a heap in the centre, and soon every avenue to the square was crowded with exulting savages. Rum was brought forth in abundance for the chiefs. Presently, slowly approaching from a distance, I heard the drums, horns, and war-bells; and, in less than fifteen minutes, a procession of women, whose naked limbs were smeared with chalk and ochre, poured into the palaver-house to join the beastly rites. Each of these devils was armed with a knife, and bore in her hand some cannibal trophy. Jen-Ken's wife, a corpulent wench of forty-five, dragged along the ground, by a single limb, the slimy corpse of an infant ripped alive from its mother's womb. As her eyes met those of her husband, the two fiends yelled forth a shout of mutual joy, while the lifeless babe was tossed in the air and caught as it descended on the point of a spear. Then came the refreshment, in the shape of rum, powder, and blood, which was quaffed by the brutes till they reeled off, with linked hands, in a wild dance around the pile of victims. As the women leaped and sang, the men applauded and encouraged. Soon the ring was broken, and, with a yell, each female leaped on the body of a wounded prisoner, and commenced the final sacrifice with the mockery of lascivious embraces. In my wanderings. in African forests, I have often seen the tiger pounce upon its prey, and, with instinctive thirst, satiate its appetite for blood and abandon the drained corpse; but these African negresses were neither as decent nor as merciful as the beast of the wilderness. Their malignant pleasure seemed to consist in the invention of tortures, that would agonize but not slay. There was a devilish spell in the tragic scene that fascinated my eyes to the spot. A slow, lingering, tormenting mutilation was practised on the living, as well as on the dead; and, in every instance, the brutality of the women exceeded that of the men. I cannot picture the hellish joy with which they passed from body to body, digging out eyes, wrenching off lips, tearing the ears, and slicing the flesh from the quivering bones; while the queen of the harpies crept amid the butchery, gathering the brains from each severed skull as a dainty dish for the approaching feast! After the last victim yielded his life, it did not require long to kindle a fire, produce the requisite utensils, and fill the air with the odor of human flesh. Yet, before the various messes were half broiled, every mouth was tearing the delicate morsels with shouts of joy, denoting the combined satisfaction of revenge and appetite! In the midst of this appalling scene, I heard a fresh cry of exultation, as a pole was borne into the apartment, on which was impaled the living body of the conquered chieftain's wife. A hole was quickly dug, the stave planted, and fagots supplied; but before a fire could be kindled, the wretched woman was dead, so that the barbarians were defeated in their hellish scheme of burning her alive. I do not know how long these brutalities lasted, for I remember very little after this last attempt, except that the bushmen packed in plaintain leaves whatever flesh was left from the orgy, to be conveyed to their friends in the forest. This was the first time it had been my lot to behold the most savage development of African nature under the stimulus of war, The butchery made me sick, dizzy, paralyzed. I sank on the earth benumbed with stupor; nor was I aroused till nightfall, when my Kroomen bore me to the conqueror's town, and negotiated our redemption for the value of twenty slaves."

- *Canot's Twenty Years of an African Slaver*, pages 384-386.

5

Slavery and the Slave-Trade in Negroland

"It seems quite natural that every one, even the most thoughtless barbarian, would feel at least some slight emotion on being exiled from his native country, and enslaved. But so far is this from being the case, that Africans, generally speaking, betray the most perfect indifference on losing their liberty, and being deprived of their relatives; while love of country is seemingly as great a stranger to their breasts as social tenderness and domestic affection."
-*Lander's Travels in Africa,* Vol. II., page 208.

"The reader must bear in mind that my observations apply chiefly to persons of free condition, who constitute, I suppose, not more than one-fourth part of the inhabitants at large; the other three-fourths are in a state of hopeless and hereditary slavery."

— *Mungo Park's 1st Journal,* page 32.

"Large families are very often exposed to absolute want, and, as the parents have almost unlimited authority over their children, it frequently happens, in all parts of Africa, that some of the lat- ter are sold to purchase provisions for the rest of the family."
- *Mungo Park's 1st Journal,* page 216.

"Every evening I observed five or six women come to the mansa's house, and receive each of them a certain quantity of corn. As I knew how valuable this article was at this juncture, I inquired of the mansa whether he maintained those poor women from pure bounty, or whether he expected a return when the harvest should be gathered in. Observe that boy,' said he, pointing to a fine child about five years of age; 'his mother has sold him to me for forty days' provision for herself and the rest of her family; I have bought another boy in the same manner."
-*Mungo Park's Travels in Africa,* page 116.

"The slave-market is held in two long sheds, one for males, the other for females, where they are seated in rows, and carefully decked out for the exhibition; the owner or one of his trusty slaves sitting near them. Young or old, plump or withered, beautiful or ugly, are sold without distinction; but, in other respects, the buyer inspects them with the utmost attention, and somewhat in the same manner as a volunteer seaman is examined by a surgeon on entering the navy; he looks at the tongue, teeth, eyes, and limbs, and endeavors to detect rupture by a forced cough. Slavery is here so common, or the mind of slaves is so constituted, that they always appeared much happier than their masters; the women, especially, singing with the greatest glee all the time they are at work."

- *Clapperton's Africa,* Vol. IV., page 36.

"The whole population of Katunga may be considered in a state of slavery, either to the king or his caboceers."
— *Clapperton's Africa,* Vol. IV., page 211.

"They had nearly a hundred slaves, the greater part female, and girls of from twelve to eighteen years of age, some of them from Nyfee, and still further to the West, of a deep copper color, and beautifully formed; but few of these were ironed. The males, who were mostly young, were linked together in couples by iron rings around their legs; yet they laughed, and seemed in good condition."
-*Denham & Clapperton's Africa,* Vol. II., page 134.

"Slaves in Africa are in proportion to the freemen of about three to one; but, although the number of individuals reduced to a state of bondage by the operation of the above causes, and the destruction created, both as regards life and property, is immense, the whole combined are but as a single grain of dust in the balance, when compared with the slavery, the destitution, and the desolation, that are daily entailed by the unceasing bloody struggles betwixt state and state. Towns and villages are then obliterated from the face of the earth; and thousands upon thou- sands of the population, of whatever age or sex, are hurried into hopeless captivity."
— *Harris's Adventures in Africa,* page 314.

"Crime, necessity arising from distress, insolvency, the inhumanity of a harsh creditor, a spirit of retaliation in petty disputes, and the sordid love of gain, for which parents will even sell their own children, severally assist in feeding the demand for slaves, the

law of every African state either tolerating or directly sanctioning the evil."
— *Harris's Adventures in Africa*, page 314.

"Not even the appearance of affection exists between husband and wife, or between parents and children. So little do they care for their offspring, that many offered to sell me any of their sons or daughters as slaves. They are, to speak the truth, in point of parental affection, inferior to brutes."
— *Duncan's Africa*, Vol. I., page 79.

"A slave in Gabun was once asked why he did not take the money, which he was known to have accumulated, and ransom himself. His reply was, 'I have as much freedom as I want, and I prefer to buy a slave to wait upon me."
— *Wilson's Africa*, page 272.

"The liability to fall into a condition of servitude is not so frightful in Africa as it is where there is a higher appreciation of personal liberty; nor does the same odium attach to the term slave as is attached to it among civilized men. The African sees very little difference between the authority exercised over him by one whom he acknowledges as his master and the petty tyranny which is exercised by most African chiefs over their subjects; and so long as he is worked moderately, and treated kindly, he has but little cause for dissatisfaction, and not infrequently by his own choice places himself in this condition."
- *Wilson's Africa*, page 156.

"Slavery exists on an immense scale in Adamawa, and there are many private individuals who have more than a thousand slaves. The only articles of export at present are slaves and ivory."
— *Barth's Africa*, Vol. II., page 190.

"With the abolition of the slave-trade all along the northern and south-western coast of Africa, slaves will cease to be brought down to the coast, and in this way a great deal of the mischief and misery necessarily resulting from this inhuman traffic will be cut off. But this, unfortunately, forms only a small part of the evil. There can be no doubt that the most horrible topic connected with slavery is slave-hunting; and this is carried on, not only for the purpose of supplying the foreign market, but, in a far more extensive degree, for supplying the wants of domestic slavery."
- *Barth's Africa,* Vol. I., page 12.

"A large number of slaves had been caught this day, and in the course of the evening, after some skirmishing, in which three Bonu horsemen were killed, a great many others were brought in; altogether they were said to have taken one thousand, and there were certainly not less than five hundred. To our utmost horror, not less than one hundred and seventy full-grown men were mercilessly slaughtered in cold blood, the greater part of them being allowed to bleed to death, a leg having been severed from the body."
— *Barth's Africa,* Vol. II., page 369.

"In times of necessity, a man will part with his parents, wives, and children, and when they fail, he will sell himself without shame. As has been observed among many tribes the uncle has a right to dispose of his nephews and nieces."
-*Burton's Africa,* page 515.

"The busiest scene is the slave-market, composed of two long ranges of sheds, one for males and another for females. These poor creatures are seated in rows, decked out for exhibition; the buyer scrutinizes them as nicely as a purchaser with us does a horse, inspecting the tongue, teeth, eyes, and limbs, making them cough and perform various movements, to ascertain if there be anything unsound."
— *Murray's African Discoveries*, page 164.

"The good qualities given to the negro by the bounty of nature, have served only to make him a slave, trodden down by every remorseless foot, and to brand him for ages with the epithet of outcast; the marked unceasing proof of a curse, as old as the origin of society, not even deserving human forbearance! And true it is, that the worst slavery is his lot, even at home, for he is there exposed to the constant peril of becoming also a victim, slaughtered with the most revolting torments. Tyrant of his blood, he traffics in slavery as it were merchandise; makes war purposely to capture neighbors, and sell even his own wives and children.".
-*Smith's Natural History of the Human Species*, page 197.

"One method of procuring slaves is by women who are maintained for the express purpose of ensnaring the unsuspecting with their blandishments, and who carry on their infamous trade with the connivance of their husbands, who frequently bestow upon them a portion of the fine or damages imposed, as a reward for their successful enterprise, and an encouragement for future infidelity. These harpies being very industrious in their vocation, and being ably seconded by the ungovernable passions of men living in a state of nature, consign a numerous body of victims to

bondage. Superstition, and the tricks and impostures of the priests, or fetichmen, contribute also their quota of slaves. The numerous and expensive observances which these prescribed, to be observed with the view of avoiding or alleviating some calamity, often oblige the applicant for priestly comfort to part with one half of his family, to secure a blessing for the other. Even death, which might be supposed calculated to terminate the family responsibility, becomes an active enslaver, on account of the expensive obsequies which it is considered the chief point of honor to perform."
- *Cruickshank's Africa,* Vol. I., page 326.

"The whole system of slave-holding by the Arabs in Africa, or rather on the coast, or at Zanzibar, is exceedingly strange, for the slaves, both in individual physical strength and in numbers, are so superior to the Arab foreigners, that if they chose to rebel, they might send the Arabs flying out of the land. It happens, how- ever, that they are spellbound, not knowing their strength any more than domestic animals."
— *Speke's Africa,* page 26.

"On arrival at the desired locality, the slave-traders disembark and proceed into the interior until they arrive at the village of some negro chief, with whom they establish an intimacy. Charmed with his new friends, the power of whose weapons he acknowledges, the negro chief does not neglect the opportunity of seeking their alliance to attack a hostile neighbor. Marching throughout the night, guided by their negro hosts, they bivouac within an hour's march of the unsuspecting village doomed to an attack about half an hour before break of day. The time arrives, and, quietly surrounding the village, while its occupants are still sleeping, they fire the grass huts in all directions, and pour volleys of musketry through the flaming thatch. Panic-stricken, the unfortunate victims rush from their burning dwellings, and the men are shot down like pheasants in a battue, while the women and children, bewildered in the danger and confusion, are kidnapped and secured. The herds of cattle, still within their kraal, or " zareeba," are easily disposed of, and are driven off with great rejoicing, as the prize of victory. The women and children are then fastened together, the former secured in an instrument called a sheba, made of a forked pole, the neck of the prisoner fitting into the fork, secured by a cross-piece lashed behind, while the wrists, brought together in advance of the body, are tied to the pole. The children are then fastened by their necks with a rope attached to the women, and thus form a living chain, in which order they are marched to the head-quarters in company with the captured herds. This is the commencement of business. Should there be ivory in any of the huts not destroyed by the fire, it is appropriated; a general plunder takes place. The trader's party dig up the floors of the hut to search for iron hoes, which are generally thus concealed, as the greatest treasure of the negroes; the granaries are overturned and wantonly destroyed, and the hands are cut off the bodies of the slain, the more easily to detach the copper and iron bracelets that are usually worn."

- *Baker's Great Basin of the Nile*, page 13.

"The Cassangas, the Banhuns, and all the other neighboring tribes and nations, punish all crimes by perpetual banishment. In such cases they consider it more advantageous to dispose of their convicts by selling them to strangers than to bear the burthen of their support. Thus they reap a rich harvest themselves, and, at the same time, encourage that detestable traffic, the slave-trade. To such an extent, indeed, does their cupidity lead them, that they outrage all the laws of justice and humanity. When any person comes

under the lash of their sanguinary laws, he himself is not alone exposed to punishment, but his whole family is involved in ruin along with him."
 - *Valdez's Africa,* Vol. I., page 293.

"A few days after my arrival at Timbuctoo I fell in with a negro, who was parading about the streets two women, whom I recollected to have been fellow-passengers with me on board the canoe. These women were not young, but their master, to give them the appearance of an age better suited to the market, had dressed them well. They wore fine white handkerchiefs, large gold ear-rings, and each had two or three necklaces of the same metal. When I passed them, they looked at me, and smiled. They did not appear in the least mortified at being exhibited in streets for sale, but manifested an indifference, which I could easily enough account for by the state of degradation to which they had been reduced and their total ignorance of the natural rights of mankind."
 - *Caillie's Africa,* Vol. II., page 63.

"No better illustration could be given of the way in which the slave system has ingrafted itself upon the life and policy of these tribes than this, that, from the sea-shore to the farthest point in the interior which I was able to reach, the commercial unit of value is a slave. As we say dollar, as the English say pound sterling, so these Africans say slave. If a man is fined for an offence, he is mulcted in so many slaves. If he is bargaining for a wife, he contracts to give so many slaves for her. Perhaps he has no slaves; but he has ivory or trade-goods, and pays of these the value of so many slaves, that is to say, as much ivory or ebony, or bar- wood, or the amount in trade-goods which would, in that precise place, buy so many slaves."
 —*Du Chaillu's Equatorial Africa,* page 380.

"High prices are a great temptation to the cupidity of the African, who, having, by custom, rights of property in his children, often does not hesitate to sell these where other produce is lacking. He finds that one of his children is not bright, that it has no sense, or that it wants to bewitch the father. Then a consultation ensues with the relatives of the mother; they are promised a share in the produce of the sale, for they have rights also in the child, and, when they are brought to consent, the unhappy child is sold off."
-*Du Chaillu's Equatorial Africa*, page 381.

"It would be a task of many pages, if I attempted to give a full account of the origin and causes of slavery in Africa. As a national institution, it seems to have existed always. Africans have been bondsmen everywhere, and the oldest monuments bear their images linked with menial toils and absolute servitude. Man, in truth, has become the coin of Africa, and the legal tender of a brutal trade. Five-sixths of the population are in chains."
- *Canot's Twenty Years of the African Slaver*, page 126. ·

6

Heathenish Superstition and Witchcraft in Negroland

"ONE of the Africans' deep-rooted superstitions is witchcraft, to the operation of which they generally ascribe disease and death, the very infirmities of age being attributed to the same influence. The doctor, being sent for upon emergencies of this nature, gives some root or drug to his patient, accompanying the administration of it with a farcical expression of countenance, and a mysterious assumption of manner, pretending to charm from the sufferer some noxious reptile, by which he alleges that the malady is occasioned, and contriving, at the same time, secretly to pro- duce one, which is supposed to have been withdrawn from the person afflicted. If the patient should happen to recover, the Igiaka is greatly commended for his skill, and obtains an adequate remuneration; if, on the contrary, the sickness should in- crease, another doctor, called the discoverer of bewitching matter,' is then summoned, who professes to discover the party supposed to have bewitched him. The guilt having been affixed, after many absurd ceremonies, upon some unfortunate wretch, a report is made to the chief, who directs torture to be inflicted on him, for the purpose of eliciting confession. The usual method of torture is by the application of heated stones to the tenderest parts of the outstretched body, the hands and feet being first made fast to four stakes at equal distances, while myriads of ants are scattered over the agonized victim, whose skin is exposed to the painful gnawing of these swarming insects. It can be no matter of surprise that innocent persons, subjected to these terrible punishments, should be induced to confess the agency of which they have been accused, and instances are on record of many individuals, perfectly guiltless, who have admitted the crime rather than to undergo the fiery ordeal, through a natural dread of its horrors."

-*Steadman's Africa*, Vol. I., page 37.

"Witchcraft is a prominent and leading superstition among all the races of Africa, and may be regarded as one of the heaviest curses which rests upon that benighted land. A person endowed with this mysterious art is supposed to possess little less than omnipotence. He exercises unlimited control, not only over the lives and destiny of his fellow-men, but over the wild beasts of the woods, over the sea and dry land, and over all the elements of nature. He may transform himself into a tiger, and keep the community in which he lives in a state of constant fear and perturbation; into an elephant, and desolate their farms; or into a shark, and devour all the fish in their rivers. By his magical arts he can keep back the showers, and fill the land with want and distress. The lightnings obey his commands, and he need only wave his wand to call forth the pestilence from its lurking- place. The sea is lashed into fury, and the storm rages

to exe- cute his behests. In short, there is nothing too hard for the machinations of witchcraft. Sickness, poverty, insanity, and almost every evil incident to human life, are ascribed to its agency."
-*Wilson's Africa*, page 222.

"Every death which occurs in the community is ascribed to witchcraft, and some one, consequently, is guilty of the wicked deed. The priesthood go to work to find out the guilty person. It may be a brother, a sister, a father, and, in a few extreme cases, even mothers have been accused of the unnatural deed of causing the death of their own offspring. There is, in fact, no effectual shield against the suspicion of it. lationship, official prominence, and general benevolence of char- acter, are alike unavailing. The priesthood, in consequence Age, the ties of re- of the universal belief in the superstition, have unlimited scope for the indulgence of the most malicious feelings, and, in many cases, it is exercised with unsparing severity."
— *Wilson's Africa*, page 223.

"The intercourse which the natives have had with white men does not seem to have much ameliorated their condition. A great number of persons are reported to lose their lives annually in different districts of Angola by the cruel superstitions to which they are addicted; and the Portuguese authorities either know nothing of them, or are unable to prevent their occurrence. The natives are bound to secrecy by those who administer the ordeal, which generally causes the death of the victim. A person, when accused of witchcraft, will often travel from distant districts, in order to assert her innocency and brave the test. They come to a river on the Cassange, called Dua, drink the infusion of a poisonous tree, and perish unknown. A woman was accused by a brother-in-law of being the

cause of his sickness while we were at Cassange. She offered to take the ordeal, as she had the idea that it would but prove her conscious innocence. Captain Neves refused his consent to her going, and thus saved her life, which would have been sacrificed, for the poison is very virulent. When a strong stomach rejects it, the accuser reiterates his charge; the dose is repeated, and the person dies. Hundreds perish thus every year in the valley of Cassange."
— *Livingstone's Africa,* page 471.

"In several tribes, a child which is said to 'tlolo' (trangress) is put to death. Tlolo,' or transgression, is ascribed to several curious cases. A child who cut the upper front teeth before the under was always put to death among the Bakaa, and, I believe, also among the Bakwains. In some tribes, a case of twins renders one of them liable to death; and an ox, which, while lying in the pen, beats the ground with its tail, is treated in the same way. It is thought to be calling death to visit the tribe. When I was coming through Londa, my men carried a great number of fowls, of a larger breed than any they had at home. If one crowed before midnight, it had been guilty of 'tlolo,' and was killed. The men often carried them sitting on their guns, and if one began to crow in a forest, the owner would give it a beating, by way of teaching it not to be guilty of crowing at unseasonable hours."
— *Livingstone's Africa,* page 618.

"When a person of influence is taken ill, or dies, the cause is eagerly sought after, not in the nature of the disease, but in some person who was at enmity with the deceased, or who had acted in some way to excite suspicion. This was very natural in them, as they did not believe in an overruling Providence. It was the universal belief, as well as their wish, that men would live alway, and that death was entirely the result of witchcraft, or medicine imparted by some malignant hand, or of some casualty, or want of food. The death of the poor excited but little sorrow; and less surmise; on the other hand, I have known instances where the domestics of a principal man have been murdered in cold blood, just because it was suspected that they had something to do with their master's sickness."

- *Moffat's Africa*, page 292.

"At the different towns and villages through which we passed, they brought to us all the sick to be cured. Nor was it the sick alone who sought advice, but men and women of all descriptions, the former for some remedy against impotency, and the latter to remove sterility. Many came for preventives against apprehended or barely possible calamities; and, in anticipation of the imaginable ills of life, resorted to us in full hope and confidence of our being able to ward them off. The women were particularly fanciful in these matters, and were frequently importunate to receive medicines that would preserve the affections of their gallants, insure them husbands, or, what was highly criminal, effect the death of some favored rival."

- *Clapperton's Africa*, Vol. III., page 239.

"At my instance, Benderachmani sent a courier to Nyffee, to endeavor to recover Mr. Hornemann's manuscripts, for which I offered him a reward of a hundred dollars; but on my return from Sackatoo I found the messenger come back with the information, that Jussuf Felatah, a learned man of the country, with whom Mr. Hornemann lodged, had been burned in his own house, to- gether with all Mr. Hornemann's papers, by the negro rabble, from a superstitious dread of his holding intercourse with evil spirits."

-*Clapperton's Africa*, Vol. IV., page 56. 66

"The Damaras have great faith in witchcraft. versed in the black art are called Omundu-Onganga, and are much sought after. Any person falling sick is immediately at- tended by one of these impostors, whose panacea is to besmear the mouth and the forehead of the patient with the ordure of the hyena, which is supposed to possess particularly healing virtues."
- *Andersson's Africa*, page 173.

"To become a witch-doctor of any importance, a person is required to be instructed by one previously well versed in the mysteries of the black art. He must begin his lessons by swallowing animal poison, be bitten by venomous reptiles, or have poison inoculated into his body. A cap, a handkerchief, or any sort of clothing worn by such a person until it has become perfectly saturated with filth, is considered the most infallible cure for all kinds of diseases, poisonous bites, etc. On emergencies, a corner of this treasure is washed, and the dirty water thus produced is given to the patient to drink.".
-*Andersson's Africa*, page 256.

"On other portions of the coast their customs are more cruel about witchcraft than among the Greboes. Any one, once accused of witchcraft, is burnt most cruelly. In some places a slow fire is made, and four posts sunk into the ground, at certain distances, the person tied hands and feet to these posts, and suspended over the fire, thus being slowly burnt; sometimes they are left to die there; at other times they are taken down before death, cast into the bush, and left to perish miserably. No one must pity a witch. Sometimes they torture them a different fashion: they are fastened down so that they cannot move, and then red-hot coals are placed on different parts of the body, and there left to eat into the flesh."

—*Brittan's Every-Day Life in Africa*, page 344.

"They are believers in witchcraft to an unlimited extent; but what they understand by the term is very difficult to say. I once obtained the character of a wizard by mixing a seidlitz-powder, and drinking it off during effervescence, for the spectators took it for granted that the water was boiling."
- *Drayson's Africa*, page 36.

"The ladies solicited amulets to restore their beauty, to preserve the affections of their lovers, and even to destroy a hated rival. The son of the Governor of Kano, having called upon Mr. Clapperton, stated it as the conviction of the whole city and his own, that the English had the power of converting men into asses, goats, and monkeys, and likewise that by reading in his book he could at any time commute a handful of earth into gold."
— *Murray's African Discoveries*, page 162.

"In times of tribulation, the magician, if he ascertains a war is projected, by inspecting the blood and bones of a fowl which he has flayed for that purpose, flays a young child, and, having laid it lengthwise on a path, directs all the warriors, on proceeding to battle, to step over his sacrifice and insure themselves victory. Another of these extra barbarous devices takes place when a chief wishes to make war on his neighbor, by his calling in a magician to discover a propitious time for commencing. The doctor places a large earthen vessel, half full of water, over a fire, and over its mouth a grating of sticks, whereon he lays a small child and a fowl side by side, and covers them over with a second large earthen vessel, just like the first, only inverted, to keep the steam in, when he sets fire below, cooks for a certain period of time, and then looks to see if his

victims are still living or dead, when, should they be dead, the war must be deferred, but, other- wise, commenced at once."
- *Speke's Africa,* page 21.

"To prevent any evil approaching their dwellings, a squashed frog, or any other such absurdity, when placed on the back, is considered a specific."
— *Speke's Africa,* page 22.

"The king was surrounded by sorcerers, both men and women. These people were distinguished from others by witch-like chaplets of various dried roots worn upon the head; some of them had dried lizards, crocodiles' teeth, lions' claws and minute tortoise- shells, added to their collection of charms. They could have subscribed to the witches' caldron of Macbeth, "Eye of newt and toe of frog, Wool of bat and tongue of dog, Adder's fork and blind worm's sting, Lizard's leg and owlet's wing, - For a charm of powerful trouble, Like a hell-broth boil and bubble."
- *Baker's Great Basin of the Nile,* page 411.

"On the 21st of June, when I was quietly sitting in my house, one of the governor's servants, who was well disposed toward me, and who used to call occasionally, suddenly made his appearance with a very serious countenance, and, after some hesitation and a few introductory remarks, delivered a message from the governor to the following effect: He wanted to know from me whether it was true (as was rumored in the town, and as the people had told him) that, as soon as a thunder-storm was gathering, and when the clouds appeared in the sky, I went out of my house and made the clouds withdraw; for they had assured him that they had repeatedly

noticed that, as soon as I looked at the clouds with a certain air of command, they passed by with- out bringing a single drop of rain."
— *Barth's Africa, Vol. II.*, page 509.

"A tree in Kukiya was remarkable on account of a peculiar charm, which testified to the many remains of pagan rites still lingering in these countries. It consisted of two earthen pots, placed one upon the other, and filled with a peculiar substance, and was supposed to guarantee prolificness to the mares of the village."
— *Barth's Africa, Vol. II.*, page 427.

"In this part of Africa are a sort of screech-owls, which in the night make a very dismal noise, and are taken by the natives for witches. If one of these birds happens to come into a town at night, the people are all up firing at it; and as I do not find that they ever had the good fortune to shoot any of them, the poor creatures still continue in the opinion of their being witches."
-*Moore's Inland Parts of Africa*, page 107.

"Black magic is usually punished by the stake. In some parts of the country, the roadside shows, at every few miles, a heap or two of ashes, with a few calcined and blackened human bones mixed with bits of half-consumed charcoal, telling the tragedy that has been enacted there. The prospect cannot be contemplated without horror. Here and there, close to the larger circles where the father and mother have been burnt, a smaller heap shows that some wretched child has shared their terrible fate, lest, growing up, he should follow in his parents' path."
-*Burton's Africa*, page 92.

"With the aid of slavery and black magic, they render their subjects' lives as precarious as they well can; no one, especially in old age, is safe from being burned at a day's notice."
-*Burton's Africa*, page 96.

"The child who cuts the two upper incisors before the lower, is either put to death, or is given away, or sold to the slave-merchant, under the impression that it will bring disease, calamity, and death into the household."
— *Burton's Africa*, page 94.

"The principal instrument of the magician's craft is one of the dirty little gourds which he wears in a bunch round his waist, and the following is the usual programme when the oracle is to be consulted: The magician brings his implements in a bag of matting; his demeanor is serious as the occasion; he is carefully greased, and his head is adorned with the diminutive antelope- horns fastened by a thong of leather above the forehead. He sits like a sultan upon a dwarf of stool in front of the querist, and be- gins by exhorting the highest possible offertory. No pay, no predict. Divination by the gourd has already been described; the magician has many other implements of his craft. Some prophesy by the motion of berries swimming in a cup full of water, which is placed upon a low stool, surrounded by four tails of the zebra or the buffalo lashed to sticks planted upright in the ground. The kasanda is a system of folding triangles not unlike those upon which plaything soldiers are mounted. Held in the right hand, it is thrown out, and the direction of the end points to the safe and auspicious route. This is probably the rudest appliance of prestidigitation. The shero is a bit of wood about the size of a man's hand, and not unlike a pair of bellows, with a dwarf handle, a projection like a nozzle, and in the circular centre

a little hollow. This is filled with water, and a grain or fragment of wood, placed to float, gives an evil omen if it tends toward the sides, and favorable if it veers toward the handle of the nozzle."
- *Burton's Africa*, page 509.

"The natives of Bihe 'are, in many particulars, very superstitious. If, on setting out on a journey, a stag or goat crosses their path, or if even a stick falls across it, they return and have re- course to their diviners, to interpret this formidable omen. Having anointed themselves with some preparation of aromatic herbs and roots, which have for a certain period been buried under their beds, they consider that they may proceed on their journey with- out danger."
-*Valdez's Africa*, Vol. II., 330. page

"Some of their practices are most ridiculous. For instance, they will take the horn of a stag, and throwing into the cavity the claws of certain birds, some feathers, and roots, cover it with the skin of a monkey. Then, taking a large horn, they throw into it three smaller ones, extracted from fawns of a month old, and fill it with a particular kind of paste. When they desire a favor from any one of their idols they whistle into the horn, ignite some gun- powder which has been thrown into it, and then dance and sing. They also preserve the powder of a certain kind of wood, the heads of certain snakes, and the claws of certain birds, — all these being considered as antidotes against disease. These customs are observed by the chiefs themselves as lawful and necessary."
— *Valdez's Africa*, Vol. II., page 330.

"Superstition seems in these countries to have run wild, and every man believes what his fancy, by some accident, most forcibly presents to him as hurtful or beneficial."

— *Du Chaillu's Equatorial Africa,* page 383.

"If the African is once possessed with the belief that he is bewitched, his nature seems to change. He becomes suspicious of his dearest friends. The father dreads his children; the son his father and mother; the man his wife; and the wives their husband. He fancies himself sick, and really often becomes sick through his fears. By night he thinks himself surrounded with evil spirits. He covers himself with fetiches and charms; makes presents to the idol, and to Abambou and Mbuirri; and is full of wonderful and frightful dreams, which all point to the fact that the village is full of wicked sorcerers. Gradually the village itself becomes infected by his fears. The people grow suspicious. Chance turns their suspicions to some unlucky individual who is supposed to have a reason for a grudge. Finally the excitement becomes too high to be restrained; and often they do not even wait for a death, but begin at once the work of butchering those on whom public suspicion is fastened. At least seventy-five per cent. of the deaths in all the tribes are murders for supposed sorcery."
— *Du Chaillu's Equatorial Africa,* page 386.

"I noticed in the village of Yoongoolapay a custom or superstition which is common to all the tribes I have visited, and the reason, or supposed reason for which, I have never been able to persuade any one to tell me. On the first night when the new moon is visible, all is kept silent in the village; nobody speaks but in an under-tone; and in the course of the evening King Alapay came out of his house and danced along the street, his face and body painted in black, red, and white, and spotted all over with spots the size of a peach. In the dim moonlight he had a frightful appearance, which made me shudder at first. I asked him why he painted thus, but he only answered by pointing to the moon, without speaking a word."

- *Du Chaillu's Equatorial Africa*, page 141.

"Greegrees are generally worn about the neck or waist; are made of the skins of rare animals, of the claws of birds, the teeth of crocodiles or leopards, of the dried flesh and brains of animals, of the feathers of rare birds, of the ashes of certain kinds of wood, of the skin and bones of serpents, etc., etc. Every greegree has a special power. One protects from sickness; another makes the heart of the hunter or warrior brave; another gives success to the lover; another protects against sorcery; some cure sterility, and others make the mother's breast abound in milk for her babe. The charmed leopard's skin, worn about the warrior's middle, is supposed to render that worthy spear-proof; and, with an iron chain about his neck, no bullet can hit him. If the charm fails, his faith is none the less firm, for then it is plain that some potent and wicked sorcerer has worked a too powerful counter- spell, and to this he has fallen a victim."

— *Du Chaillu's Equatorial Africa*, page 385.

"Guessing the rascals had killed the poor old man, whom they denounced as a wizard, and turning my step toward the river, I was met by the crowd returning, every man armed with axe, knife, cutlass, or spear, and these weapons and their own hands, and arms, and bodies, all sprinkled with the blood of their victim. In their frenzy they had tied the poor wizard to a log near the river bank, and then deliberately hacked him into many pieces. They finished by splitting open his skull and scattering the brains in the water."

-*Du Chaillu's Equatorial Africa*, page 63.

"One of the hunters had shot a wild bull, and when the carcass was brought in, the good fellow sent me an abundant supply of the best portions. The meat is tough, but was most welcome for a change. I had a great piece boiled for dinner, and expected King Quengueza to eat as much as would make several hungry white men sick. Judge of my surprise, when, coming to the table and seeing only the meat, he refused to touch it. I asked why. It is roondah for me,' he replied. And then, in answer to my question, explained that the meat of the bos brachicheros was forbidden to his family, and was an abomination to them, for the reason that many generations ago one of their women gave birth to a calf instead of a child. I laughed, but the king replied very soberly that he could show me a woman of another family whose grandmother had given birth to a crocodile, for which reason the crocodile was roondah to that family. Quengueza would never touch my salt beef, nor even the pork, fearing lest it -had been in contact with the beef. Indeed they are all religiously scrupulous in this matter; and I found, on inquiry afterward, that scarce a man can be found to whom some article of food is not 'roondah.' Some dare not taste crocodile, some hippopotamus, some monkey, some boa, some wild pig, and all from this same belief. They will literally suffer the pangs of starvation rather than break through this prejudice; and they firmly believe that if one of a family should eat of such forbidden food, the women of the same family would surely miscarry, and give birth to monstrosities in the shape of the animal which is roondah, or else die of an awful disease."

-*Du Chaillu's Equatorial Africa*, page 355.

"When we stopped for breakfast next day, I noticed a little way from us an extraordinary tree, quite the largest in height and circumference I ever saw in Africa. It was a real monarch of even this great forest. It rose in one straight and majestic trunk, entirely branchless, till the top reached far above all the surrounding trees. There at the top the branches were spread out some- what like an umbrella, but could not give much shade, being so high. I found that this tree was highly venerated by the people, who call it the oloumi. Its kind is not common even here, where its home is said to be. Its bark are said to have certain healing properties, and is also in request from a belief that if a man going off on a trading expedition washes himself first all over in a de- coction of its juices in water, he will be lucky and shrewd in mak- ing bargains. For this reason great strips were torn off this tree to the height of at least twenty feet."

- *Du Chaillu's Equatorial Africa,* page 308.

"The morning before we set out, we accidentally stumbled across one of those acts of barbarism which chill the blood of a civilized man, though but slightly regarded by the negroes. I was hunting in the woods near the village, and saw sitting on a tree at some distance a pair of beautiful green pigeons, which I wanted much for my collection of birds. By dint of much exertion, I penetrated the jungle to the foot of the tree, and here a ghastly sight met my eyes. It was the corpse of a woman, young evidently, and with features once mild and good. She had been tied up here on some infernal accusation of witchcraft, and tortured. The torture consisted in lac- erations of the flesh all over the body, and in the cuts red peppers had been rubbed. This is a common mode of tormenting with these people, and as devilish in ingenuity as anything could well be.. Then the corpse was deserted. I could only hope the poor girl died of her wounds, and had not to wait for the slower process of agonized starvation to which such victims are left. Will the reader think hard of me that I felt it in my heart to go back to the village and shoot every man who had a hand in this monstrous barbarity?"

—*Du Chaillu's Equatorial Africa,* page 156.

7

Fetichism, Priestcraft, and Idolatry in Negroland

"WHEN the Congo priest appears in public he walks on his hands, with his body straight and his feet in the air. He can walk in this manner, through constant practice, with great ease and rapidity. He is the medicine-man or fetich-doctor, and is consulted in cases of sickness and witchcraft. To the cunning of this priest may easily be traced that superstition which I have de- scribed as prevalent in Equatorial Africa, that no one dies a natural death. If any one dies in spite of the medicines of the priest, he preserves his reputation by declaring that the patient has been bewitched, and obtains more money by discovering the sorcerer. There is still another priest, who officiates as rain-maker; for this, a knowledge of the seasons, which in Congo never vary more than a few days, is all that is required. The ceremony of rain- making is that of covering mounds with branches of trees and ornaments of fetich, and of walking round these, muttering incantations."

—*Reade's Savage Africa*, page 288.

"Idol worship in Africa confines the idolater to no particular idol; as he attributes his prosperity to the protecting care of his fetich, he will, as long as his prosperity continues, remain stead- fast to the worship of that particular fetich; but when difficulties arise, and he is beset with perplexities, he will range at will, as fancy directs him, to a thousand different objects, and make them the gods of his gross idolatry. The prosperous man is therefore confined in his worship to fewer idols and observances than the unfortunate. The former has faith in the power of his idol, while the latter cannot rest until he has found a relief from his troubles; and hence the multiplication of his idols and of his modes of worship."

— *Cruickshank's Africa*, Vol. II., page 132.

"When any calamity is general, such as a drought, a dearth, a pestilence, or want of success in war, the whole population or their representatives, with their chiefs and head men, repair to the chief boossum to make their offerings and sacrifice, and to seek, through the intercession of the priests, a mitigation and a release from their sufferings. These priests, aware of the necessity of making a deep impression upon such momentous occasions, sur- round the whole of their proceedings with a fearful secrecy and mysterious solemnity, calculated to awe the minds of the supplicants, and they deliver their oracles in such enigmatical language as may be capable of a double interpretation."

– *Cruickshank's Africa*, Vol. II., page 130.

"There is one peculiar form, which the fetich worship of a family about to be separated takes, which deserves to be recorded, as in it we have no external representation of an idol. In view of a separation which will most probably prevent them from ever again worshipping the boossum, to which they have made their devotions hitherto, they repair to the priest, or sofoo, and having explained their wants, he pounds up some fetich substance, and mixes it with water into a drink, which the whole family swallow together. While partaking of this strange communion, the priest declares to them that his boossum commands that none of this family shall ever after partake of such and such an article of food, naming, perhaps, fowl, mutton, beef, pork, eggs, milk, or any-thing which he may choose to mention at the time. The fetich edict once pronounced against a particular article of food under such circumstances, no one of the family ever tastes it more; and thus we find one who will not taste a bit of chicken, another an egg, a turkey, and so on; and this abstinence from a particular species of food descends to the children, who are under the necessity of observing a similar abstinence."
-*Cruickshank's Africa*, Vol. II., page 133.

"The Fans have a great reverence for charms and fetiches, and even the little children are covered with these talismans, duly consecrated by the doctor or greegree man of the tribe. They place especial value on charms which are supposed to have the power to protect their owner in battle. Chief among these is an iron chain, of which the links are an inch and a half long by an inch wide. This is worn over the left shoulder, and hanging down the right side. Besides this, and next to it in value, is a small bag, which is suspended round the neck or to the side of the warrior. This bag is make of the skin of some rare animal, and contains various fragments of others,

such as dried monkeys' tails, the bowels and claws of other beasts, shells, feathers of birds, and ashes of various beasts."
-Du Chailly's Equatorial Africa, page 128.

"Their religion, if it may be called so, is the same in all tribes. They all believe in the power of their idols, in charms, fetiches, and in evil and good spirits. Mahommedanism has not penetrated into this vast jungle. They all believe in witchcraft, which I think is more prevalent in the West than in the East, causing an untold amount of slaughter."
- Du Chaillu's Ashango-Land, page 428.

"Their fetiches consisted of fingers and tails of monkeys, of human hair, skin, teeth, bones; of clay, old nails, copper chains, shells, feathers, claws, and skulls of birds; pieces of iron, copper, or wood; seeds of plants; ashes of various substances; and I cannot tell what more. From the great variety and plenty of these objects on their persons, I suppose these Fan to be a very superstitious people."
- Du Chaillu's Equatorial Africa, page 93.

"This evening I went to see the village idol (the patron saint as it may be called), and to witness a great ceremony in the sacred house. As with the Aviia and other tribes, the idol was a monstrous and indecent representation of a female figure in wood. I had remarked that the further I travelled toward the interior, the coarser these wooden idols were, and the more roughly they were sculptured. This idol was kept at the end of a long, nar- row, and low hut, forty or fifty feet long, and ten feet broad, and was painted in red, white, and black colors. When I entered the hut it was full of Ashango people, ranged in order on each side, with lighted torches stuck in the ground before them. Amongst them were conspicuous two priests, dressed in clothes of vegeta- ble fibre, with their skins painted grotesquely in various colors, one side of the face red, the other white, and in the middle of the breast a broad yellow stripe; the circuit of the eye was also daubed with paint. These colors are made by boiling various kinds of wood, and mixing the decoction with clay. The rest of the Ashangos were also streaked and daubed with various colors, and, by the light of their torches, they looked like a troop of dev- ils assembled in the lower regions to celebrate some diabolical rite. Around their legs were bound white leaves from the heart of the palm-tree; some wore feathers, others had leaves twisted in the shape of horns behind their ears, and all had a bundle of palm-leaves in their hands."

-*Du Chaillu's Ashango-Land*, page 313.

"As we came away from Mouina's village, a witch-doctor, who had been sent for, arrived, and all Mouina's wives went forth into the fields that morning fasting. There they would be compelled to drink an infusion of a plant named 'goho,' which is used as an ordeal. This ceremony is called 'muavi,' and is performed in this way: When a man suspects that any of his wives has be- witched him, he sends for the witch-doctor; and all the wives go forth into the field, and remain fasting till that person has made an infusion of the plant. They all drink it, each one holding up her hand to heaven in attestation of her innocency. Those who vomit it are considered innocent, while those whom it purges are pronounced guilty, and put to death by burning."

- *Livingstone's Africa*, page 666.

"At different points in our course we came upon votive offerings to the Barimo. These usually consisted of food; and every deserted village still contained the idols and little sheds with pots of medicine

THE NEGROES IN NEGROLAND | 73

in them. One afternoon we passed a small frame house, with the head of an ox in it as an object of worship. The dreary uniformity of gloomy forests and open flats must have a depressing influence on the minds of the people. Some villages appear more superstitious than others, if we may judge from the greater number of idols they contain."

— *Livingstone's Africa,* page 503.

"We passed two small hamlets, surrounded by gardens of maize and manioc, and near each of these I observed, for the first time, an ugly idol, common in Londa, the figure of an animal, resembling an alligator, made of clay. It is formed of grass, plastered over with soft clay. Two cowrie-shells are inserted as eyes, and numbers of the bristles from the tail of an elephant are stuck in about the neck. It is called a lion, though, if one were not told so, he would conclude it to be an alligator. It stood in a shed, and the Balonda pray and beat drums before it all night in cases of sickness."

-*Livingstone's Africa,* page 304.

"I was disturbed this evening from my repose, on the dry sand, under the pale moonlight, by the most unearthly noises, coming from a group of our black servants. On getting up to see what it was, I found that one of our negresses, a wife of one of the servants, was performing Boree, the Devil,' and working herself up into the belief that his satanic majesty had possession of her. She threw herself upon the ground in all directions, and imitated the cries of various animals. Her actions were, however, some- what regulated by a man tapping upon a kettle with a piece of wood, beating time to her wild manœuvres. After some delay, believing herself now possessed, and capable of performing her work, she went forward to half a dozen of our servants, who were squatting down on their

hams, ready to receive her. She then took each by the head and neck, and pressed their heads between her legs, they sitting, she standing, not in the most decent way, and made over them, with her whole body, certain inelegant motions, not to be mentioned."
 - *Richardson's Africa,* Vol. I., page 286.

"At the back of our hut stands a fetich god, in a small thatched hut, supported by four wooden pillars, which is watched continually by two boys and a woman. We were desired to roast our bullock under him, that he might enjoy the savory smell of the smoking meat, some of which he might also be able to eat, if he desired. We were particularly enjoined to roast no yams under him, as they were considered by the natives too poor a diet to offer to their deity."
— *Lander's Travels in Africa,* Vol. II., page 163.

"This day a long and gay procession, formed by the female followers of the ancient religion of the country, passed through the town, walking and dancing alternately, with large-spreading branches of trees in their hands. The priestess, at the time we saw her, had just swallowed fetich water, and was carried on the shoulders of one of the devotees, who was assisted by two female companions, supporting the trembling hands and arms of their mistress. Her body was convulsed all over, and her features shockingly distorted, while she stared wildly and vacantly on the troop of enthusiasts and other objects which surrounded her. The priestess was then believed to be possessed with a demon. Indeed, to us they all appeared to be so, for not one of them seemed in their sober senses, so indescribably fantastic were their actions, and so unseemly did they deport themselves. A younger woman was likewise borne on the shoulders of a friend, and carried along in the same manner as her mistress; but she was by no means so uncouth a figure, nor was her agitation so great as that of the priestess, by whom she was preceded. The whole of the women forming this strange procession might amount to be tween ninety and a hundred. Their motions were regulated at times by the sound of drums and fifes, and to this music they joined their wild, shrill voices. They were arranged in couples, and, with the branches of trees shaking in the air, presented one of the most extraordinary and grotesque spectacles that the human mind can conceive."

-*Lander's Travels in Africa,* Vol. I., page 322.

"Immediately opposite to the first square, which forms the entrance to the chief's residence, stands a small tree, profusely decorated with human skulls and bones. This tree is considered by the people as fetich, or sacred; and is supposed to possess the virtue of preventing the evil spirit from entering the chief's residence. Near the tree stands the house which is inhabited by fetich priests, a class of beings certainly in the most savage condition of nature that it is possible to imagine. The fetich priests of Brass town chalked themselves from head to foot, besides dressing after a fashion of their own; but these fellows outdo them by far, and make themselves the most hideous and disgusting objects possible. Whether it may be with the idea of personifying the evil spirit they are so afraid of, I could not learn; but they go about the town with a human skull fastened over their face, so that they can see through the eye-holes; this is surmounted by a pair of bullock's horns; their body is covered with net, made of stained grass; and, to complete the whole and give them an appearance as ridiculous behind as they are hideous before, a bullock's tail protrudes through the dress and hangs down to the ground, rendering them altogether the most uncouth-looking beings imaginable. Sometimes a cocked-hat is substituted for the horns, and the skull of a dog or monkey used, which renders their appearance, if possible, still more grotesque. Thus equipped they are ready to perform the mysteries of their profession, which I had not sufficient opportunity to inquire into, but which are quite enough to enslave the minds of the people."

-*Lander's Travels in Africa*, Vol. II., page 318.

"Becoming obese by age and good living, Fundikira, Chief of the Unyannvezi, fell ill in the autumn of 1858, and, as usual, his relations were suspected of compassing his end by black magic. In these regions the death of one man causes many. The priest was summoned to apply the usual ordeal. After administering a mystic drug, he broke the neck of a fowl, and, splitting it into two lengths, inspected the interior. If blackness or blemish appear about the wings, it denotes the treachery of children, relations, and kinsmen; the backbone convicts the mother and grand- mother; the tail shows that the criminal is the wife, the thighs the concubines, and the injured shanks or feet the other slaves. Hav- ing fixed upon the class of the criminals, they are collected to- gether by the priest, who, after similarly dosing a second hen, throws her up into the air above the heads of the crowd, and singles out the person upon whom she alights. Confession is ex- torted by tying the thumb backward till it touches the wrist, or by some equally barbarous mode of question. The consequence of condemnation is certain and immediate death; the mode is chosen by the priest. Some are speared, others are beheaded or clubbed; a common way is to bind the cranium between two stiff pieces of wood, which are gradually tightened by cords till the brain bursts out from the sutures. For women they practise a peculiarly horrible kind of impalement. These atrocities continue until the chief recovers or dies, at the commencement of his attack, in one household eighteen souls, male and female, had

been destroyed; should his illness be protracted, scores will precede him to the grave, for the magician must surely die.".
-*Burton's Africa*, page 300.

"The Shangalla have but one language, and of a very guttural pronunciation. They worship various trees, serpents, the moon, planets, and stars in certain positions, which I never could so perfectly understand as to give any account of them. A star passing near the horns of the moon denotes the coming of an enemy. They have priests, or rather diviners; but it would seem that these are looked upon as servants of the evil being, rather than of the good. They prophesy bad events, and think they can afflict their enemies with sickness, even at a distance.".
-*Bruce's Travels*, Vol. II., page 554.

"At Whydah I found the natives addicted to a very grovelling species of idolatry. It was their belief that the good as well as the evil spirit existed in living iguanas. In the home of the man with whom I dwelt, several of these large lizards were constantly fed and cherished as gods; nor was any one allowed to interfere with their freedom, or to harm them even when they grew insufferably offensive. The death of one of these crawling deities is considered a calamity in the household, and grief for the reptile becomes as great as for a departed parent."
- *Canot's Twenty Years of an African Slaver*, page 266.

"When the King of Whydah, in 1694, heard that Smith, the chief of the English factory, was dangerously ill with fever, he sent his fetichman to aid in the recovery. The priest went to the sick man, and solemnly announced that he came to save him. He then marched to the white man's burial-ground with a provision of brandy, oil, and rice, and made a loud oration to those that slept there: 'O you dead white people, you wish to have Smith among you; but our king likes him, and it is not his will to let him go to be among you.' Passing on to the grave of Wyburn, the founder of the factory, he addressed him: You, captain of all the whites who are here! Smith's sickness is a piece of your work. You want his company, for he is a good man; but our king does not want to lose him, and you can't have him yet.' Then digging a hole over the grave, he poured into it the articles which he had brought, and told him that if he needed these things, he gave them with good-will, but he must not expect to get Smith. The factor died notwithstanding.".

-*Foote's Africa and the American Flag*, page 58.

"A musket among those tribes is an object of almost supernatural dread; individuals have been seen kneeling down before it, speaking to it in whispers, and addressing to it earnest supplications."

- *Murray's African Discoveries*, page 127.

"The purposes for which fetiches are used are almost without number. One guards against sickness, another against drought, and a third against the disasters of war. One is used to draw down rain, another secures good crops, and a third fills the sea and rivers with fishes, and makes them willing to be taken in the fishermen's net. Insanity is cured by fetiches, the sterility of women is removed, and there is scarcely a single evil incident to human life which may not be overcome by this means; the only condition annexed is that the right kind of fetich be employed. Some are intended to preserve life, others to destroy it. One in- spires a man with courage, makes him invulnerable in war, or paralyzes the energy of an adversary. They have also national fetiches to protect their towns from fire, pestilence, and from surprise by enemies. They have others to procure rain, to make fruitful seasons, and to cause abundance of game in their woods, and fish in their waters. Some of these are suspended along the highways, a larger number are kept under rude shanties at the entrances of their villages; but the most important and sacred are kept in a house in the centre of the village, where the high-priest lives and takes care of them. Most of these, and especially those at the entrances of their villages, are of the most uncouth forms, representing the heads of animals or human beings, and almost always with a formidable pair of horns. One of the first things which salutes the eyes of a stranger, after planting his feet upon the shores of Africa, is the symbols of this religion. He steps forth from the boat under a canopy of fetiches, not only as a security for his own safety, but as a guaranty that he does not carry the elements of mischief among the people; he finds them suspended along every path he walks; at every junction of two or more roads; at the crossing-place of every stream; at the base of every large rock or overgrown forest-tree; at the gate of every village; over the door of every house, and around the neck of every human being whom he meets. They are set up on their farms, tied around their fruit-trees, and are fastened to the necks of their sheep and goats to prevent them from being stolen. If a man trespasses upon the property of his neighbor, in defiance of the fetiches he has set up to protect it, he is confidently expected to suffer the penalty or his temerity at some time or other. If he is overtaken by a formidable malady or lingering sickness after- ward, even should it be after the lapse of twenty, thirty, or forty years, he is known to be suffering the consequence of his own rashness. "And not only are these fetiches regarded as having power to protect or punish men, but they are equally omnipotent to shield themselves from violence. White men are frequently challenged to test their invulnerability, by shooting at them; and if they are destroyed in this way (and this is a very common occurrence), the only admission is, that that particular fetich had no special virtues, or it would have defended itself."

— *Wilson's Africa*, page 212.

"On the Gold Coast there are stated occasions, when the people turn out *en masse* (generally at night) with clubs and torches, to drive away the evil spirits from their towns. At a given signal, the whole community start up, commence a most hideous howling, beat about in every nook and corner of their dwellings, then rush into the streets, with their torches and clubs, like so many frantic maniacs, beat the air, and scream at the top of their voices, until some one announces the departure of the spirits through some gate of the town, when they are pursued several miles into the woods, and warned not to come back. After this the people breathe easier, sleep more quietly, have better health, and the town is once more cheered by an abundance of food. Demoniacal possessions are common, and the feats performed by those who are supposed to be under such influence are certainly not un- like those described in the New Testament. Frantic gestures, convulsions, foaming at the mouth, feats of supernatural strength, furious ravings, bodily lacerations, gnashing of teeth, and other things of a similar character, may be witnessed in most of the cases which are supposed to be under diabolical influences."

- *Wilson's Africa*, page 217.

"On some parts of the Gold Coast the crocodile is sacred; a certain class of snakes, on the Slave Coast, and the shark at Bonny, are all regarded as sacred, and are worshipped, not on their own account, perhaps, but because they are regarded as the temples, or dwelling-places of spirits. Like every other object of the kind, however, in the course of time the thing signified is for- gotten in the

representative, and these various animals have long since been regarded with superstitious veneration, while little is thought of the indwelling spirit."
- *Wilson's Africa*, page 218.

"In the afternoon, nearly all the principal persons in the town were dressed in their gayest attire; a large group of them was collected under the fetich-tree, to see and hear the fetichman, while he made his orations, and danced to the sound of several drums which were played by females. The appearance of the fetichman was very much like that of a clown; his face was daubed with white clay; he had a large iron chain hanging around his neck, which seemed to be worn as a necklace; around his legs were tied bunches of fetich; and he held in his hand an immense knife, about fifteen inches long, and two and half broad. Some- times he danced with many frantic gestures; and at other times stood gazing around him with every indication of a vacant mind. While I was at a distance looking at him, he set out, and ran to a distance of about a hundred yards. Anxious to keep him in sight, I walked forward, past a small shed, which would have concealed him from me, and saw him standing with a musket at his shoulder, taking aim at a turkey-buzzard on a tree hard by."
— *Freeman's Africa*, page 26.

"Worship is not confined to any particular species of serpent, but is extended generally to all. A woman was seen one day worshipping a small serpent, and overheard praying to it the unique and selfish prayer, 'Give rain to my garden, let me have plenty; and let there be nobody in the world but you and me.' On meeting a serpent in the road, a woman will take off some of her beads and offer them as a present or sacrifice, in token of ven- eration. They are regarded as representing, in some way, their departed ancestors; and hence, one has been heard addressing a serpent, and saying, 'Ah, I see in your eyes my former chief.' These are additional facts which serve to illustrate the doctrine of the almost universal worship of serpents, one of the strangest anomalies in the religious history of mankind."

— *Freeman's Africa*, page 279.

"The chief objects of worship in Whydah are snakes and a large cottonwood-tree. There is a snake-house which I used to go often to see. The snakes are of the boa species, and are from five to fifteen feet in length. You can almost always see them crawling about the streets. When the natives see them they fall down and kiss the earth. They are perfectly harmless, as I have often seen the natives take them up and carry them back to the fetich-house. It is not at all unfrequent to find them on the mat alongside of you in the morning, as the huts are without doors. I had my lodging in what was once an English fort, but is now in ruins, and is a favorite resort of the snakes. I never found one in my room, but one morning, upon looking in the room adjoining mine, I found one almost seven feet long. The penalty for killing one is for a white person-the price of sixty slaves; for a native, he is shut up in a bamboo house, and then the house is set on fire. The poor fellow has the privilege of getting out if he can, and running for the lagoon, a distance of two miles, followed by the mob, and if he reaches the water he is free. But very few can ever avail themselves of this water cure. It is a great dodge with the fetich- man, if he knows that you are peculiarly averse to this kind of god, to bring them near your house and put them down, knowing they will enter, and he will be sent for to come and take them away, for which he gets a few strings of cowries."

— *West's African Correspondence of the Boston Post,* 1859.

"We passed along a narrow path some distance, till we came to two sticks, stuck up, one on each side of the path, with a small piece of white cotton rag on the top of each. The boys declared that it would be at the peril of my life if I proceeded any further in that direction, for this was the road to a fetich-house; and the fetichman had stuck up those sticks as a warning not to attempt to proceed any further. I pretended, however, not to comprehend their palaver, and walked on till I was some distance past the spot, when I looked round, and ordered them to come on; but they stood trembling, watching, expecting to see me drop down dead. After many assurances of the absurdity of such superstition, they were at last induced to follow me. Such is the infatuation of the people all along the West Coast, and, in fact, in most places I have yet visited in the interior."

-*Duncan's Africa,* Vol. I., page 174.

"The snake is also a fetich or idol here; and houses are built in several parts of the town for the accommodation of snakes, where they are regularly fed. These houses are about seven feet high in the walls, with conical roof, about eight feet diameter, and circular. The snakes are of the boa-constrictor tribe, and are considered quite harmless, although I have my doubts upon it. They generally leave this house at intervals; and, when found by any of the natives, are taken up and immediately conveyed back to the fetich-house, where they are placed on the top of the wall, under the thatch. It is disgusting to witness the homage paid to these reptiles by the natives. When one of them is picked up by any one, others will prostrate themselves as it is carried past, throwing dust on their heads, and begging to be rubbed over the body with the reptile."

— *Duncan's Africa,* Vol. I., page 126.

8

Rain-Doctors and Other Doctors in Negroland

"THE natives, finding it irksome to sit and wait until God gives them rain from heaven, entertain the more comfortable idea that they can help themselves by a variety of preparations, such as charcoal made of burned bats, inspissated renal deposit of the mountain cony, the internal parts of different animals, - jackals' livers, baboons' and lions' hearts, and hairy calculi from the bowels of cows, · serpents' skins and vertebræ, and every kind of tuber, bulb, root, and plant to be found in the country. Although you disbelieve their efficacy in charming the clouds to pour out their refreshing treasures, yet, conscious that civility is useful everywhere, you kindly state that you think they are mistaken as to their power. The rain-doctor selects a particular bulbous root, pounds it, and administers a cold infusion to a sheep, which, in five minutes afterward, expires in convulsions. Part of the same bulb is converted into smoke, and ascends toward the sky; rain follows in a day or two. The inference is obvious."

-*Livingstone's Africa*, page 24.

"The modes in which the rain-makers propitiate the clouds are various. The one most commonly practised is by collecting a few leaves of each individual variety of tree in the forest, which they allow to simmer in large pots over a slow fire, while a sheep is killed by pricking it in the heart with a long sewing-needle, while the rain-maker is employed in performing a variety of absurd incantations. The steam arising from the simmering leaves is sup- posed to reach and propitiate the clouds, and the remainder of the day is spent in dances, which are joined in by all the tribe, and kept up till midnight, being accompanied with songs having a long-continued chorus, in which all join, and the burden of which is the power and praises of the rain-maker; but the fields of young corn become parched and withered."

- *Cumming's Africa*, Vol. II., page 63.

"When the rain-makers fail to fulfil their promises, they always ascribe their want of success to the presence of some mysterious agency, which has destroyed the effect of their otherwise infallible nostrums. One of the anti-rain-making articles is ivory, which is believed to have great influence in driving away rain, in consequence of which, in the summer season, they produce it only as the sun goes down, at which time it is brought for the trader's inspection, carefully wrapped in a kaross. I remember on one occasion incurring the censure of a whole tribe, who firmly believed me to have frightened the rain from their dominions by exposing a quantity of ivory at noon-day; and, on another occasion, the chief of a certain tribe commanded a missionary, with whom I am acquainted, to

remove all the rafters from the roof of his house, these having been pointed out by the rain-maker as obstructing the success of his incantations.".
-*Cumming's Africa*, Vol. II., page 64.

"It occurred some time ago, while the Rev. Mr. Lemne was residing here, that a horse died at the village, at a time when rain was much wanted. Mr. Lemne very properly had the carcass of the animal dragged away to a great distance, to avoid the evils arising from its putrefaction in so hot a climate. This act became a matter of great consultation, and it was decided in some way that this dragging to a distance the remains of the dead horse prevented the rain coming; and the chief above named actually sent men, with leathern cords, to drag it again to the village, and there it was placed, at no great distance from Mr. Lemne's house, and left to decay!"
- *Freeman's Africa*, page 269.

"They are subject to a variety of diseases which baffle the skill of their medical advisers, who, in such cases, have recourse to smearing the patient with cow-dung, and keeping up his spirits with the constant excitement of dancing and singing within his hut."
-*Steedman's Africa*, Vol. I., page 267.

"The Kru candidate for medical honors is not subject to formal examination by a board of trustees, but is required to evince his proficiency in a different way. The head of a chicken is secretly deposited in one of a number of earthen jars provided for the occasion, and he is required to go and point out the one in which it is secreted. If he does this promptly, it is conclusive proof of his qualification to be a doctor, and is the occasion of unbounded exultation on the part of his friends. His head is then shorn, and the hair is carefully folded

up, and kept as an indispensable means of success, and is sometimes pawned as a security for his good behavior and faithful discharge of duty. The doc- tor's badge of office is a monkey's skin, which he carries in the form of a roll wherever he goes, and of which he is quite as proud as his white brother is of his sheep-skin diploma."
 - *Wilson's Africa,* page 134.

"When all ready for the trial, I went down to look at the Ouganga doctor, who looked literally like the devil. I never saw a more ghastly object. He had on a high head-dress of black feathers. His eyelids were painted red, and a red stripe, from the nose upward, divided his forehead in two parts. Another red stripe passed round his head. The face was painted white, and on each side of the mouth were two round red spots. About his neck hung a necklace of grass, and also a cord, which held a box against his breast. This little box is sacred, and contains spirits. A number of strips of leopard and other skins crossed his breast and were exposed about his person; and all these were charmed, and had charms attached to them. From each shoulder down to his hands was a white stripe; and one hand was painted quite white. To complete this horrible array, he wore a string of little bells around his body. "He sat on a box or stool, before which stood another box containing charms. On this stood a looking-glass, beside which lay a buffalo-horn containing some black powder, and said, in addition, to be the refuge of many spirits. He had a little basket of snake-bones, which he shook frequently during his incantations, as also several skins, to which little bells were attached. Near by stood a fellow beating a board with two sticks. All the people of the village gathered about this couple, who, after continuing their incantations for quite a while, at last came to the climax. Jombuai was told to call over the names of persons in the village, in order that the doctor might ascertain if any one of those named did the sorcery. As each name was called, the old cheat looked in the glass to see the result. During the whole operation, I stood near him, which seemed to trouble him greatly. At last, after all the names were called, the doctor declared that he could not find any witch-man,' but that an evil spirit dwelt in the village, and many of the people would die if they continued there."

-*Du Chaillu's Equatorial Africa*, page 282.

"A celebrated doctor had been sent for from a distance, and appeared in the morning, decked out in the most fantastic manner. Half his body was painted red and the other half white; his face was daubed with streaks of black, white, and red; and, of course, he wore around his neck a great quantity of fetiches. The villagers were assembled, and the doctor had commenced his divinations, when I arrived at the place, a witness once again of this gloomy ceremony, which was diffcrent from that of the Commi people seen formerly by me, as related in 'Adventures in Equatorial Africa.' The doctor counterfeited his voice when speaking, in order to impress on the people a due sense of his supernatural powers of divination; all the painting, dressing, and mummery have the same object in view, namely, to strike awe into the minds of the people. A black earthenware vessel filled with water, and surrounded by charmed ochre and fetiches, served the purpose of the looking-glass used by the coast tribes. The doctor, seated on his stool, looked intently and mysteriously into the water, shook his head, then looked into a lighted torch, which he waved over it, made contortions with his body, trying to look as ugly as he could, then repeated the mummer- ies over again, and concluded by pronouncing that the persons who were bewitch- ing the village were people belonging to the place."

-*Du Chaillu's Ashango-Land*, page 173.

"Whilst I am on the subject of native doctoring, I must relate what I saw afterwards in the course of Mayolo's illness. I knew the old chief had been regularly attended by a female doctor, and often wondered what she did to him. At length, one morning I happened to go into his house when she was administering her cures, and remained an interesting spectator to watch her operations. Mayolo was seated on a mat, submitting to all that was done with the utmost gravity and patience. Before him was extended the skin of a wild animal. The woman was engaged in rubbing his body all over with her hands, muttering all the while, in a low voice, words which I could not understand. Having continued this wholesome friction for some time, she took a piece of alumbi chalk and made with it a broad stripe along the middle of his chest and down each arm. This done, she chewed a quantity of some kind of roots and seeds, and, having well charged her mouth with saliva, spat upon him in different places, but aiming her heaviest shots at the parts most affected. Finally, she took a bunch of a particular kind of grass, which had been gathered when in bloom and was now dry, and, lighting it, touched with the flame the body of her patient in various places, beginning at the foot and gradually ascending to the head. I could perceive that Mayolo smarted with the pain of the burns, when the torch remained too long. When the flame was extinguished, the woman applied the burnt part of the torch to her patient's body, and so the operations ended."

— *Du Chaillu's Ashango-Land,* page 169.

9

Nakedness, Shamelessness, and Prostitution in Negroland

"CLOSE to the place where we stood, was a circle of naked savage women, all black as a coal, who were performing the oddest antics imaginable; and still nearer stood a wild-looking group of their male companions, resting on their tall spears and participating in the frolic with all their hearts. A three-cornered rush or straw hat, having a high peak, but without a brim, was the only article of dress worn by these men."
-*Lander's Travels in Africa*, Vol. I., page 307.

"The Shangalla of both sexes, while single, go entirely naked; the married men, indeed, have a very slender covering about their waist, and married women the same. Young men and young women, till long past the age of puberty, are totally uncovered, and in constant

conversation and habits with each other, in woods and solitudes, free from constraint, and without any punishment annexed to the transgression."
— *Bruce's Africa*, Vol. II., page 558.

"The natives came down to the boats. They are something superlative in the way of savages; the men as naked as they came into the world; their bodies rubbed with ashes, and their hair stained red by a plaster of ashes and cow's urine. These fellows are the most unearthly-looking devils I ever saw, - there is no other expression for them. The unmarried women are also entirely naked; the married have a fringe made of grass around their loins."
-*Baker's Great Basin of the Nile*, page 42.

"There is little difficulty in describing the toilet of the natives, —that of the men being simplified by the sole covering of the head, the body being entirely nude. It is curious to observe among these wild savages the consummate vanity displayed in their head-dresses. Every tribe has a distinct and unchanging fashion for dressing the hair; and so elaborate is the coiffure that hair- dressing is reduced to a science. European ladies would be startled at the fact, that to perfect the coiffure of a man requires a period of from eight to ten years."
-Baker's Great Basin of the Nile, page 42.

"Among the worst characteristics of Kaffir society, is its great incontinence. Most young women are frequently and forcibly violated before marriage; and widows are considered public property. When the chiefs wish to carry any particular point, they seize a number of young women, and give them up to their wild warriors. This I do not think has been noticed before in any account of the

Kaffirs; and, with wholesale and periodical rape,' constitutes a very black feature in their character. Adultery also is frequent among them; and the fine is merely a cow. The following I know to be a fact: A Kaffir coveted a handsome cow, or one with a musical voice, the property of his neighbor; he ordered his wife to throw herself in his neighbor's way; the guilty pair were detected; and the injured husband secured the object of his desires."
-*Alexander's Africa*, Vol. I., page 397.

"The women clothe themselves better than the Balonda, but the men go in puris naturalibus. They walk about without the smallest sense of shame. They have even lost the tradition of the 'fig-leaf.' I asked a fine, large-bodied old man if he did not think it would be better to adopt a little covering. He looked with a pitying leer, and laughed with surprise at my thinking him at all indecent; he evidently considered himself above such weak superstition. I told him that, on my return, I should have my family with me, and no one must come near us in that state. 'What shall we put on, we having no clothing? It was considered a good joke when I told them that, if they had nothing else, they must put on a bunch of grass."
- *Livingstone's Africa*, page 590.

"There is no difference between the sexes during their early years. A sense of shame or modesty seems altogether unknown or disregarded; nor is it unusual to find ten or a dozen of both genders huddled promiscuously beneath a roof whose walls are not more than fifteen feet square. True to his nature, a Vey bushman rises in the morning to swallow his rice, and crawls back to his mat, which is invariably placed in the sunshine, where he basks till noontide, when another wife serves him a second meal. The remainder of the daylight is passed either in gossip or a second siesta, till, at sundown,

his other wives wash his body, furnish a third meal, and stretch his wearied limbs before a blazing fire to refresh him for the toils of the succeeding day. In fact the slaves of a household, together with its females, form the entire working class of Africa."
— *Canot's Twenty Years of an African Slaver*, page 430.

"Women in Africa will frequently bathe in public, and before strangers, without the slightest shame. Young men erroneously suppose that there is something voluptuous in the ex- cessive dishabille of an equatorial girl. On the contrary, nothing is so moral and so repulsive as nakedness. Dress must have been the invention of some clever woman to ensnare the passions of men."
-*Reade's Savage Africa,* page 424.

"The women in all the tribes are much given to intrigue, and chastity is an unknown virtue."
—*Du Chaillu's Equatorial Africa*, page 382.

"Some of their customs are so obscene that even the record of them would be inadmissible here."
-*Valdez's Africa,* Vol. II., page 163.

"This freedom of the women I did not much relish, and desired my servants to ask them what they wanted. They replied that their object was to obtain a dram of rum, and offer themselves as wives, saying that every great man had a number of wives, and, knowing me to be a stranger with no wife, they supposed that of course I wanted a few."
-Duncan's Africa, Vol. I., page 172.

"The women of Inasamet not only made the first advances, but, what is worse, they were offered even by the men, their brethren or husbands. Even those among the men whose behavior was least vile and revolting did not cease urging us to engage with the women, who failed not to present themselves soon afterwards. It could scarcely be taken as a joke. Some of the women were immensely fat, particularly in the hinder regions."
- *Barth's Africa,* Vol. I., page 408.

"The chief just mentioned was in a certain degree subject to the rulers of Bornu; but it seemed rather an ironical assertion that this prince would be pleased with the arrival of the expedition. While describing his reception at the court of the chief, the scout indulged in a lively description of the customs prevalent among these people. His majesty, he said, used to indulge in amorous intercourse with his female slaves, of whom he had two hundred, before the eyes of his people, an account which was rather confirmed by Belal, who had been his host several times. Belal, who was a very jovial old fellow, also stated that this little prince was not jealous of the favors bestowed by his female partners upon his guests, but, on the contrary, that he himself voluntarily gave them up to them."
-*Barth's Africa,* Vol., II., page 216.

"The people in general are very libidinous, but their ability answers not their desire; however, their too frequent actions and their dealing with variety of women draw upon them no small inconveniences. Nor do the women fall short of the men in their unchastity, wholly giving themselves up to venereal exercises; and if continually troubled with a furor uterinus, at all times chew and eat such herbs and barks of trees as are the greatest incentives to heighten their desires to almost hourly congresses."

—*Ogilby's Africa*, page 390.

10

Drunkenness and Debauchery in Negroland

"THE large quantity of palm-trees in and around the village furnishes the inhabitants of Mokaba with a ready supply of their favorite drink, palm-wine; for, as I have said before, they are a merry people, and make a regular practice of getting drunk every day, as long as the wine is obtainable. I often saw them climb the trees in early morning, and take deep draughts from the calabashes suspended there. Like most drunken people they be- come quarrelsome; and being a lively and excitable race, many frays occur. Happily the palm-wine season lasts only a few months in the year; it was the height of the drunken season when I was at Mokaba. I saw very few men who had not scars, or the marks of one or more wounds, received in their merry- making scrimmages. Their holidays are very frequent. Un- limited drinking is the chief amusement, together with dancing, tam-tamming, and wild uproar, which last all night."

— *Du Chaillu's Ashango-Land,* page 260.

"The king, as usual, was drunk when I arrived. Indeed, he was too tipsy to stand on his legs; nevertheless, he was bullying and boasting in a loud tone of voice. I had not been in his place long before he ordered another calabash full of palm-wine, and drank off about a gallon of it. This finished him up for the day; he fell back into the arms of his loving wives, ejaculating many times, I am a big king! I am a big king!' The voice soon be- came inaudible, and he fell asleep."

— *Du Chaillu's Ashango-Land,* page 41.

"The king's usual way of living is to sleep all day, till toward sunset; then he gets up to drink, and goes to sleep again till mid- night; then he rises and eats, and if he has any strong liquors, will sit and drink till daylight, and then eat, and go to sleep again. When he is well stocked with liquor, he will sit and drink for five or six days together, and not eat one morsel of anything in all that time. It is to that insatiable thirst of his after brandy that his subjects' freedom and families are in so precarious a situation; for he very often goes with some of his troops by a town in the daytime, and returns in the night, and sets fire to three parts of it, and sets guards at the fourth to seize the people as they run out from the fire. He then ties their arms behind them, and marches them to the place where he sells them into slavery."

-Moore's Inland Parts of Africa, page 87.

"The virtue of chastity I do not believe to exist in Wawa. Even the widow Zuma lets out her female slaves for hire, like the rest of the people of the town. Neither is sobriety held as a virtue. I never was in a place in my life where drunkenness was so general.

Governor, priest, and layman, and even some of the ladies, drink to excess. I was pestered for three or four days by the governor's daughter, who used to come several times in a day, painted and bedizened in the highest style of Wawa fashion, but always half tipsy. I could only get rid of her by telling her that I prayed and looked at the stars all night, and never drank any- thing stronger than water. She always departed in a flood of tears.

- *Clapperton's Africa,* page 129.

11

Night Carousals, and Noisy and Nonsensical Actions in Negroland

"THE people usually show their joy and work off their excitement in dances and songs. The dance consists of the men standing nearly naked in a circle, with clubs or small battle-axes in their hands, and each roaring at the loudest pitch of his voice, while they simultaneously lift one leg, stamp heavily twice with it, then lift the other and give one stamp with that; this is the only movement in common. The arms and head are often thrown about, also, in every direction; and all this time the roaring is kept up with the utmost possible vigor; the continual stamping makes a cloud of dust ascend, and they leave a deep ring in the ground where they stood. If the same were witnessed in the lunatic asylum it would be nothing out of the way, and quite appropriate even, as a means of letting off the excessive excitement of the brain; but here gray-headed men joined

in the performance with as much zest as others whose youth might be an excuse for making the perspiration stream off their bodies with the exertion."
- *Livingstone's Africa,* page 245.

"The villagers, especially in the remoter districts, were even more troublesome, noisy, and inquisitive than the Wagogo. A 'notable passion of wonder' appeared in them. We felt like baited bears; we were mobbed in a moment, and scrutinized from every point of view by them. The inquisitive wretches stood on tiptoe; they squatted on their hams; they bent sideways; and they thrust forth their necks like hissing geese to vary the prospect."
-*Burton's Africa,* page 359.

"On the spot were the people assembled, with every instrument capable of making a noise which could be procured in the whole town. They had formed themselves into a large treble circle, and continued running round with amazing velocity, crying, shouting, and groaning with all their might. They tossed and flung their heads about, twisted their bodies into all manner of contortions, jumped into the air, stamped with their feet on the ground, and flourished their hands above their heads. No scene in the romance of Robinson Crusoe was so wild and savage as this. Little boys and girls were outside the ring, running to and fro, and clashing empty calabashes against each other; groups of men were blowing on trumpets, which produced a harsh and discordant sound; some were employed in beating old drums; others again were blowing on bullock's horns; and, in the short intervals between the rapid succession of all these fiend-like noises, was heard one more dismal than the rest, proceeding from an iron tube, accompanied by the clinking of chains, indeed, every. thing that could increase the uproar was put in requisition on this memorable occasion; nor did it cease till midnight. Never have we witnessed so extraordinary a scene as this. If a European, a stranger to Africa, were to be placed of a sudden in the midst of these people, he would imagine himself to be among a legion of demons, holding a revel over a fallen spirit, so peculiarly un- earthly, wild, and horrifying was the appearance of the dancing group, and the clamor which they made."

-*Lander's Travels in Africa*, Vol. I., page 366.

12

Inhospitality to Strangers, Begging, Extortion, and Robbery in Negroland

"GRATITUDE with the African is not even a sense of prospective favor. He looks upon a benefit as the weakness of his benefactor and his own strength; consequently he will not recognize even the hand that feeds him. He will, perhaps, lament for a night the death of a parent or a child, but the morrow will find him thoroughly comforted. The name of hospitality, except for interested motives, is unknown to him. 'What will you give me?' is his first question. To a stranger entering a village the worst hut is assigned, and, if he complain, the answer is that he can find encamping-ground outside. Instead of treating him like a guest, which the Arab Bedouin would hold to be a point of pride, of honor, his host compels him to pay and prepay every article ; otherwise he might starve in the midst of plenty."

- *Burton's Africa*, page 490.

"The curiosity of these people, and the little ceremony with which they gratify it, are, at times, most troublesome. stranger must be stared at; total apathy is the only remedy; if the victim lose his temper, or attempt to dislodge them, he will find it like disturbing a swarm of bees. They will come for miles to 'sow gape-seed.' If the tent-fly be closed, they will peer and peep from below, complaining loudly against the occupant; and, if further prevented, they may proceed to violence. On the road hosts of idlers, especially women, boys, and girls, will follow the caravan for hours. It is a truly offensive spectacle, these un- couth figures, running at a gymnastic pace,' half clothed, except with grease, with pendent bosoms shaking in the air, and cries that resemble the howls of beasts more than any effort of human articulation."

-*Burton's Africa*, page 496.

"To travellers, the African is, of course, less civil than to merchants, from whom he expects to gain something. He will refuse a mouthful of water out of his abundance to a man dying of thirst; utterly unsympathizing, he will not stretch out a hand to save another's goods, though worth thousands of dollars."

— *Burton's Africa*, page 491.

"The traveller cannot practise pity; he is ever in the dilemma of maltreating or being maltreated. Were he to deal civilly and liberally with this people, he would starve; it is vain to offer a price for even the necessarys of life; it would certainly be re- fused, because more is wanted, and so on beyond the bounds of possibility."

- *Burton's Africa,* page 88.

"The Wagogo are importunate beggars, who specify their long list of wants without stint or shame; their principal demand is tobacco, which does not grow in the land; and they resemble the Somal, who never sight a stranger without stretching out the hand for 'bori.' The men are idle and debauched, spending their days in unbroken revelry and drunkenness, while the girls and women hoe the fields, and the boys tend the flocks and herds."
— *Burton's Africa,* page 215.

"In proportion as the traveller advances into the interior, he finds the people less humane, or rather less human. The Wavinza, the Wajiji, and other lakist tribes, much resemble one another. They are extortionate, violent, and revengeful barbarians; no Muyamwezi dares to travel alone through their territories, and small parties are ever in danger of destruction."
-*Burton's Africa,* page 498.

"From the highest to the lowest, all classes are most pertinacious beggars. Whatsoever is seen is surely demanded, — guns, knives, scissors, beads, cloth, mirrors, and dollars. The love of acquiring property stifles every sense of shame; and no compunction is felt in asking for the cloak from off the back, or in carrying it away during a pitiless storm."
- *Harris's Adventures in Africa,* page 299.

"They are a people remarkable for their disregard for truth, wickedness which I regret to state I found very prevalent in Southern Africa. They are also great beggars, generally commencing by soliciting for 'trexels,' a trexel being a pound of tea or coffee.

Knowing the gallantry of our nation, they affirm this to be a present for a wife or daughter, whom they represent as being poorly. If this is granted, they continue their importunities, successively fancying your hat, neckcloth, and coat."

-*Cumming's Africa*, Vol. I., page 128.

"I was extremely anxious to get away from this place, as I was sorely pestered by begging parties, the inhabitants of Wuruo and Sokoto being the most troublesome beggars in the world."

-*Barth's Africa*, Vol. III., page 137.

"The people are in general faithless and very covetous, and they never make a present without expecting to receive three times as much in return."

-*Valdez's Africa*, Vol. II., page 208.

"I retired to my hut in disgust. This afternoon a messenger arrived from the king with twenty-four small pieces of straw, cut into lengths of about four inches. These he laid carefully in a row, and explained that Speke had given that number of presents, whereas I had only given ten, the latter figure being carefully exemplified by ten pieces of straw; he wished to know why I did not give him the same number as he had received from Speke.' This miserable, grasping, lying coward, is nevertheless a king, and the success of my expedition depends upon him."

-*Baker's Great Basin of the Nile*, page 313.

"True to his natural instincts, the king commenced begging, and being much struck with my Highland costume, he demanded it as a proof of friendship, saying, that if I refused I could not be his friend. My watch, compass, and double Fletcher rifle were asked for in their turn; all of which I refused to give him. He appeared much annoyed, therefore I presented him with a pound-canister of powder, a box of caps, and a few bullets. He replied, 'What's the use of the ammunition, if you won't give me your rifle ?' I explained that I had already given him a gun, and that he had a rifle of Speke's. Disgusted with his importunity, I rose to depart, telling him that I should not return to visit him, as I did not believe he was the real Kamrasi. I had heard that Kamrasi was a great king, but that he was a mere beggar, and was doubtless an impostor."

-*Baker's Great Basin of the Nile*, page 386.

"Nothing seems to us so incommensurable with the trouble, fatigue, and danger of African travel as the small success which usually rewards the explorer of this impenetrable continent. In other countries it has been said you ought to travel alone on foot, or as a grand seigneur, if you wish to understand the people or their customs. In Africa either method is impossible to any purpose. In its savage equatorial districts no European can travel alone; his necessary baggage calls for a small company of followers. He must trade and he must defend his goods. He cannot avoid arousing the cupidity of every tribe with which he comes in con- tact, and yet he must depend upon their good-will for his chance of seeing any other. Infinitely more strange to them than they can be to him, he is at once associated with any misfortune which has happened to them, either shortly before his arrival, during his stay with them, or following close upon his departure. He becomes the object of con- stant intrigues, and of unceasing, if simple efforts at extortion. How can it be otherwise? He carries about with him what, in the eyes of the savages by whom he is surrounded, is wealth greater than that in Aladdin's cave. Only by the rarest good fortune can he hope to escape from some contingency which will rob him not only of all

he possesses, but also of most of the tangible results of his labors, if not of his life."
-Westminster Review, 1867.

"When they can no longer ask, they begin to borrow, with the firm resolution of never repaying; and, what is worst of all, when they make a present, they hold it a deadly offence not to receive at least double the value in return."
-Murray's African Discoveries, page 69.

"In begging, the South Africans are most ceaseless and importunate. At Mr. Burchell's first entrance, they observed a certain degree of ceremony, and only one solitary cry for tobacco was heard; but this feeling of delicacy or decorum soon gave way. Mattivi himself made a private request that the presents intended for him should not be seen by the people at large, by whom they would soon be all begged away. They seemed to have more pride in what they procured by solicitation than in a thing of greater value if received as a spontaneous gift."
— *Murray's African Discoveries*, page 222.

"Tjopopa would spend whole days at our camp in the most absolute idleness and apathy, teasing us with begging for everything Like all Damaras, he had a perfect mania for tobacco, and considered no degradation too deep provided he could obtain a few inches of narcotic weed. . . . He was supposed to have no less than twenty wives, — two of whom, I found to my astonishment, were mother and daughter. I have since ascertained that it is by no means an unusual practice amongst this demoralized nation."
- *Andersson's Africa*, page 135.

"It often came about that our house was like a shop where there are customers in abundance, except that in our case they were customers who wished to have everything for nothing. One wanted a hatchet, another a garment, a third needles, a fourth a dollar, a fifth salt or pepper, a sixth physic; and so, in one day, we sometimes had fifteen or twenty applicants, all begging, and often after a very cunning fashion."
-*Krapf's Africa*, page 175.

"The chief now said something to his boys, and then retired out of sight. Immediately a dozen or more boys were in chase of an unfortunate rooster; every boy or girl who came up was pressed into service, so that soon nearly all the children of the town were engaged in the chase. Finally the rooster was captured, and taken to the chief, who now came forward and, with a low bow, presented it to me. We were now allowed to proceed. You may be sure, if you are acquainted with the African character, that the chief did not fail to pay me a visit soon after, when I had to make him a return present of four or five times the value of his fowl. Nor was this sufficient, but he must come four or five times, giving me to understand he wanted something."
-*Scott's Day Dawn in Africa*, page 108.

"Both men and women give themselves wholly up, as it were, to wantonness; and toward strangers they are churlish and uncivil, not only exacting from them beyond reason, but defrauding them by many subtle and sly inventions."
— *Ogilby's Africa*, page 521.

"I was about to take my leave, when the King of Bondou, desiring me to stop awhile, began a long preamble in favor of the whites, extolling their immense wealth and good dispositions. He next proceeded to an eulogium on my blue coat, of which the yellow buttons seemed particularly to catch his fancy; and he concluded by entreating me to present him with it, assuring me, for my consolation under the loss of it, that he would wear it on all public occasions, and inform every one who saw it of my great liberality toward him. The request of an African prince, in his own dominions, particularly when made to a stranger, comes little short of a command. It is only a way of obtaining by gentle means what he can, if he pleases, obtain by force; and, as it was against my interest to offend him by a refusal, I very quietly took off my coat, the only good one in my possession, and laid it at his feet."

- *Mungo Park's Travels in Africa*, page 44.

"Another drew his knife, and, seizing upon a metal button which remained upon my waistcoat, cut it off and put it in his pocket. Their intentions were now obvious, and I thought that the easier they were permitted to rob me of everything, the less I had to fear. I, therefore, allowed them to search my pockets without resistance, and examine every part of my apparel, which they did with the most scrupulous exactness. But observing that I had one waistcoat under another, they insisted that I should cast them both off; and at last, to make sure work, they stripped me quite naked. Even my half boots (though the sole of one of them was tied on to my foot with a broken bridle-rein) were minutely inspected. While they were examining the plunder, I begged them, with great earnestness, to return my pocket-compass; but when I pointed it out to them, as it was lying on the ground, one of them, thinking I was about to take it up, cocked his musket, and swore that he would lay me dead on the spot if I presumed to put a hand upon it. After this, some of them went away with my horse, and the remainder stood considering whether they should leave me quite naked, or allow me something to shelter me from the sun. They returned me the worst of the two shirts and a pair of trousers; and, as they went away, one of them threw back my hat, in the crown of which I kept my memorandums; and this was probably the reason he did not wish to keep it. After they were gone, I sat for some time looking around me with amazement and terror. Whichever way I turned, nothing appeared but danger and difficulty. I saw myself in the midst of a vast wilderness, in the depth of the rainy season, naked and alone, surrounded by savage animals, and men still more savage. I was five hundred miles from the nearest European settlement. All these circumstances crowded at once on my recollection, and I confess that my spirits began to fail me. I considered my fate as certain, and that I had no alternative but to lie down and perish."

— *Mungo Park's Travels in Africa*, page 113.

13

Wrangling, Lawlessness, Penury, and Misery in Negroland

"AFRICA from the earliest ages has been the most conspicuous theatre of crime and of wrong; where social life has lost the traces of primitive simplicity, without rising to order, principle, or refinement; where fraud and violence are formed into national systems, and man trembles at the sight of his fellow-man. For centuries this continent has seen thousands of her unfortunate children dragged in chains over its deserts and across the ocean, to spend their lives in foreign and distant bondage. Superstition, tyranny, anarchy, and the opposing interests of numberless petty states, maintain a constant and destructive warfare in this suffering portion of the earth."
— *Murray's African Discoveries,* page 21.

"Grumbling and dissatisfied, they never do business without a grievance. Revenge is a ruling passion, as the many rancorous fratricidal wars that have prevailed between kindred clans, even for a generation, prove. Retaliation and vengeance are, in fact, their great agents of moral control. Judged by the test of death, the East African is a hard-hearted man, who seems to ignore all the charities of father, son, and brother. Their squabbling and clamor pass description; they are never happy except when in dispute. After a rapid plunge into excitement, the brawlers alternately advance and recede, pointing the finger of threat, howling and screaming, cursing and using terms of insult which an inferior ingenuity, — not want of will, - --- causes to fall far short of the Asiatic's model vituperation. After abusing each other to their full, both parties usually burst into a loud laugh or a burst of sobs. After a cuff, a man will cover his face with his hands and cry as if his heart would break."
— *Burton's Africa*, page 492.

"The children have all the frowning and unprepossessing look of their parents; they reject little civilities, and seem to spend life in disputes, biting and clawing like wild-cats. There appears to be little family affection in this undemonstrative race."
-*Burton's Africa*, page 323.

"Property among them is insecure; a man has always a vested right in his sister's children, and when he dies his brothers and relations carefully plunder his widow and orphans."
-*Burton's Africa*, page 97.

"All the natives, escorts, guides, carriers, slaves, and villagers, are as bad as bad can be; idle, cowardly, thievish, full of every kind of trick and deception. Your own hired people are insubordinate, quarrelsome, and ready to desert at a moment's notice. They stop when they please, hurry on when you wish them to go slow, and creep when you want them to hasten, always grumbling, and getting drunk whenever they can."

— *Maebrair's Africa*, page 352.

"The Bushman, who has lost his wife by elopement, walks out with his gun and shoots the first man whom he meets. He then proclaims that he has done this because a man has run away with his wife. The clansmen of the murdered man are enraged, not against the husband, who has simply complied with a usage of society, but because the duty of the avenger is now cast upon them. As the gay Lothario is out of their reach, they kill a man belonging to the next village; his friends retaliate on their unsuspecting neighbors; and so rolls on this ball of destruction till the whole country is on the alert. The gates of all the villages are closed and barricaded, and some luckless clan can gain no opportunity of washing out their wrong in somebody's else blood. The chief of that clan then summons a council, and puts forward his claim against the man who has run away with the wife. The husband has no longer anything to do with the matter. The chief of the culprit's clan offers pecuniary compensation, and general concord is restored.

-*Reade's Savage Africa*, page 217.

"Everything that comes in their way, which they cannot appropriate on the spot to their own use, is destroyed, that it may not be of advantage to others. If they discover an ostrich's nest, and circumstances do not permit their continuing on the spot till all they find there is consumed, they eat as much as they can, but the rest of the eggs are destroyed. Do they meet a large flock of springboks, they wound as many as possible, although six or eight are sufficient to last them several days; the rest are left to die, and rot on the ground."

-*Lichtenstein's Africa,* Vol. II., page 50.

"On attacking a place, it is the custom of the country instantly to fire it; and as they are all composed of straw huts only, the whole is shortly devoured by the flames. The unfortunate inhabitants fly quickly from the destructive element, and fall immediately into the hands of their no less merciless enemies, who surround the place; the men are quickly massacred, and the women and children lashed together, and made slaves."

— *Denham and Clapperton's Africa,* Vol. II., page 120.

"In the whole district of Taganama, where so many different nationalities border close together, the greatest insecurity reigns, and the inhabitants of one town cannot safely trust themselves to those of a neighboring place without fear of being sold as slaves, or at least of being despoiled of the little they have."

- *Barth's Africa,* Vol. I., page 548.

"With the acquisition of their liberty the people of Pundi soon lost the little sense of right and wrong which they once had; and, having no leader for whom they cared, and no law which they obeyed, they threw off all manner of restraint, and, from robbing each other, they turned to plundering the property of their neighbors, and waylaying every unprotected stranger or traveller that had occasion to pass through their country. The same unruly, outrageous, and turbulent spirit, and desperate conduct prevail among the natives of Pundi to the present time, and similar acts of rapacity and violence are consummated by them every day, so that their country is dreaded and shunned by every one acquainted with their character and habits."

— *Lander's Travels in Africa*, Vol. I., page 335.

"Like the natives of Yarriba, the inhabitants of Layaba appear to bestow scarcely a moment's reflection either on public misery or individual distress, upon their own misfortunes or the calamities of their neighbors. Nature has moulded their minds to enjoy the life they lead; their grief, if they grieve at all, is but for a moment; sorrow comes over them and vanishes like the lightning's flash; they weep, and, in the same breath, their spirits re-gain their elasticity and cheerfulness; they may well be said to drink of the waters of Lethe whenever they please. As long as they have food to eat, and health to enjoy their frivolous pastimes, they seem contented, happy, and full of life. They think of little else. "Thought would destroy their paradise.""

- *Lander's Travels in Africa*, Vol. II., page 40.

"There are instances of parents throwing their tender offspring to the hungry lion, who stands roaring before their cavern, refusing to depart till some peace-offering be made to him. In general their children cease to be the objects of a mother's care as soon as they are able to crawl about in the field."

- *Kicherer, quoted in Moffat's Africa*, page 49.

"On our return we saw a child, about eight years old, standing in the middle of the street weeping, and, being almost a skeleton, it attracted our attention. We inquired respecting its disease; when the women told us, the child was well enough, and that want of food had brought it into that state, that the father and mother were poor, that he had gone away with another woman, and was hunting in the south; that the mother was gone to the westward, searching for food. Neither the men, women, nor children present seemed by their countenances to express the least sympathy or feeling for this forsaken, starving child. They said, laughing, that we might take the child with us if we pleased. I am certain that the sight of this little girl in the streets of Lon- don would have excited pity in the hearts of thousands. We took the child to our wagons, desiring the people to inform its mother, when she returned, where she might find her. When some meat was given to the child, she devoured it with the voracity of a tiger."

-*Campbell's Africa*, page 266.

"I thanked God that I was not a native African. These poor people lead dreadful and dreary lives. Not only have they to fear their enemies among neighboring tribes, as well as the various acci- dents to which a savage life is especially liable, such as starvation, the attacks of wild beasts, etc., but their whole lives are saddened and embittered by the fears of evil spirits, witchcraft, and other kindred superstitions under which they labor."

— Du Chaillu's *Equatorial Africa*, page 102.

"The chief's daughter was the best-looking girl that I have seen among the blacks; she was about sixteen. Her clothing consisted of a piece of dressed hide, about a foot wide, slung across her shoulders, all other parts being exposed. All the girls of this country wear merely a circlet of little iron jingling orna- ments around their waists. They came in numbers, bringing small bundles of wood to exchange for a few handfuls of corn. Most of the men are tall, but wretchedly thin; the children are mere skeletons, and the entire tribe appears thoroughly starved."

- Baker's *Great Basin of the Nile*, page 48.

"The people of the Kytch tribe are mere apes, trusting entirely to the productions of nature for their subsistence; they will spend hours in digging out field-mice from their burrows, as we should for rabbits. They are the most pitiable set of savages that can be imagined; so emaciated, that they have no visible posteriors; they look as though they had been planed off, and their long, thin legs and arms give them a peculiar gnat-like appearance. At night they crouch close to the fires, lying in the smoke to escape the clouds of mosquitoes. At this season the country is a vast swamp, the only dry spots being the white ant-hills; in such places the natives herd like wild animals, simply rubbing them- selves with wood ashes to keep out the cold. So miserable are the natives of this tribe, that they devour both skins and bones of all dead animals; the bones are pounded between stones, and when reduced to powder they are boiled to a kind of porridge; nothing is left even for a fly to feed upon, when an animal either dies a natural death, or is killed."

-*Baker's Great Basin of the Nile,* page 49.

14

Theft as a Fine Art Among the Africans

"SHOW me a black man, and I will show you a thief."
— *Hutchinson's Western Africa*, Vol. II., page 280.

"We found the people thieves to a man."
-*Mungo Park's 2d Journal*, page 201.

"The most prominent defect in their character was that insurmountable propensity, which the reader must have observed to prevail in all classes of them, to steal from me the property of which I was possessed.".
-*Mungo Park's 1st Journal*, page 193.

"The Africans are all of them thieves. They have no sense of honor in that respect. I have never yet had a negro servant (and I have had a great many) who did not rob me of some trifling article, whether he was pagan or Christian. The Africans tell a lie more readily than they tell the truth. Falsehood, like petty larceny, is not recognized among them as a fault."

- *Reade's Savage Africa,* page 447.

"The ladies of the principal persons of the country visited me, accompanied by one or more female slaves. They examined everything, even to the pockets of my trousers; and more inquisitive ladies I never saw in any country; they begged for every- thing, and nearly all attempted to steal something; when found out, they only laughed heartily, clapped their hands, together, and exclaimed, Why, how sharp he is! Only think! Why, he caught us!"

- *Denham's Africa,* Vol. III., page 24.

"The thievish propensities of the people of Logon are very remarkable, and the first intimation which I received of it was an official caution given to me to beware of the slaves of my house."

-*Barth's Africa,* Vol. II., page 444.

"From the king to the slave, theft is a prevailing vice with the Bechuanas; and, from what I have seen of them, I am confident that the wealthiest and the most exalted amongst them would not hesitate to steal the shirt off one's back, could he effect it without being compromised. Their pilfering habits know no bounds; and they carry on the game with much dexterity. When grouped about our camp fires, I have known them to abstract the tools with which we have been working; nay, indeed, the very knives and forks from our plates. Once, they actually took the meat out of the pot, as it was boiling on the fire, substituting a stone. They will place their feet over any small article lying on the ground, burying it in the sand with their toes; and, if unable to carry it away at the time, they return to fetch it at a more convenient period."

-*Andersson's Africa,* page 372.

"Polygamy is here unlimited, and depravity of every description to an extraordinary extent. The longer I reside here, the more am I convinced, however, that the most predominant passion of the African is theft. The more they are taught, the more accomplished rogues they become."

— *Duncan's Africa,* Vol. I., page 141.

"Another innate quality they have is to steal anything they can lay their hands upon, especially from foreigners, and among themselves; then make boast thereof, as an ingenious piece of subtlety; and so generally runs this vicious humor through the whole race of blacks, that great and rich merchants do sometimes practise small filching; for being come to the trading ships they are not at rest till they have taken away something, though it be but nails, or lead; which no sooner done, than with a singular slight of hand they convey it from one to another; but if they chance to be trapped, they all leap instantly overboard for fear of a beating; but if caught, and soundly bastinadoed, then, as past doubt of other punishment, they never avoid the ship, but come again the next day as usual to trade."

— *Ogilby's Africa,* page 452.

"The men naturally incline to cheating and thieving, but not so much among themselves as toward strangers, to whom they are also bloody, barbarous, and unnatural."

-*Ogilby's Africa,* page 486.

"The people of the Grain Coast are very envious of all strangers, and steal from them whatever they can lay their hands on; so that it behooves all dealers to have a circumspect eye over their goods; and, in some places, they must be careful of themselves, for, being cannibals, they eat whomsoever they can get into their power."
- *Ogilby's Africa*, page 415.

'I witnessed to-day a striking instance of the inborn cunning and deceit of the native African. My people had spread out on mats, in front of my hut, a quantity of ground-nuts which we had bought, when I observed from the inside of the hut a little urchin, about four years old, slyly regaling himself with them, keeping his eyes on me, and believing himself unnoticed. I suddenly came out; but the little rascal, as quick as thought, seated him-self on a piece of wood, and dexterously concealed the nuts he had in his hand under the joints of his legs and in the folds of his abdominal skin; then looked up to me with an air of perfect innocence. This, thought I, is a bright example of the unsophisticated children of nature, whom some writers love to describe, to the disadvantage of the corrupted children of civilization! Thieving, in these savage countries, is not considered an offence against the community; for no one complains but he who has been robbed. My precocious little pilferer would, therefore, have no teaching to prevent him from becoming an accomplished thief as he grew older."
—Du Chaillu's *Ashango-Land*, page 190.

15

Lying as an Accomplishment Among the Africans

"THE truth is not in them, and to be detected in a lie is not the smallest disgrace; it only causes a laugh."
— *Clapperton's Africa,* page 184.

"Almost every African is guilty of gross exaggeration in his statements, and too many of them are confirmed liars."
-*Lander's Travels in Africa,* Vol. I., page 375.

"Lying is thought an enviable accomplishment among all the tribes, and a more thorough and unhesitating liar than one of these negroes is not to be found anywhere."
— *Du Chaillu's Equatorial Africa,* page 437.

"Lying being more familiar to their constitution than truth-saying, they are forever concocting dodges with the view, which they glory in, of successfully cheating people."

- *Speke's Africa,* page 28.

"They little esteem any promises made to foreigners, but break them if they can see any advantage in it; in brief, they are a treacherous, perjured, subtle, and false people, only showing friendship to those they have most need of."

— *Ogilby's Africa,* page 452.

16

Duplicity and Venality of the Negroes in Negroland

"It seems it was a custom in this country (and not yet entirely repealed) that whatever commodity a man sells in the morning, he may, if he repents his bargain, go and have the things returned to him again, on his paying back the money any time before the setting of the sun the same day; and this custom is still in force very high up the river, but here below it is at present pretty well worn out. However, I shall here give an account how a gentleman, who had the honor of being at the head of the company's affairs here, was served at this very town of Nackway. Not above twelve years ago, he went up in a sloop on a trading voyage to Nackway, where he got a hut built, and took his goods ashore to trade with. It happened that one morning a man brought a cow to sell to him, which he bought for an iron barr. Soon after he bought it, he cut the cow's tail off, which being carried to the ears of the fellow that sold the cow, he resolved to make a handle of it, in order to extort money from the governor. Accordingly, about noon the same day, he came to the port of Nackway, in a seeming good-humor, and a great number of people with him, with a plausible story, that, as he was going the next day to marry one of his daughters to a young man for whom he had a great regard, and had nothing to make him a present of, he therefore had thought better of it, and was not willing to sell his cow, as he intended, and so desired he might have it re- turned to him. The governor, not dreaming of the plot, immediately ordered one of his servants to bring the cow, and return it to the person who brought it. Accordingly, the cow was produced, at which the fellow seemed surprised, and told the governor that that was not his cow. The governor told him it was. 'How can that be?' says he; 'my cow had a tail on when I brought her to you this morning.' It is very true,' quoth the governor; when I bought her, she had a tail; but, when I had paid for her, I cut the tail off.' 'How,' says the fellow, 'durst you have the assurance to cut off my cow's tail without my leave? I value the cow and her tail at three hundred barrs, and that sum you shall pay me before you stir from this place.' The governor was very much out of humor, and endeavored to prove that after he had paid for the cow she belonged to him; but it was all to no purpose, for every one present gave it against him (expecting to come in for a snack of the money), and so he was obliged to go to his store and pay the fellow three hundred barrs for only docking the cow's tail."

-*Moore's Inland Parts of Africa*, page 122.

"In morality, according to the more extended sense of the word, the East African is markedly deficient. He has no benevolence, but little veneration (the negro race is ever irreverent), and, though his cranium rises high in the region of firmness, his futility prevents his being firm. The outlines of law are faintly traced upon his heart.

The authoritative standard of morality, fixed by a revelation, is in him represented by a vague and varying custom, derived traditionally from his ancestors; he follows in their track for old sake's sake. The accusing conscience is unknown to him. His only fear, after committing a treacherous murder, is that of being haunted by the angry ghost of the dead; he robs as one doing a good deed, and he begs as if it were his calling. His depravity is of the grossest; intrigue fills up all the moments not devoted to intoxication."

— *Burton's Africa*, page 496.

"The queen has slandered and defamed the character of her brother to us most shamefully. In more civilized or rather more polished countries, among the reasonable part of mankind, a mutual interchange of benevolent intentions produces a reciprocity of kind feeling; and we would hope that the present of yams from her brother would excite the queen's more generous and affectionate sentiments for him. Yet this despicable vice of slander is universal in Africa; the people all speak ill of each other, from the monarch to the slave."

— *Lander's Travels in Africa*, Vol. I., page 343.

17

Revolting Voracity and Gluttony of the Negroes in Negroland

"HUNGER compels them to feed on everything edible. Ixias, wild garlic, mysembryanthemums, the core of aloes, gum of acacias, and several other plants and berries, some of which are extremely unwholesome, constitute their fruits of the field; while almost every kind of living creature is eagerly devoured, lizards, locusts, and grasshoppers not excepted. The poisonous, as well as innoxious serpents they roast and eat. They cut off the head of the former, which they dissect, and carefully extract the bags, or reservoirs of poison, which communicate with the fangs of the upper jaw. They mingle it with the milky juice of the euphorbia, or with that of a poisonous bulb. After simmering for some time on a slow fire, it acquires the consistency of wax, with which they cover the points of their arrows."

— Moffat's Africa, page 47.

"Every animal is entrapped and eaten. Gins or snares are seen on both sides of the path, every ten or fifteen yards, for miles together. The time and labor required to dig up moles and mice from their burrows would, if applied to cultivation, afford food for any amount of fowls or swine; but the latter are seldom met with."
-*Livingstone's Africa,* page 490.

"When a horde has taken anything in the chase, or by plunder, it is concealed as much as possible from all the others; since whoever learns that there is something to be eaten, comes without any ceremony, or waiting for an invitation to partake of it. As everything is common property, the booty cannot be withheld, or a part of it at least, from any one who requires it. Thence the incredible voracity with which they immediately devour whatever they catch in the chase."
— *Lichtenstein's Africa,* Vol. II., page 50.

"The Bagos are great eaters, and their diet principally consists of dry fish, swimming in palm oil, which renders it so disgusting that a European could not touch it. When they kill a sheep, they mix the skin and entrails, unwashed, with the stews which they make; they also eat snakes, lizards, and monkeys."
— *Caillie's Africa,* Vol. I., page 166.

"The Kaffirs eat like ogres, but at a pinch they can easily go three days without food. I once saw a clever mischievous Kaffir lad, named April, hide inside an elephant we had shot that day. He caught two vultures by the legs as they were tearing away at the carcass, pulled the first inside, and shoved him forward into the vacant space where the Masaras had taken out the elephant's heart, and then proceeded to capture his mate."

  -*Baldwin's Africa*, page 306.

"Hosts of savages by whom we were attended quickly cleared away the carcasses of the game we slew, and then quarrelled for the entrails. I hope the reader has understood that these barbarians generally devour the meat raw, although when at leisure they do not object to its being cooked. They usually seize a piece of flesh by the teeth, cutting a large mouthful of it with a knife close to the lips, before masticating it, which they do with a loud sput- ter and noise. The meal being finished they never fail to wipe their hands on their bodies, and then being generally gorged they lay themselves down to repose."

  —*Harris's Expedition into Southern Africa*, page 150.

18

Dislike of their Own Color by the Negroes in Negroland

"THE whole of the colored tribes consider that beauty and fairness are associated, and women long for children of light color so much, that they sometimes chew the bark of a certain tree, in hopes of producing that effect. To my eye the dark color is much more agreeable than the tawny hue of the half-caste, which that of the Makoloto ladies closely resembles. The women generally escape the fever, but they are less fruitful than formerly; and to their complaint of being undervalued on account of the disproportion of the sexes, they now add their regrets at the want of children, of whom they are all excessively fond."

— *Livingstone's Africa*, page 204.

"Katema, the ruler of the village, asked if I could not make a dress for him like the one I wore, so that he might appear as a white man when any stranger visited him."
— *Livingstone's Africa*, page 517.

"The people under Bango are divided into a number of classes. There are his councillors, as the highest, who are generally head men of several villages, and the carriers, the lowest freemen. One class above the last obtains the privilege of wearing shoes from the chief by paying for it; another, the soldiers or militia, pay for the privilege of serving, the advantage being that they are not afterward liable to be made carriers. They are also divided into gentlemen and little gentlemen, and, though quite black, speak of themselves as white men, and of others who may not wear shoes, as 'blacks.' The men of all these classes trust to their wives for food, and spend most of their time in drinking the palm-toddy."
-*Livingstone's Africa*, page 445.

"The negro feels that, in energy of character, in scope of understanding, in the exercise of mechanical skill, and in the practice of all the useful acts of life, he is hopelessly distanced by the white man."
- *Wilson's Africa*, page 343. 99

"The whole court, which was large, was filled, crowded, crammed with people, except a space in front, where we sat, into which his highness led Mr. Houston and myself, one in each hand; and there we performed an African dance, to the great delight of the surrounding multitude. The tout ensemble would doubtless have formed an excellent subject for a caricaturist, and we regretted the absence of Captain Pearce, to sketch off the old black caboceer, sailing majestically around in his damask robe, with a train-bearer behind him, and every now and then turning up his old, withered face, first to myself, then to Mr. Houston; then whisking round on one foot; then marching slowly, with solemn gait; twining our hands in his, —proud that a white man should dance with him."

- *Clapperton's Africa,* Vol. IV., page 199.

"Zuma, a rich widow of Wava, the owner of a thousand slaves, told me that her husband had been dead these ten years; that she had only one son, and he was darker than herself; that she loved white men, and would go to Boussa with me."

- *Clapperton's Africa,* Vol. IV., page 222.

"The Foulahs evidently consider all the negro natives as their inferiors; and, when talking of different nations, always rank themselves among the white people."

— *Mungo Park's Travels in Africa,* page 23.

"Observing the improved state of our manufactures, and our manifest superiority in the arts of civilized life, Harfa, the intelligent negro merchant, would sometimes appear pensive, and ex- claim, with an involuntary sigh, Fato fing inta feng,' — black men are good for nothing."

— *Mungo Park's 1st Journal,* page 259.

"The women are well disposed toward strangers of fair complexion, apparently with the permission of their husbands."

-*Burton's Africa,* page 216.

"The Kaffirs believe that white men can do anything.".

-*Baldwin's Africa,* page 266.

"The negro Mohammedans worship God under the name of Allah; they acknowledge Mohammed as a prophet, but do not pay him divine honors; they have, some traditions respecting Jesus Christ, whom they call Nale, the son of Malek, and whom they speak of as a great prophet, who had wrought wondrous miracles. They denounce as impious the doctrine that God could have carnal conversation with a woman, but have a prophecy of their own that some day they shall be all subdued by a white people."
-*Reade's Savage Africa*, page 354.

"The European stranger, travelling in their country, is expected to patronize their wives and daughters; and they feel hurt, as if dishonored, by his refusing to gratify them. The custom is very prevalent along this coast. At Gaboon, perhaps it reaches the acme; there a man will in one breath offer the choice between his wife, sister, and daughter. The women of course do as they are bid by the men, and they consider all familiarity with a white man a high honor."
— *Hutchinson's Western Africa*, Vol. II., page 24.

"I know the white men, too, said the prince, - they are good men; in fact I have reason to speak well of them, for I also am a white man, and therefore I am of opinion that they are of the same blood as ourselves.' It is in this manner that Falatahs endeavor to claim relationship with Europeans, though these people are either of a swarthy complexion or black as soot; and this passion to be considered fair is often carried to a most ridiculous height. White men, how sorry soever their outward appearance may be, are certainly considered, not only by Falatahs, but by the native blacks, as a superior order of beings, in all respects more excel- lent than themselves. At Yaoorie we recollect having overheard a conversation between two men, who were quarrelling in the very height of passion. What!' exclaimed one of them to his fellow, thou pitiful son of a black ant! dost thou presume to say that a horse was my father? Look at these Christians! for as they are, I am; and such were my ancestors; answer me not, I say, for I am a white man!' The speaker was a negro, and his skin was the color of charcoal."

— *Lander's Travels in Africa*, Vol. II., page 79.

19

Courtship, Marriage, and Concubinage

"THE highest aspiration to which an African ever rises is to have a large number of wives. His happiness, his reputation, his influence, his position in society, all depend upon this. The consequence is, that the so-called wives are little better than slaves. They have no other purpose in life than to administer to the wants and gratify the passions of their lords, who are masters and owners, rather than husbands. It is not a little singular, however, that the females, upon the burden of whom this degrading institution mainly rests, are quite as much interested in its continuance as the men themselves. A woman would infinitely prefer to be one of a dozen wives of a respectable man, than to be the sole representative of a man who had not force of character to raise himself above the one-woman level. That such a state of feeling should exist in the mind of a heathen woman is not surprising. She has never seen any other state of society; nor has she had any moral or intellectual training that would

render such a position revolting to her better feelings. On the contrary, such is the degradation of her moral character, that she would greatly prefer the wider margin of licentious indulgence that she would enjoy as one of a dozen wives, than the closer inspection to which she would be subjected as the only wife of her household."
— *Wilson's Africa*, page 112.

"The wife is always purchased; and as this is done, in the great majority of cases, when she is but a child, her wishes, as a matter of course, are never consulted in this most important affair of her whole life. The first overture must be made to the mother. Her consent is to be won by small presents, such as beads, plates of dried fish, or a few leaves of tobacco. When this is accomplished the way is prepared for opening negotiations with the father and his family, who are the real owners of the child. The main question to be settled, and indeed the only one about which there is much negotiation, is whether the applicant is able to pay the dowry, and will be likely to do so without giving much trouble. The character of the man, his position in society, his family connections, or circumstances in life, are seldom taken into the account. The price of a wife is usually three cows, a goat or a sheep, and a few articles of crockery ware or brass rods, the whole of which would scarcely exceed twenty dollars. The goat and the smaller articles go to the mother's family, and the cows belong to the family of the father, which pass out of their hands without much delay in payment for a wife for some other member of the family. Bullocks may be seen passing from village to village, almost every day, in fulfilment of these matrimonial arrangements."
- *Wilson's Africa*, page 113.

"When a man has a large number of wives he can of course bestow but a moderate portion of his time upon any one of them. If it is necessary for him to watch his wives, they in turn are not less jealous of any superabundant attentions that he might confer upon any one of their own number. The chief business of his domestic life is to adjust these petty jealousies, and, to a still greater extent, the quarrels and strifes which are hourly springing up among the children of the different branches of the same house-hold."

-*Wilson's Africa*, page 144.

"The present King of Dahomey has appropriated no less than three thousand women to his own use. The number belonging to his head warriors depends upon their bravery, but no one is allowed to have a number large enough to suggest most remotely any idea of rivalry with the king. It is well known that many of the wives of the king must be sacrificed at the death of their lord, and this, no doubt, is a powerful motive to induce them to take the best care of him, and prolong his life as much as possible, but never deters any from freely entering into this honored relationship."

-*Wilson's Africa*, page 202.

"The Ashantee wife is not placed on a footing of social equality with her husband. Her position is a menial one, and she seldom aspires to anything higher than merely to gratify the passions of her husband. She never takes a seat at the social board with him. Indeed it would be regarded as a degradation on the part of the husband. The different women of his household, at a given concert among themselves, bring each their quota of food, and set it before their lord, each one taking up a small portion of their respective dishes and eating it in his presence, as evidence that they have not used poison in the preparation of his food, then retire to their

respective houses, while he partakes of his repast alone. His smaller children, and generally those of the wives who have provided his food, gather around him with their little wooden bowls to receive at his hands a portion of the superabundant sup- ply that has been set before him."
- *Wilson's Africa*, page 182.

"Polygamy is a favorite institution with the Ashantees, and, like everything of the kind, it is carried to an extravagant length. A man's importance in society is rated according to the number of his wives and slaves; and, naturally enough, the only limit known to the multiplication of them in a country where both can be had for money, is a man's ability to purchase. In Ashantee the law limits the king to three thousand three hundred and thirty-three. Whether it requires him to come up to this mark is not known. No one is permitted to see the wives of the king except female relatives, or such messengers as he may send, and even these must communicate with them through their bamboo walls. Some times they go forth in a body through the streets, but are always preceded by a company of boys, who warn the people to get out of the way, and avoid the unpardonable offence of seeing the king's wives. The men especially, no matter what their rank, must get out of the way, and, if they have not had sufficient time to do this, they must fall flat on the ground and hide their faces until the procession has passed. To see one of the king's wives, even accidentally, is a capital offence; and the scene of confusion which occasionally takes place in the public market, in consequence of the unexpected approach of the royal cortege, is said to be ludicrous beyond all description."
- *Wilson's Africa*, page 180.

"Married women are extremely superstitious in having their beds covered with the skins of particular animals when their husbands visit them; and never fail to predict the fate and fortune of a child in consequence of these arrangements. A panther or a leopard's skin is sure to produce a boy, or nothing. Should the father be a soldier, and a chief, the boy will be a warrior, bold, and bloody. A lion's skin is said to prevent child-bearing altogether; yet exceptions to this rule sometimes occur. It is then always a boy, and a wonderful one. He puts his foot on the necks of all the world, and is alike brave, generous, and fortunate."

- *Denham and Clapperton's Africa,* Vol. III., page 182.

"Yano, Chief of Kiama, asked me if I would take his daughter for a wife. I said 'Yes.' The old woman went out, and I followed with the king's head man. I went to the house of the daughter, which consists of several coozies separate from those of the father, and I was shown into a very clean one; a mat was spread; I sat down; and the lady coming in and kneeling down, I asked her if she would live in my house, or I should come and live with her; she said, whatever way I wished; very well, I said, I would come and live with her, as she had the best house."

-*Clapperton's Africa,* Vol. IV., page 215.

"Assulah, the Chief of Chaki, inquired how many wives an Englishman had. Being told only one, he seemed much aston- ished, and laughed greatly, as did all his people. 'What does he do,' said he, when one of his wives has a child? Assulah has two thousand.'"

- *Clapperton's Africa,* Vol..IV., page 204.

"Of wives, the Chief of Katunga said, he himself had plenty, he did not exactly know how many, but he was sure that, hand to hand, they would reach from Katunga to Jannah."
— *Clapperton's Africa*, Vol. IV., page 212.

"So little tenderness or sociability exists between a married couple, particularly if they should happen to be slaves, that they have nothing in common; and, though they eat and sleep in the same hut, they seek a separate livelihood. Perhaps it would be speaking within compass to say that four-fifths of the whole population in this country are slaves."
-Lander's Travels in Africa, Vol. I., page 377

"The king solicited a charm of us to-day, to preserve his house from the effects of fire, and cause him to become rich; while one of his elderly wives made a doleful complaint of having been likely to become a mother for the last thirty years, and begged piteously for medicine to promote and assist her accouchement. We could satisfy the old man easily enough, but his wife's hypochondriacal complaint we conceived too dangerous to be meddled with by un- professional hands. Poor woman, she is much to be pitied, for the odd delusion under which she has been laboring so long a time has given her considerable uneasiness, so that life it- self has become a burden to her. All that we could do for her was to soothe her mind, by telling her that her distemper was very common, and not at all dangerous; and promising that on our return this way, should noth- ing transpire in her favor in the mean time, we would endeavor to remove the cause of her com- plaint. This comforted the aged matron exceedingly, and, in the fulness of her heart, she burst into tears of joy, dropped on her knees to express her acknowledgment, and pressed us to accept of a couple of goora-nuts."

— *Lander's Travels in Africa,* Vol. I., page 193.

"The chief recreations of the natives of Angola are marriages and funerals. When a young woman is about to be married she is placed in a hut alone, and anointed with various unguents, and many incantations are employed in order to secure good fortune and fruitfulness. Here, as almost everywhere in the south, the height of good fortune is to bear sons. They often leave a husband altogether if they have daughters only. In their dances, where any one may wish to deride another, in the accompanying song a line is introduced, 'So and so has no children, and never will get any." She feels the insult so keenly that it is not un- common for her to rush away and commit suicide."

-*Livingstone's Africa*, page 446.

"Female virtue is held in so little esteem that opportunities of infidelity are often afforded by husbands to some of his less favorite wives, for the purpose of extorting money and get- ting rid of her. The common price of a wife here and at Cape Coast is sixteen dollars. A wife is very seldom purchased when more than twenty years old; but generally when five or six years younger, so that very old men have frequently ten or a dozen wives much younger than their own daughters."

— *Duncan's Africa*, Vol. I., page 79.

"In Maopongo it was a prevailing practice that before marriage the two parties should live together for some time, and make trial of each other's tempers and inclinations, before they formed the final engagement. To this system of probation the people were most obstinately attached, and the missionaries in vain denounced it, calling upon them at once either to marry or to separate. The young ladies were always the most anxious to have the full benefit of this experimental process, and the mothers, on being referred to, refused to incur responsibility, and ex- pose themselves to the reproaches of their daughters, by urging them to an abridgment of the trial, of which they might after- ward repent. The missionaries seem to have been most diligent in the task, as they call it, of 'reducing strayed souls to matrimony.' Father Benedict succeeded with no less than six hundred, but he found it such laborious work' that he fell sick and died in consequence."

- *Murray's African Discoveries,* page 55.

"The Bushmen use no form in their marriages. A young man courts the object of his affection; teazes her in the night time to take him to be her husband, and will sometimes pull her out of the hut while asleep, and teaze her till he obtains her consent. He need not ask the consent of her parents, or even tell them, but at marriage he makes a feast for them, when he gives them a present of a bow and arrows, or a skin sack.".

-*Campbell's Africa,* page 439.

"As the Bosjesman lives without a home, and without property, he must be without the great medium of moral refinement, - the social union. A horde commonly consists of the different members of one family only, and no one has any power or distinction above the rest. Every difference is decided by the right of the strongest; even the family tie is not sanctioned by any law or regulation. The wife is not indissolubly united to her husband; but, when he gives her permission, she may go whither she will, and associate with any other man; nay, the stronger man will sometimes take away the wife of the weaker, and compel her, whether she will or not, to follow him."

— *Lichtenstein's Africa*, Vol. II., page 48.

"I have, on a former occasion, in my remarks upon the languages of these savages, observed, as a thing worthy of notice, that they seem to have no idea of the distinction of girl, maiden, and wife; they are all expressed by one word alone. I leave every reader to draw from this single circumstance his own inference with regard to the nature of love, and every kind of moral feeling among them."
- *Lichtenstein's Africa*, Vol. II., page 48.

"When the Muata Cazembe falls in love with a female, either from personal observation or from a report of her attractions, he causes her to be conveyed to his gauda, where she is compelled to discover all the objects of her former amours, who, by order of the Muata, are immediately put to death, and all their property confiscated. When all objects of jealousy are thus removed by the Cata-Dofo, or high commissioner of the seraglio, who is the chief agent in carrying out the orders of the Muata, the new ob- ject of his passion is sent to join the other ladies of the seraglio. The introduction of a new wife into the harem is thus always the signal for a number of deaths; and, indeed, to so great an excess is this carried, that the occasion is often laid hold of as a pretext for the jealous to wreak their vengeance on the unsuspecting victims of their hatred."
- *Valdez's Africa*, Vol. II., page 253.

"The palavers were numerous and difficult to settle. related either to runaway wives (a fertile source of ill-will and blood-shed) or to homicides. When a man is killed here, if only by accident, satisfaction must be given. Deaths by accident are not more excusable than wilful murder. As regards run- away wives, the laws are very severe. Any wife refusing to remain with her husband, or running away, is condemned to have her ears and nose cut off. Any man debauching his neighbor's wife has to give a slave to the injured husband, and, if he cannot pay this fine, he must have his ears and nose cut off. They have no laws to punish robbery."

— *Du Chaillu's Ashango-Land*, page 74.

"A man pays goods or slaves for his wife, and regards her, therefore, as a piece of merchandise. Young girls- even children in arms - are married to old men for political effect. The idea of love, as we understand it, seems unknown to the Africans. On the sea-shore a man will hire you his mother, wife, or sister, for the vilest uses, and the women are never averse if they can only obtain the wages of prostitution."

-*Du Chaillu's Equatorial Africa*, page 75.

"Obedience is the wife's first duty, and it is enforced without mercy. A whip is made of the hide of the hippopotamus or manatu, and is a barbarous weapon, as stiff, and hard, and heavy as iron. This is laid on with no light hand, the worthy husband crying out, Rascal, do you think I paid my slaves for you for nothing?' The wives are more harshly treated than the slaves; a stroke of the whip often leaves a lifelong mark; and I saw very few women in my travels who had not some such marks on their persons."

-*Du Chaillu's Equatorial Africa*, page 382.

"With usual African hospitality, my kingly friend offered me a wife on my arrival at his place. This is the common custom when the negroes wish to pay respect to their guests; and they cannot understand why white men should decline what they consider a mere matter of course."

-*Du Chaillu's Equatorial Africa*, page 71.

"I had now grown to such sudden importance among the natives, that the neighboring chiefs and kings sent me daily messages of friendship, with trifling gifts that I readily accepted.. One of these lords, more generous and insinuating than the rest, hinted several times his anxiety for a closer connection in affection as well as trade, and, at length, insisted upon becoming my father-in-law. I had always heard that it was something to receive the hand of a princess, even after long and tedious wooing; but now that I was surrounded by a mob of kings, who absolutely thrust their daughters on me, I confess I had the bad taste not to leap with joy at the royal offering. Still I was in a difficult position, as no graver offence can be given a chief than to reject his child. It is so serious an insult to refuse a wife, that, high-born natives, in order to avoid quarrels or war, accept the tender boon, and as soon as etiquette permits, pass it over to a friend or relation. As the offer was made to me personally by the king, I found the utmost difficulty in escaping. Indeed, he would receive no excuse. When I declined on account of the damsel's youth, he laughed incredulously. If I urged the feebleness of my health and tardy convalescence, he insisted that a regular life of matrimony was the best cordial for an impaired constitution."

-*Canot's Twenty Years of an African Slaver*, page 110.

"During the whole time that the old lady was at work she was uttering disjointed remarks to me, and at length proposed, in the most shameless and barefaced manner, that I should marry her daughter. I requested to know which of the damsels then pres- ent was the proposed bride, and was shown a young lady about twelve years old, who had very much the appearance of a picked Cochin-China fowl. I concealed my laughter, and told the old lady that when this lassie became taller, and very fat, I might then think more seriously of her proposition; but as at present I had not six cows (the required price) handy, I could not entertain the subject. The old lady told me she would get the skin and bone adorned with fat by the time I came on another visit, and, for all I know, this black charmer may be now waiting in disappointed plumpness."

— *Drayson's Africa*, page 227.

"The husband is always expected to provide a separate house for each of his wives; but even this precaution cannot prevent the quarrels and strife which are continually occurring among the different wives and children. The wives are never treated as equals. They are not allowed to sit down to a meal with their husbands; but after they have prepared their food, they are required in their presence to taste it, to show that it has not been poisoned. This process is called 'taking off the witch.'"

- *Scott's Day Dawn in Africa*, page 50.

"A man must marry because it is necessary to his comfort, consequently the woman becomes a marketable commodity. Her father demands for her as many cows, cloths, and brass-wire bracelets as the suitor can afford; he thus virtually sells her, and she belongs to the buyer, ranking with his other live-stock. The husband may sell his wife, or, if she be taken from him by another man, he claims her value, which is ruled by what she would fetch in the slave-market. Polygamy is unlimited, and the chiefs pride themselves upon the number of their wives, varying from twelve to three hundred. It is no disgrace for an unmarried woman to become the mother of a family."

— *Burton's Africa*, page 493.

"There is no such thing as love in those countries, the feeling is not understood, nor does it exist in the shape in which we understand it. Everything is practical, without a particle of romance. Women are so far appreciated as they are valuable animals. They grind the corn, fetch the water, gather firewood, cement the floors, cook the food, and propagate the race; but they are mere servants, and as such are valuable. The price of a good-looking, strong, young wife, who could carry a heavy jar of water, would be ten cows; thus a man, rich in cattle, would be rich in domestic bliss, as he could command a multiplicity of wives. The simple rule of proportion will suggest that if one daughter is worth ten cows, ten daughters must be worth a hundred, therefore a large family is the source of wealth; the girls produce the cows, and the boys milk them. All being perfectly naked (I mean the girls and the boys), there is no expense, and the children act as herdsmen to the flocks as in the patriarchal times."
— *Baker's Great Basin of the Nile,* page 148.

"One of Katchiba's wives had no children, and she came to me to apply for medicine to correct some evil influence that had lowered her in her husband's estimation. The poor woman was in great distress, and complained that Katchiba was very cruel to her because she had been unable to make an addition to his family, but that she was sure I possessed some charm that would raise her to the standard of his other wives. I could not get rid of her until I gave her the first pill that came to hand from my medicine-chest, and with this she went away contented."
— *Baker's Great Basin of the Nile,* page 216.

"When a man becomes too old to pay sufficient attention to his numerous young wives, the eldest son takes the place of his father and becomes his substitute." — Baker's Great Basin of the Nile, page 50. - - And she is "Negro women can gratify the desire of a libertine, but they can never inspire a passion of the soul, nor feed that hunger of love which must sometimes gnaw the heart of a refined and cultivated man. The negress has beauty, - beauty in spite of her black skin, — which might create a furore in our demi-monde, and for which fools might fling their fortunes to the dogs. gentle, and faithful, and loving in her own poor way. But where is the coy glance, the tender sigh, the timid blush? Where is the intellect, which is the light within the crystal lamp, the genius within the clay? No, no, the negress is not a woman; she is a parody of woman; she is a pretty toy, an affectionate brute, - that is all."

-*Reade's Savage Africa,* page 240.

"When the King of Congo takes a fresh concubine, her husband is put to death. She is forced to give the names of her lovers (for it seems that all the married women have lovers), and these are also executed."

-*Reade's Savage Africa,* page 286.

"It is curious that the Equatorial savages of Africa should have a remarkable antipathy to widows. Women never marry twice; they are compelled to go on the town on the death of their hus- band, and to pay all their earnings to their brothers. That a husband should offer one of his wives to a visitor, as he offers him a seat in his house and at his table, argues a want of refinement only. But the husband who uses his wife, as is done all over Africa, to decoy young men to ruin, slavery, and death, practises a vice which seldom occurs among civilized nations."

-*Reade's Savage Africa,* page 218.

"In many parts of Africa, no marriage can be ratified till a jury of matrons have pronounced a verdict of purity on the bride and of capability on the husband. In other parts, especially in the malarious localities, where women are so frequently sterile, no one cares to marry a girl till she has produced a child. This has given rise to a supposition that they prefer a wife who has earned a little experience in dissipation. The real reason is, that if they marry they must pay a high price for their wife. This price they hope to regain by the sale of the children which she will bear."

-*Reade's Savage Africa,* page 425.

20

Mumbo Jumbo in Negroland

"ON the 6th of May, at night, I was visited by a Mumbo Jumbo, an idol, which is among the Mandingoes a kind of a cunning mystery. It is dressed in a long coat made of the bark of trees, with a tuft of fine straw on the top of it, and when the person wears it, it is about eight or nine feet high. This is a thing invented by the men to keep their wives in awe, who are so ignorant (or at least are obliged to pretend to be so) as to take it for a wild man; and indeed no one but he who knows it would take it to be a man, by reason of the dismal noise it makes, and which but few of the natives can manage. It never comes abroad but in the night time, which makes it have the better effect. When- ever the men have any dispute with the women, this Mumbo Jumbo is sent for to determine it; which is, I may say, always in favor of the men. Whoever is in the coat, can order the others to do what he pleases, either fight, kill, or make prisoner; but it must be observed, that no one is allowed to come armed into its presence. When the women hear it coming, they run away and hide themselves; but if you are acquainted with the person who has the coat on, he will send for them all to come and sit down, and sing or dance, as he pleases to order them; and if any refuse to come, he will send the people for them, and then whip them. When a man has been a day or two from home, the wife salutes him on her knees at his return, and, in the same posture, she always brings him water to drink. This, I believe, is the effect of, what I before mentioned, Mumbo Jumbo."

-*Moore's Inland Parts of Africa*, page 116-122.

"Among the Mandingoes, if a married woman is suspected of being unfaithful to her husband, the aid of Mumbo Jumbo is put in requisition. This mysterious personage, so frightful to the whole race of African matrons, is a strong, athletic man, disguised in dry plantain leaves, and bearing a rod in his hand, which he uses on proper occasions with most unsparing severity. When invoked by an injured husband, he appears about the outskirts of the village at dusk, and commences all sorts of pantomimes. After supper, he ventures to the town hall, where he commences his antics, and every grown person, male or female, must be present, or subject themselves to the suspicion of having been kept away by a guilty conscience. The performance is kept up until midnight, when Mumbo suddenly springs with the agility of the tiger upon the offender, and chastises her most soundly, amidst the shouts and laughter of the multitude, in which the other women join more heartily than anybody else, with the view, no doubt, of raising themselves above the suspicion of such infidelity."

- *Wilson's Africa*, page 76.

21

Funeral and Burial Rites in Negroland

"DRUMS were beating, horns blowing, and people were seen all running in one direction. The cause was a funeral dance, and I joined the crowd, and soon found myself in the midst of the entertainment. The dancers were most grotesquely got up. About a dozen huge ostrich feathers adorned their helmets; either leopard or the black and white monkey skins were suspended from their shoulders, and a leather tied round the waist covered a large iron bell, which was strapped upon the loins of each dancer like a woman's old-fashioned bustle. This they rung to the time of the dance by jerking their posteriors in the most absurd man- ner. Every dancer wore an antelope's horn suspended round the neck, which he blew occasionally in the height of his excitement. These instruments produced a sound partaking of the braying of a donkey and the screech of an owl. Crowds of men rushed round and round in a sort of 'galop infernel,' brandishing their lances and iron-headed maces, and keeping tolerably in line five or six deep, following the leader who headed them, dancing back- wards. The women kept outside the line, dancing a slow, stupid step, and screaming a wild and most inharmonious chant."

- *Baker's Great Basin of the Nile*, page 165.

"I had noticed, during the march from Latome, that the vicinity of every town was announced by heaps of human re- mains. Bones and skulls formed a Golgotha within a quarter of a mile of every village. Some of these were in earthenware pots, generally broken; others lay strewn here and there, while a heap in the centre showed that some form had originally been observed in their disposition. This was explained by an extraordinary custom most rigidly observed by the Latookas. Should a man be killed in battle the body is allowed to remain where it fell, and is devoured by the vultures and hyenas; but should he die a natural death, he or she is buried in a shallow grave within a few feet of his own door, in a little court-yard that surrounds each dwelling."

— *Baker's Great Basin of the Nile*, page 142.

"The chiefs of Unyamwezi generally are interred by a large assemblage of their subjects with cruel rites. A deep pit is sunk, with a kind of vault or recess projecting from it; in this the corpse, clothed with skin and hide, and holding a bow in the right hand, is placed sitting, with a pot of pombe, upon a dwarf- stool, while sometimes one, but more generally three, female slaves, one on each side and the third in front, are buried alive to preserve their lord from the horrors of solitude. A copious libation of pombe upon the heaped-up earth concludes the ceremony."

-*Burton's Africa,* page, 296.

"The great headmen of Wadoc are buried almost naked, but retaining their bead-ornaments, sitting in a shallow pit, so that the fore-finger can project above the ground. With each man are interred alive a male and a female slave, the former holding a bill-hook, wherewith to cut fuel for his lord in the cold death-world, and the latter, who is seated upon a little stool, supports his head in her lap."
- *Burton's Africa,* page 98.

"At this funeral, the women having first appeared and formed a circle, one advanced into the midst, having a child tied on her back, and went wriggling about on her heels, with her head and hands inclined toward the ground. Her companions sang Fantee songs; some struck pieces of iron together, three others clashed in their hands calabashes surrounded with a loose net-work of beads; and meanwhile, men beat drums with their fingers in the background. Next half a dozen wild-looking men appeared, who seemed to be under the excitement of liquor, and their waist- cloths trailing in the dust. They roared out songs; rushed madly ten or a dozen yards up the street, twisting violently their shoulders, arms, and legs; then wheeled round and returned, stopping and circling on their hams, whilst musicians beat drums and dry sticks, and loudly joined in the chorus."
-*Alexander's Africa*, Vol. I., page 188.

"The Kaffirs differ very materially from all the neighboring nations in their manner of disposing of the dead. Funeral rites are bestowed only on the bodies of their chiefs, and of their children. The first are generally interred very deep in the dung of their own cattle accumulated in the kraals or places where they are pent up at nights; and the bodies of infants are most commonly deposited in the ant-hills that have been excavated by the ant-eaters. The common people are exposed to be devoured by wolves. As these animals drag them away immediately into their dens, the relations of the deceased are in no danger of being shocked or disgusted with the sight of the mangled carcass. A Kaffir, in consideration of this piece of service holds the life of a wolf to be sacred, at least, he never endeavors to destroy it; the consequence of which is, that the country swarms with this voracious and destructive animal."

-*Barrow's Africa,* Vol. I., page 174.

"On our way home, I saw the corpse of a young slave, about twelve years of age, slung to a pole, and carried by two men. This led to the disclosure of a fact, of which I had hitherto been ignorant; namely, that all slaves, except a few favored ones, are considered not worth the trouble of a decent burial, and are consequently taken, and thrown into the water which runs round the town, where they are eaten by the thousands of fishes which the river contains."

- *Freeman's Africa,* page 135.

"Every one is buried under the floor of his own house, without monument or memorial; and among the commonalty the house continues occupied as usual; but among the great there is more refinement, and it is ever after abandoned. The bodies of slaves are dragged out of town, and left a prey to vultures and wild beasts. In Kano they do not even take the trouble to convey them beyond the walls, but throw the corpse into the morass or nearest pool of water."

— *Clapperton's Africa,* Vol. IV., page 55.

"A death had occurred in a village about a mile off, and the people were busy beating drums and firing guns. There is noth- ing more heartrending than their death-wails. When the natives turn their eyes to the future world, they have a view cheerless enough of their own utter helplessness and hopeless- ness. They fancy themselves completely in the power of the disembodied spirits, and look upon the prospect of following them as the greatest of misfortunes. Hence they are constantly deprecating the wrath of departed souls, believing that, if they are appeased, there is no other cause of death but witchcraft, which may be averted by charms."

- *Livingstone's Africa,* page 477.

"One never expects to find a grave nor a stone of remembrance set up in Africa; the very rocks are illiterate."

— *Livingstone's Africa,* page 233.

22

Indolence and Improvidence of the Negroes

"THE natives are so lazy that at times the merchants cannot, without great difficulty, get men to load or unload their ships. This is a very serious grievance, and often exposes our merchants to great difficulties as well as loss. One English laborer, on an average, does more work than any twelve Africans; and the provision of the latter being so cheap (ane penny per day is sufficient for their support), they have always plenty to eat. I am writing from actual observation, having had for three months a number of hired men under my charge. If a man is urged to do anything like a tenth part of a day's work, he will go away, and steal sufficient to maintain him for some time; consequently, the towns on the coast abound with thieves and vagabonds, who will not work."

— Duncan's Africa, Vol. I., page 40.

"Even the free negroes labor merely to acquire the means of gratifying their animal enjoyment. Negroes are indolent by nature, and therefore indisposed to labor. They perform their tasks carelessly, and have no idea of attention and punctuality, two qualities indispensable for a good servant. If a service is asked of a negro, he commonly shows great readiness to undertake it, being stimulated with the hope of reward, but he has no idea that a service quickly executed has double value. He returns in as many hours as he should have taken minutes, and is quite surprised at being found fault with for his slowness. He will make no secret of his having in the mean time taken a stroll, visited a friend, stopped at an inn, or perhaps performed some other work. The negro thinks it is quite enough to have per- formed the service; as to when or how, he considers that a matter of no moment."
— *Burmeister's Black Man*, page 15.

"Laziness is inherent in these people, for which reason, although extremely powerful, they will not work unless compelled to do so. They have no love for truth, honor, or honesty."
-*Speke's Africa*, page 27.

"The negro has been, and still is, thoroughly misunderstood. However severely we may condemn the horrible system of slavery, the results of emancipation have proved that the negro does not appreciate the blessings of freedom, nor does he show the slightest feeling of gratitude to the hand that broke the rivets of his fetters. His narrow mind cannot embrace that feeling of pure philanthropy that first prompted England to declare herself against slavery, and he only regards the anti-slavery movement as a proof of his own importance. In his limited horizon he is himself the important object, and as a sequente to his self-conceit, he imagines that the whole world is at issue concerning the black The negro, therefore, being the important question, must be an important person, and he conducts himself accordingly, he is far too great a man to work. Upon this point his natural character exhibits itself most determinedly. Accordingly, he resists any attempt at coercion; being free, his first impulse is to claim an equality with those whom he lately served, and to usurp a dignity with absurd pretensions, that must inevitably insure the disgust and abhorrence of the white community."

-*Baker's Great Basin of the Nile*, page 197.

"My next effort was to procure laborers, for whom I invoked the aid of Fana-Foro and the neighboring chiefs. During two days, forty negroes, whom I hired for their food and a per diem of twenty cents, wrote faithfully under my direction; but the constant task of felling trees, digging roots, and clearing ground was so unusual for savages, that the entire gang, with the excep- tion of a dozen, took their pay in rum and tobacco, and quitted me. A couple of days more devoted to such endurance drove off the remaining twelve, so that on the fifth day of my philanthropic enterprise I was left in my solitary hut with a single attendant. I had, alas! undertaken a task altogether unsuited to people whose idea of earthly happiness and duty is divided between palm oil, concubinage, and sunshine. I found it idle to remonstrate with -the king about the indolence of his subjects, Fana-Toro enter- tained very nearly the same opinion as his slaves. He declared and perhaps very sensibly-that white men were fools to work from sunrise to sunset every day of their lives; nor could he com- prehend how negroes were expected to follow their example; nay, it was not the fashion of Africa;' and, least of all, could his majesty conceive how a man possessed of so much merchan- dise and property, would voluntarily undergo the toils I

was pre- paring for the future. For a while I tried the effect of higher wages; but an increase of rum, tobacco, and coin, could not string the nerves or cord the muscles of Africa. Four men's labor was not equivalent to one day's work in Europe or America. The negro's philosophy was both natural and self-evident: - why should he work for pay when he could live without it?"
— *Canot's Twenty Years of an African Slaver*, page 417.

"A writer in the Southern Planter and Farmer' states that a gentleman in Charlotte county, Virginia, thus tested the comparative results of white and black labor. He furnished thirteen negroes with mules and implements and provisions to raise a crop, and at the same time furnished an outfit to two white men. negroes raised ninety-four barrels of corn, seven stacks of oats, and five thousand pounds of tobacco. The two white men, with a little negro girl to cook for them, raised one hundred and twelve and a half barrels of corn, ten stacks of oats, and eight thousand pounds tobacco. The negroes returned the mules in a poor, emaciated condition. The white men turned theirs over fat and sleek. The negroes worked four mules, the whites two. The gentleman referred to will, this year, work white men exclusively. To show the improvidence of the negroes, he said the cart and mules were at their service to haul wood; yet they preferred to burn rails."
-*Raleigh (N. C.) Register*, Jan. 17, 1868.

"Civilization hitherto has made very tardy progress in these African wilds; the black inhabitants of which are so indisposed to labor, and so wedded to their nomadic habits, that it is difficult to get them to settle down to industrious habits, either as agriculturists or as artisans; to say nothing of the colonist being obliged to be at all times prepared to oppose their predatory incursions."

- *Valdez's Africa,* Vol. II., page 109.

"The great national vice of the Africans is their indolence, They have no athletic sports. They wonder at the white man who walks to and fro from the mere love of walking.'

-*Reade's Savage Africa,* page 448.

"I saw a man afflicted with palsy in his head. He applied to me for a remedy, but I could only recommend him to bathe him- self every day in warm water, which will never be done; for these people are too indolent to perform any labor of this kind, even if it be to save their lives."

— *Richardson's Africa,* Vol. II., page 303.

23

Timidity and Cowardice of the Negroes

"IN their warfare, cunning has a most important part. They laugh at the courage of the white man, who faces his enemy, and delight most in ambushes and sudden surprises. If one has a quarrel with another, he lies in wait for him, shoots him as he is passing by the way, and immediately retreats. Then, of course, the dead man's friends take up his quarrel; then ensue other am- bushes and murders; frequently a dozen villages are involved in the palaver, and the killing and robbing goes on for months and even years, each party acting as occasion offers."
— *Du Chaillu's Equatorial Africa,* page 195.

"The warriors of this part of Africa-with the exception of the Fans and Osheba are not overstocked with courage. They applaud tricks that are inhumanly cruel and cowardly, and seem to be quite incapable of open hand-to-hand fight. To surprise man, woman, or child in sleep, and kill them then; to lie in am- bush in the woods for a single man, and kill him by a single spear- thrust before he can defend himself; to waylay a woman going to the spring for water, and kill her; or to attack on the river a canoe much smaller and weaker than the attackers, - these are the warlike feats I have heard most praised, and seen oftenest done in this part of Africa."

-*Du Chaillu's Equatorial Africa*, page 131.

"In war, they show no bravery, although on the hunt they are certainly brave enough. They despise boldness and admire cunning; prefer to gain by treachery, if possible; have no mercy or consideration for the enemy's women and children; and are cruel to those who fall in their power."

-*Du Chaillu's Equatorial Africa*, page 379.

"Besides cowardice, their principal fault is thieving, -a disposition which they never fail to evince; and nothing comes amiss to them, from wholesale robbery to petty prigging. Like the true coward, too, they are bullies when they meet those more timid than themselves."

— *Hutchinson's Africa*, Vol. II., page 22.

"During the war, which has continued these four months, the loss on the part of the Yaoorie has been about a half-dozen men killed, and the slaughter on the part of the rebels, it is said, has been no less. This sanguinary contest is a specimen of their war-fare, so that there will never be any great danger of depopulation from foreign wars or domestic broils. The 'great war,' • for which there was said to have been such mighty preparations in Nouffie, and which caused so much consternation in this city. an evening or two ago, has terminated in the capture of a herd of the King of Wowow's bullocks near the walls of his town."

-*Lander's Travels in Africa,* Vol. I., pages 273, 275.

"About two o'clock, as I was lying asleep upon a bullock's hide behind the door of the hut, I was awakened by the screams of women, and a general clamor and confusion among the inhabitants. At first I suspected that the Bambawans had actually entered the town; but observing my boy upon the top of one of the huts, I called to him to know what was the matter. He informed me that the Moors were come a second time to steal the cattle, and that they were now close to the town. I mounted the roof of the hut, and observed a large herd of bullocks coming toward the town, followed by five Moors on horseback, who drove the cattle forward with their muskets. When they had reached the wells, which are close to the town, the Moors selected from the herd sixteen of the finest beasts, and drove them off at a gallop. During this transaction the town people, to the number of five hundred, stood collected close to the walls of the town; and when the Moors drove the cattle away, though they passed within pistol-shot of them, the inhabitants scarcely made a show of resistance. I saw only four muskets fired, which, being loaded with gunpowder of the negroes' own manufacture, did no execution."

- *Mungo Park's 1st Journal,* page 85.

"In an attempt to storm or subdue Cooniah, the capital of the rebellious province of Ghoober, the number of fighting men brought before the town could not, I think, have been less than fifty or sixty thousand, horse and foot, of which the foot amounted to more than nine-tenths. For the depth of more than two hundred yards, all round the walls, was a dense circle of men and horses. The horse kept out of the reach of bow-shot, while the foot went up, as they felt courage or inclination, and kept up a struggling fire with about thirty muskets and the shooting of arrows. 'These fellows, whenever they fired their pieces, ran out of bow-shot to load. All of them were slaves; not a single Felatah had a musket. The enemy kept up a sure and slow fight, seldom throwing away their arrows, until they saw an opportunity of letting fly with effect. Now and then a single horseman would gallop up to the ditch, and brandish his spear, taking care to cover himself with his large leathern shield, and return as fast as he went, generally calling out lustily, when he got among his own party, Shields to the wall!' 'You people of Godado, why don't you hasten to the wall?' To which some voices would call out, 'Oh! you have a good large shield to cover you!' The cry of 'Shields to the wall!' was constantly heard from the several chiefs to their troops; but they disregarded the call, and neither chiefs nor vassals moved from the spot. At the conclusion of this memorable battle, in which nothing was concluded, the whole army set off in the greatest confusion, men and quadrupeds tum- bling over each other, and upsetting everything that fell in their way."

- *Clapperton's Africa,* Vol. IV., page 242.

"These unfortunate people seldom think of defending their habitations, but rather give them up, and by that means gain time to escape."

-*Denham and Clapperton's Africa*, Vol. II., page 121.

"It is only self-interest that makes the African brave. I have seen a small cow, trotting up with tail erect, break a line of one hundred and fifty men carrying goods not their own."

- *Burton's Africa,* page 242.

"It is confidently stated by the missionaries that the King of Kongo raised the incredibly large army of nine hundred thousand men. They say very little, however, for the bravery or discipline of this immense army, when they add that the main di- vision of it was entirely routed by four hundred Portuguese musketeers."
— *Wilson's Africa*, page 322.

"Twenty whites will put to flight a thousand Congoans."
-*Ogilby's Africa*, page 533.

"I was fortunately enabled to buy two camels instead of sumpter oxen, which give great trouble on the road during the dry season, especially if not properly attended to, and prepared every- thing for my journey; but the people in these countries are all cowards, and as I was to go alone without a caravan, I was un- able to find a good servant."
- *Barth's Africa*, Vol. I., page 503.

"I witnessed their drill exercise a short time before leaving Port Royal, and it was truly amusing. During the exercises, they practised them in the manual of arms, and loading and firing blank cartridge; and when the command, 'Fire,' was given, nearly one half of the line squatted and dropped down, frightened at the noise of the guns in their own hands. I also conversed with several of them. They told me they never expected it of the Yankees to make them fight; that they could not fight; 'Me drap right down gone dead, I get so skeered."
- Correspondence of a Michigan officer to the National Intelligencer, August 13, 1862.

Of the negroes at Harper's Ferry, and especially of those negroes who were more immediately concerned with John Brown n his Harper's Ferry raid, and who were afterward captured and punished, the general newspaper accounts of that time concur in representing them all (so very unlike their fearless but misguided Anglo-American leaders) as the complete victims of cowardice and trepidation. Thus :-

"The blacks made no resistance, but begged for mercy. They ran with all the swiftness that their fears could excite. Green, the negro, is a large man, with a very bad countenance and expression, and a most arrant coward. He cringes and begs to every person who approaches him."

How the negro troops behaved on the occasion of the attempt to blow up Petersburg, Virginia, on the 30th of July, 1864, may be seen by reference to the following Federal account from the regular army correspondent of a New York newspaper:—

"The rebels, exasperated at sight of the negroes, fought with the fury of devils, and, reinforcements coming to their aid, the tide of battle turned. The colored troops gave way and broke in con- fusion, when the rebels, having repulsed their charge, charged them in turn, and then they ran, a terror-stricken, disordered mass of fugitives, to the rear of our white troops. In vain their officers endeavored to rally them with all the persuasion of tongue, sabre, and pistol. Whatever discredit attaches to the negroes them- selves, their white officers are beyond reproach."

24

African Anecdotes

"So long as the negro can laugh, he cares little against whom the joke goes."
— *Du Chaillu's Equatorial Africa*, page 330.

"The enraged wife rushed out to seek her supposed rival, and a battle ensued. Women's fights in this country always begin by their throwing off their dengui, that is, stripping themselves entirely naked. The challenger having thus denuded herself, her enemy showed pluck and answered the challenge by promptly doing the same; so that the two elegant figures immediately went at it, literally tooth and nail, for they fought like cats, and between the rounds reviled each other in language the most filthy that could possibly be uttered. Mayolo being asleep in his house, and no one seemingly ready to interfere, I went myself and separated the two furies."
-*Du Chaillu's Ashango-Land*, page 187.

"No one can rely upon them even for a moment. Dog wit, or any silly remark, will set them giggling. Any toy will amuse them. Highly conceited of their personal appearance, they are forever cutting their hair in different fashions, to surprise a friend; or if a rag be thrown away, they will all in turn fight for it to bind on their heads, then on their loins or spears, peacocking about with it before their admiring comrades."
-*Speke's Africa*, page 29.

"Should one happen to have anything specially to communicate to his master in camp, he will enter giggling, sidle up to the pole of a hut, commence scratching his back with it, then stretch and yawn, and gradually, in bursts of loud laughter, slip down to the ground on his stern, when he drums with his hands on the top of a box until summoned to know what he has at heart, when he delivers himself in a peculiar manner, laughs and yawns again, and, saying it is time to go, walks off in the same way as he came."
-*Speke's Africa*, page 29.

"Proceeding to another court, we sat in the shade together, when the women returned again, but were all dumb, because my interpreters dared not for their lives say anything, even on my account, to the king's women. Getting tired, I took out my sketchbook and drew Lubuga, the pet, which amused the king immensely, as he recognized her cockscomb. Then twenty naked virgins, the daughters of Wakungu, all smeared and shining with grease, each holding a small square of calico for a fig-leaf, marched in a line before us, as a fresh addition to the harem, whilst the happy fathers floundered, yauzigging on the ground, delighted to find their darlings appreciated by the king. Seeing this done in such a quiet, mild way before all my men, who dared not lift their heads to see it, made me burst into a roar of laughter, and the king, catching the infection from me, laughed as well; but the laughing did not end there, - for the pages, for once giving way to nature, kept bursting, my men chuckled in sudden gusts, while even the women, holding their mouths for fear of detection, responded, and we all laughed together. Then a sedate old dame rose from the squatting mass, ordered the virgins to right- about, and marched them off, showing their still more naked reverses."

— *Speke's Africa*, page 357.

"A negro dwarf, who measured three feet all but an inch, the keeper of Princess Miram's keys, sat before her with the insignia of office on his shoulder, and richly dressed in Soudan tobes. This little person afforded us a subject of conversation and much laughter. Miram inquired whether we had such little fellows in my country; and when I answered in the affirmative, she said, 'Ah, gieb! what are they good for? Do they ever have children?' I answered, 'Yes; that we had instances of their being fathers to tall and proper men.' Oh, wonderful!' she replied; 'I thought so; they must be better than this dog of mine; for I have given him eight of my handsomest and youngest slaves, but it is all to no purpose. I would give a hundred bullocks and twenty slaves to the woman who would bear this wretch a child.' The wretch, and an ugly wretch he was, shook his large head, grinned, and slobbered copiously from his extensive mouth, at this flattering proof of his mistress' partiality."

— *Denham's Africa*, Vol. III., page 3.

"Their supreme happiness consists in having an abundance of meat. Asking a man, who was more grave and thoughtful than his companions, what was the finest sight he could desire, he instantly replied, 'A great fire covered with pots full of meat,' adding, 'How ugly the fire looks without a pot!'"

-*Moffat's Africa*, page 306.

"They are very superstitious in some things, one of which is, that if they know anybody boils the sweet milk which they buy of them, they will not, for any consideration, sell that person any more, because they say that boiling the milk makes the cows dry."-

-*Moore's Inland Parts of Africa*, page 35.

"During my absence, a French captain, who was one of our most attentive friends, had left a donkey, which he brought from the Cape de Verds, for my especial delectation. I at once resolved to bestow the 'long-eared convenience' on Prince Freeman, not only as a type, but a testimonial; yet, before a week was over, the unlucky quadruped reappeared at my quarters, with a message from the prince, that it might do well enough for a bachelor like me, but its infernal voice was enough to cause the miscarriage of an entire harem, if not of every honest women throughout his jurisdiction. The superstition spread like wildfire. The women were up in arms against the beast; and I had no rest till I got rid of its serenades by despatching it to Monrovia, where the dames and damsels were not afraid of donkeys of any dimensions."

- *Canot's Twenty Years of an African Slaver*, page 375.

"The women, in order not to accustom themselves to much talking or scolding, take every morning, betimes, a little water in their mouths, which they keep there till all their household work is done; but then putting it out, give their tongues free liberty."

-*Ogilby's Africa*, page 364.

"When the chief arrived, I was busy preparing some skins of birds and snakes, which caused no small amount of jesting amongst his followers. One fellow, more inquisitive and impertinent than the rest, approached close to me, and, seizing one of the reptiles by the tail, held it up before the multitude, which were now thronging my tent to inconvenience, and, addressing to it some unintelligible words, the whole assembly burst out into a deafening roar of laughter. Indeed, the mirth became so outrageous as to throw the party into convulsions, many casting themselves at full length on the ground, with their hands tightly clasped across their stomachs as if in fear of bursting, whilst their greasy cheeks became furrowed with tears trickling down in streams."

-*Andersson's Africa*, page 345.

"The ideas of a Namaqua, as to the formation and rotary motion of the heavenly bodies, if not very profound, are unquestionably very original. The sun, by some of the people of this benighted land, is considered to be a mass of fat, which descends nightly to the sea, where it is laid hold of by the chief of a white man's ship, who cuts away a portion of tallow, and, giving the rest a kick, it bounds away, sinks under the wave, goes round below, and then comes up again in the east."

-*Andersson's Africa*, page 257.

25

Utter Failure and Inutility of All Missionary Enterprises in Negroland

"THE Austrian mission-station of St. Croix consists of about twenty grass huts on a patch of dry ground close to the river. The church is a small hut, but neatly arranged. Herr Morlang, chief of the establishment, acknowledged, with great feeling, that the mission was absolutely useless among such savages; that he had worked with much zeal for many years, but that the natives were utterly impracticable. They were far below the brutes, as the latter show signs of affection to those who are kind to them; while the natives, on the contrary, are utterly obtuse to all feelings of gratitude. He described the people as lying and deceitful to a superlative degree; the more they receive the more they desire, but in return they will do nothing. Twenty or thirty of these disgusting, ash-smeared, stark-naked brutes, armed with clubs of hard wood brought to a point, were lying idly about the station. Near by are the graves of several members of the mission, who have left their bones in this horrid land, while not one convert has been made from the mission of St. Croix."

- *Baker's Great Basin of the Nile*, page 53.

"The state of the East-African heathen, their indifference toward all that is spiritual, or to any progress in mere human affairs (they are, as Rebmann rightly says, profitable in nothing, either to God or to the world'), may easily beget in the heart of a missionary a mood of disappointment, in which he would say, with Isaiah, I have labored in vain; I have spent my strength for nought, and in vain.'"

— *Krapf's Africa*, page 507.

"From this time forward the king began to develop his treacherous character, promising, in the hope of presents, to promote my journey to Uniamesi, while all the while he had resolved to prevent it. Extortion, too, followed upon extortion,-his magician, Wessiri, speaking and acting in the king's name. I saw the stock of goods which I had intended for Uniamesi gradually melting away; and when, by order of the king, I was obliged to part with piece after piece of the calico which I had reserved for my further journey, I could not suppress my tears. The king observed them, and asked the cause. Wessiri replied that I wept because of the loss of my goods; when I rejoined that I was not weeping on that account, but because the things had been given me by good people at home, who wished to send the Book of Life to all Africans, with which object I had made the journey; whereas I was now deprived of my property, and the good design of my friends was defeated"

- *Krapf's Eastern Africa,* page 260.

"A clergyman of the Church of England, the Rev. Thomas Thompson, proceeded to the Gold Coast in 1751, with the view of attempting the introduction of the Christian religion. He remained chaplain at the Castle for four years, and brought home a few natives for education, one of whom, Philip Quacoe, was educated at Oxford, and was afterward chaplain at Cape Coast for the long space of fifty years. No result followed his labors. It is even said that, at the approach of death, he had recourse to fetich practices."
— *Cruickshank's Africa,* Vol. I., page 183.

"The most important and interesting portion of the last number of the 'Journal of the Anthropological Society of London' is the discussion before the Anthropological Society on the efforts of missionaries among savages, a discussion inaugurated by Mr. Winwood Reade, author of Savage Africa,' who stated, as the result of his observation in Equatorial Africa, that missionary ef- forts were total failures, even when directed by men eminently qualified for the task. So far from professing Christians' among negroes being better than the heathen, they were, if possible, worse. 'In plain words,' said Mr. Reade, 'I found that every Christian negress was a prostitute, and that every Christian negro was a thief.' Mr. Walker, of fourteen years' Gaboon experience, confirmed this testimony. Captain Burton, in a very forcible speech, followed suit, giving the result of his observations, not merely in Africa, but in Western India, the prairie tribes ofspeaking and acting in the king's name. I saw the stock of goods which I had intended for Uniamesi gradually melting away; and when, by order of the king, I was obliged to part with piece after piece of the calico which I had reserved for my further journey, I could not suppress my tears. The king observed them, and asked the cause. Wessiri replied that I wept because of the loss of my goods; when I rejoined that I was not weeping on that account, but because the things had been given me by good people at home, who wished to send the Book of Life to all Africans, with which object I had made the journey; whereas I was now deprived of my property, and the good design of my friends was defeated"

- *Krapf's Eastern Africa*, page 260.

"A clergyman of the Church of England, the Rev. Thomas Thompson, proceeded to the Gold Coast in 1751, with the view of attempting the introduction of the Christian religion. He remained chaplain at the Castle for four years, and brought home a few natives for education, one of whom, Philip Quacoe, was educated at Oxford, and was afterward chaplain at Cape Coast for the long space of fifty years. No result followed his labors. It is even said that, at the approach of death, he had recourse to fetich practices."

— *Cruickshank's Africa*, Vol. I., page 183.

"The most important and interesting portion of the last number of the 'Journal of the Anthropological Society of London' is the discussion before the Anthropological Society on the efforts of missionaries among savages, a discussion inaugurated by Mr. Winwood Reade, author of Savage Africa,' who stated, as the result of his observation in Equatorial Africa, that missionary ef- forts were total failures, even when directed by men eminently qualified for the task. So far from professing Christians' among negroes being better than the heathen, they were, if possible, worse. 'In plain words,' said Mr. Reade, 'I found that every Christian negress was a prostitute, and that every Christian negro was a thief.' Mr. Walker, of fourteen years' Gaboon experience, confirmed this testimony. Captain Burton, in a very forcible speech, followed suit, giving the result of his observations, not merely in Africa, but in Western India, the prairie tribes of America, and tropical Africa generally; missionary efforts, he said, being failures all. The following is characteristic : :- 'A VERY DEAR PERSON TO US.' - With the last African or Mombas mission I am personally acquainted. Years ago this ill-fated establishment had spent a sum of £12,000, and what were the results ? In 1857, when calling at the mis- sionary station of Rabbai Mpia, near Mombas, I was informed that a wild-looking negro, whose peculiar looks caused me to get my bowie-knife handy, was a very dear person to us; he is our first and only convert.' 'Yes,' added the husband, with an amount of simplicity which might provoke a smile but for the melancholy thought that it breeds, and he was prepared for Christianity by an attack of insanity, caused by the death of all his relations, and lasting five years."

— *London Dispatch*, July 16, 1865.

"Mr. Phillips, of Abeokuta, with the rest of the missionaries in Central Africa, have been expelled from the country, suffering the loss of their entire property. Mr. Phillips is at Lagos in a destitute condition."

- *New York Tribune*, February 11, 1868.

"The Catholic missionaries threatened the natives with hell fire if they refused to adopt the marriage system of the Christians. The natives replied that they were quite content to go where their fathers had gone before them. But the firmest opponents of these innovations were the women; and, as every one knows, a priesthood is only powerful when supported on female pillars. The ladies of the court, who despised the monks on account of their chastity, determined to take advantage of this pious weakness. Accordingly they chose a rivulet, which flowed before the garden of the

missionaries, as their place of bathing, and there exhibited themselves during the whole day, often in very indecent attitudes. The afflicted fathers laid their distress before the king, but soon found the evil doubled by this proof of the effect which it had produced."
-*Reade's Savage Africa*, page 442.

"They dread a superhuman power, and they fear and worship it as being a measureless source of evil. It is scarcely correct to call this devil-worship, for this is a title of contrast, presuming that there has been a choice of the evil in preference to the good. The fact in their case seems to be, that good in will, or good in action, are ideas foreign to their minds. Selfishness cannot be more intense, nor more exclusive of all kindness and generosity or charitable affection, than it is generally found among these barbarians. The inconceivableness of such motives to action has often been found a strong obstacle to the influence of the Christian missionary. They can worship nothing good, because they have no expectation of good from anything powerful. They have mysterious words or mutterings, equivalent to what we term incantations, which is the meaning of the Portuguese word from which originated the term 'fetich.'"
— *Foote's Africa and the American Flag,* page 55.

"Soon an aged woman, to whom the missionary had often spoken of the glorious gospel, joined the little praying-circle. The change in this old woman, Yuwa, was very striking. She had seemed to be one of the most unpromising characters in the town of Nyaro, and the first time the missionary, who had charge of the town,, asked her why she did not regularly attend the chapel, she replied, 'Me go to church, and you no pay me!'"
-*Scott's Day Dawn in Africa*, page 89.

"A missionary at Maopongo having met one of the queens, and finding her mind inaccessible to all his instructions, deter- mined to use sharper remedies, and, seizing a whip, began to apply it to her majesty's person. The effect he describes as most auspicious; every successive blow opened her eyes more and more to the truth, as she at length declared herself wholly unable to resist such affecting arguments in favor of the Catholic doctrine."

- *Murray's African Discoveries,* page 54.

"I am not to be understood as intimating that any of the numerous tribes are anxious for instruction; they are not the inquiring spirits we read of in other countries; they do not desire the gospel, because they know nothing about either it or its benefits."

- *Livingstone's Africa,* page 544.

"The town swarmed with thieves and drunkards, whose only object in life was sensual gratification. Nowhere else had I met with so many impudent and shameless beggars. When a missionary attempted to preach to a crowd in the streets or market, it was very common for some of them to reply by laying their hands on their stomachs, and saying, ' White man, I am hungry."

- *Bowen's Central Africa,* page 101.

"All missionaries praise the African for his strict observance of the Sabbath. He would have three hundred and sixty-five Sabbaths in the year, if possible, and he would as scrupulously observe them all."

— *Burton's Wanderings in West Africa,* Vol. I., page 266.

"In the negroes' own country the efforts of the missionaries for hundreds of years have had no effect; the missionary goes away and the people relapse into barbarism. Though a people may be taught the arts and sciences known by more gifted nations, unless they have the power of progression in themselves, they must inevitably relapse in the course of time into their former state."

-*Du Chaillu's Ashango-Land,* page 436.

26

Miscellaneous Peculiarities, Habits, Manners, and Customs of the Negroes in Negroland

"THEIR mode of salutation is quite singular. They throw themselves on their backs on the ground, and, rolling from side to side, slap the outside of their thighs as expressions of thankfulness and welcome, uttering the words, Kina bomba.' This method of salutation was to me very disagreeable, and I never could get reconciled to it. I called out, Stop-stop! I don't want that!' but they, imagining I was dissatisfied, only tumbled about more furiously, and slapped their thighs with greater vigor. The men being totally unclothed, this performance imparted to my mind a painful sense of their extreme degradadation."

— *Livingstone's Africa,* page 590.

"They fear all manner of phantoms, and have half-developed ideas and traditions of something or other, they know not what. The pleasures of animal life are ever present to their minds as the supreme good."
— *Livingstone's Africa*, page 477.

"Sambanza gave us a detailed account of the political affairs of the country, and of Kolimbota's evil doings, and next morning performed the ceremony called 'Kasendi,' for cementing our friendship. It is accomplished thus: The hands of the parties are joined (in this case Pitsane and Sambanza were the parties engaged); small incisions are made on the clasped hands, on the pits of the stomach of each, and on the right cheeks and foreheads. A small quantity of blood is taken off from these points in both parties by means of a stalk of grass. The blood from one person is put into a pot of beer, and that of the second into another; each then drinks the other's blood, and they are supposed to be- come perpetual friends or relations."
- *Livingstone's Africa*, page 525.

"The chieftainship is elective from certain families. Among the Bangalas of the Cassange valley the chief is chosen from three families in rotation. A chief's brother inherits in preference to his The sons of a sister belong to her brother; and he often sells his nephews to pay his debts. By this and other unnatural customs, more than by war, is the slave-market supplied. The prejudices in favor of these practices are very deeply rooted in the native mind. Even at Loanda they retire out of the city in order to perform their heathenish rites without the cognizance of the authorities. Their religion, if such it may be called, is one of dread. Numbers of charms are employed to avert the evils with which they feel themselves to be encompassed. Occasionally you meet a man, more cautious or more timid than the rest, with twenty or thirty charms round his neck. He seems to act upon the principle of Proclus, in his prayer to all the gods and goddesses; among so many he surely must have the right one. The disrespect which Europeans pay to the objects of their fear is to their minds only an evidence of great folly."

— *Livingstone's Africa*, page 471.

"All the Batoka tribes follow the curious custom of knocking out the upper front teeth at the age of puberty. This is done by both sexes; and though the under teeth, being relieved from the attrition of the upper, grow long and somewhat bent out, and thereby cause the under lip to protrude in a most unsightly way, no young woman thinks herself accomplished until she has got rid of the upper incisors. This custom gives all the Batoka an uncouth, old-man-like appearance. Their laugh is hideous; yet they are so attached to it than even Sebituane was unable to eradicate the practice. He issued orders that none of the children living under him should be subjected to the custom by their parents, and disobedience to his mandates was usually punished with severity; but, notwithstanding this, the children would ap- pear in the streets without their incisors, and no one would con- fess to the deed. When questioned respecting the origin of this practice, the Batoka reply that their object is to be like oxen, and those who retain their teeth they consider to resemble zebras. Whether this is the true reason or not, it is difficult to say; but it is noticeable that the veneration for oxen which prevails in many tribes should here be associated with hatred to the zebra, as among the Bakwains; that this operation is performed at the same age that circumcision is in other tribes; and that here that ceremony is unknown. The custom is so universal that a person who has his teeth is considered ugly, and occasionally, when the Batoka borrowed my looking-glass, the disparaging remark would be made respecting boys or girls who still retained their teeth, Look at the great teeth!' Some of the Makololo give a more facetious explanation of the custom: they say that the wife of a chief having in a quarrel bitten her husband's hand, he, in revenge, ordered her front teeth to be knocked out, and all the men in the tribe followed his example; but this does not explain why they afterward knocked out their own."

— *Livingstone's Africa*, page 571.

"I have already noticed some peculiar customs of the Marghi; but I must say a few words about their curious ordeal on the holy granite rock of Kobshi. When two are litigating about a matter, each of them takes a cock which he thinks the best for fighting, and they go together to Kobshi. Having arrived at the holy rock, they set their birds a-fighting, and he whose cock prevails in the combat is also the winner in the point of litigation. But more than that, the master of the defeated cock is punished by the divinity whose anger he has thus provoked, and on returning to his village he finds his hut in flames."

— *Barth's Africa*, Vol. II., page 216.

"All over Bornu no butter is prepared except with the dirty and disgusting addition of some cow's urine, and it is always in a fluid state."

-*Barth's Africa*, Vol. I., page 580.

"There are no ceremonies on birth occasions, and no purification of women among these people. When the mother perishes in childbirth, the parents claim a certain sum from the man that killed their daughter.' Twins, here called wapacha, are usually sold, or exposed in the jungle, as among the Ibos of West Africa. If the child die, an animal is killed for a general feast, and in some tribes the mother does a kind of penance. Seated outside the village, she is smeared with fat and flour, and exposed to the derision of people who surround her, hooting and mocking with offensive jests and gestures. To guard against this calamity, the Wazaramo and other tribes are in the habit of vowing that the babe shall not be shaved till manhood, and the mother wears a number of talismans- bits of wood tied with a thong of snake's round her neck, and beads of different shapes round her head."

— *Burton's Africa,* page 93.

"When meat is not attainable and good water is scarce, the African severs one of the jugulars of a bullock and fastens upon it like a leech. This custom is common in Karagwah and the other northern kingdoms; and some tribes, like the Wamjika, near Moinbasah, churn the blood with milk."

-*Burton's Africa*, page 463

"All the thoughts of the negroids are connected with this life. 'Ah!' they exclaim, 'it is bad to die! to leave off eating and drinking, never to wear a fine cloth!' As in the negro race gen- erally, their destructiveness is prominent; a slave never breaks a thing without an instinctive laugh of pleasure; and, however care- ful he may be of his own life, he does not value that of another, even of a relative, at the price of a goat. During fires in the town of Zanzibar, the blacks have been seen adding fuel, and singing and dancing, wild with delight. On such occasions they are shot down by the Arabs like dogs."

- *Burton's Africa*, page 493.

"In the absence of all refined pleasures, various rude sports are pursued with eagerness, and almost with fury. The most favor. ite is wrestling, which the chiefs do not practise in person, but train their slaves to exhibit in it as our jockeys do game-cocks, taking the same pride in their prowess and victory. Death or maiming, however, is no unfrequent result of these encounters. The ladies, even of rank, engage in another very odd species of contest. Placing themselves back to back, they cause particular parts to strike together with the most violent collision, when she who maintains her equilibrium, while the other lies stretched, is proclaimed victor with loud cheers."

- *Murray's African Discoveries*, page 145.

"After the heat of the day was over, Yano, Chief of Kiama, came, attended by all his train. The most extraordinary persons in it were himself and the bearers of his spears, which, as before, were six naked young girls, from fifteen to seventeen years of age. The only thing they wore was a fillet of white cloth round the forehead, about six inches of the ends flying behind, and a string of beads round their waists; in their right hands they carried three light spears each. Their light form, the vivacity of their eyes, and the ease with which they appeared to fly over the ground, made them appear something more than mortal as they flew along- side of his house, when he was galloping and making his horse curvet and bound. A man with an immense bundle of spears remained behind at a little distance, apparently to serve as a magazine for the girls to be supplied from when their master had expended those they carried in their hands."

- *Clapperton's Africa*, Vol. IV., page 214.

"At that moment one of their lucky omens took place. My servant, who had assisted in bringing the presents, got up to receive the Goora nuts presented to me by the governor's orders; and in rising he overturned a pot of honey which had also been given to us, but without breaking it, the honey running out on the floor. Had the pot been broken, the omen would have been unfortunate. As it was, the governor was highly elated, and graciously ordered the poor to be called in to lick up the honey. They immediately made their appearance, equally rejoiced at the lucky omen; and, upon their knees, quickly despatched the honey, not, however, without much strife and squabbling. One man came off with a double allowance, happening to have a long beard, which he carefully cleaned into his hand for a bonne bouche, after the repast on the ground was finished."

-*Clapperton's Africa*, Vol. III., page 242.

"The ceremony of prostration before the king is required from all. The chiefs who come to pay their court, cover themselves with dust, and then fall flat on their bellies, having first practised the ceremony, in order to be perfect."

- *Clapperton's Africa*, Vol. IV., page 208.

"The Bomonese have twenty cuts or lines on each side of the face, which are drawn from the corners of the mouth toward the angles of the lower jaw and the cheek-bone; and it is quite distressing to witness the torture the poor little children undergo who are thus marked, enduring not only the heat, but the attacks o millions of flies. They have also one cut on the forehead in the centre, six on each arm, six on each leg and thigh, four on each breast, and nine on each side, just above the hips. They are, however, the most humble of females, never approaching their husbands except on their knees."

— *Denham and Clapperton's Africa*, Vol. III., page 175.

"His Highness vouchsafed this day to sleep in my tent, and yesterday he did the Germans the honor of slaughtering lice in theirs. It is a grand piece of etiquette in this country, that every man has the privilege of murdering his own lice. If you pick a louse off a man's slave, you must deliver it up instantly to him to be murdered, as his undoubted right and privilege."

—*Richardson's Africa*, Vol. II., page 89.

"Before they sit down to eat meat in company, the Kaffirs are very careful to immerse their hands in fresh cow-dung, wiping them on the grass, which is considered the perfection of cleanliness. Except an occasional plunge in a river, they never wash themselves, and consequently their bodies are covered with vermin."

-*Steedman's Africa*, Vol. I., page 265.

"It is very common among the Hottentots to catch a serpent, squeeze out the poison from under his teeth, and drink it. They say it only makes them a little giddy; and they imagine it pre- serves them afterwards from receiving any injury from the sting of that reptile."

— *Campbell's Africa*, page 401.

"As for the people of Namacqua, when their sons are declared to be men, they erect a shade, kill an animal, and tie its fat on his head and round his neck, which, according to custom, he must wear till it gradually rots and falls off. They likewise cut several strokes on his breast with a sharp instrument. The entrails of the animal which was killed at the commencement of the ceremony, being dried and pounded into a powder, are now mixed with water, with which he is rubbed all over, and he is then declared to be a man in the presence of the whole kraal. He who does not submit to this ceremony eats only with women, and is despised."

— *Campbell's Africa*, page 430.

"A curious custom, originating in the superstitious belief of the people of the Gold Coast, prevails among them, in reference to a girl after conception. As soon as it becomes generally apparent that she is with child, her friends and neighbors set upon her, and drive her to the sea, pelting her with mud and covering her with dust. During this operation they abuse her vehemently; and conclude the ceremony by tumbling her over among the waves. She returns unmolested to her house; and the fetich- woman binds charms of strings and parrots' feathers about her wrists, ankles, and neck, muttering a dark spell all the while, to keep away bad luck and evil spirits. Without passing through this ordeal, they believe that her childbirth would be unfortunate."

-*Cruickshank's Africa*, Vol. II., page 200.

"The Africans pay no attention either to domestic or wild animals; even the dog or horse, the two most sagacious of all the animal creation, excite in them no interest whatever. If not driven to it, they will suffer a horse to stand for days, tied up without food or water. In fact, in no case do they exhibit any feeling, either of regard or affection, to merit even a comparison with any of the lower animals, being also selfish in the extreme."

– *Duncan's Africa*, Vol. I., page 90.

THE NEGROES IN NEGROLAND | 191

"His prime minister and four others next in rank, who were conducting me to his majesty's presence, desired me to halt till they paid their compliment to his majesty, forming line in front of me. They completely prostrated themselves at full length, rubbing both sides of their faces on the ground and kissing it. They then raised themselves on their knees, where they remained till they had completely covered themselves with dust, and rubbed their arms over with dirt as high as the shoulders."
-*Duncan's Africa,* Vol. I., page 220.

"Much neglect seems to prevail at the time of the birth of male children, respecting the separation of the umbilical cord. Many boys, and even men, may be seen with protruding navels as large as a duck's egg."
— *Duncan's Africa*, Vol. I., page 80.

"Very little systematic control is exercised by either parent; and the children are, for the most part, utterly disobedient and reckless of parental authority. As they are taught in their earliest infancy to steal and lie, and to indulge in other gross vices, nothing better could be expected. One most cruel punishment inflicted upon their children, when they can no longer bear with them, is to rub red pepper in their eyes."
-*Scott's Day Dawn in Africa,* page 49.

"The Obbo natives are similar to the Bari in some of their habits. I have had great difficulty in breaking my cow-keeper of his disgusting custom of washing the milk-bowl with cow's urine, and even mixing some with the milk; he declares that, unless he washes his hands with such water before milking, the cow will lose her milk."
— *Baker's Great Basin of the Nile*, page 258.

"The entire crowd were most grotesquely gotten up, being dressed in either leopard or white monkey skins, with cows' tails strapped on behind, and antelopes' horns fitted upon their heads, while their chins were ornamented with false beards, made of the bushy ends of cows' tails sewed together. Altogether, I never saw a more unearthly set of creatures; they were perfect illustrations of my childish ideas of devils, — horns, tails, and all, excepting the hoofs; they were our escort! furnished by King Kamrasi to accompany us to the lake.".

-*Baker's Great Basin of the Nile*, page 321.

"The women continue to perform the severest labors until the very last moment of their time. They give birth to children without uttering a complaint, and one would almost believe that they are delivered without pain, for on the following day they resume their usual occupations."

-*Caillie's Africa*, Vol. I., page 351.

"The women of Bambara, who were exceedingly dirty, have all a bit of calabash, or a thin slip of wood, stuck into the under lip. I could scarcely persuade myself that this was a mere matter of taste, and questioned my guide upon the subject; he assured me that it was the fashion of the country. I was equally at a loss to conceive how this bit of wood, which was merely stuck through the lip, could keep its place. The women allowed me to see that this curious ornament was brought through to the inner part of the lip, and they laughed heartily at my astonishment. I asked one of them to remove the piece of wood from her lip; but she told me that if she did so the saliva would run through the hole. In short, I was quite amazed that coquetry could induce them to disfigure themselves in this manner;

yet it is the general custom of this country. I saw young girls eight or ten years of age, who had in their lower lip little pieces of wood of the circumference of a pen-holder pointed at one end and stuck into the flesh. They renew it frequently, and every time use a larger bit of wood, which gradually widens the hole, until it becomes large enough to admit a piece of wood of the size of a half-crown piece. I observed that this singular and inconvenient ornament contributed to their uncleanliness."

-*Caillie's Africa*, Vol. I., page 374.

"The male Mandingoes are circumcised between the age of fifteen and twenty. The excision which females should undergo when they are marriageable, is often delayed until they are promised in marriage. I even saw a married woman, who, after having a child, submitted to this operation. It is always performed by women, and on several patients at once, who are thereby ren- dered for some time unable to work. In this state they are taken care of by their mothers, who bathe the wound several times a day with an indigenous caustic, with the use of which they are acquainted."

- *Caillie's Africa*, Vol. I., page 351.

"In Guinea, some of the customs practised on women, after their confinement, are most barbarous and inhuman. The mother is separated from her husband for a period of three years, that she may give undivided attention to her offspring; and, in the mean time, the husband supplies himself with another partner."

-*Valdez's Africa*, Vol. I., page 218.

"Their dances are mere steppings and turnings, in which there is nothing graceful, accompanied by the clapping of hands, and various distortions and gestures."

—*Valdez's Africa*, Vol. II., page 344.

"On our walk to the house, we first saw a woman of the Bosjesman race, and had ocular conviction of the truth of all we had previously heard respecting the uncommon ugliness of these people, particularly of the females. She sat more than half-naked, at the entrance of a miserable straw hut, near a fire of fresh brushwood, which exhaled a terrible smoke and vapor, and was occupied in skinning a lean hare. The greasy swarthiness of her skin, her clothing of animal hides, as well as the savage wildness of her looks, and the uncouth manner in which she handled the hare, presented altogether a most disgusting spectacle. She took no further notice of us than now and then to cast a shy leer to- ward us."
— *Lichtenstein's Africa*, Vol. I., page 56.

"They generally eat their flesh raw, and chew it very little. If they dress it, they scarcely make it hot through, and bite it with their teeth the moment it is taken out of the ashes. The incisive teeth, therefore, of the old Bosjesmans are commonly half worn away, and have one general flat edge. They drink out of the rivers and streamlets, lying down flat on their bellies, even when the bank is very steep, so that they are obliged to support them- selves in a fatiguing manner with their arms, to avoid falling into the water.".
—*Lichstentein's Africa*, Vol. II., page 48.

"The queen, who accompanied her lord, and who was decidedly the ugliest woman I ever saw, and very old, was called Mashumba. She was nearly naked, her only article of dress being a strip of the Fan cloth, dyed red, and about four inches wide. Her entire body was tattooed in the most fanciful manner; her skin, from long exposure, had become rough and knotty. She wore two enormous iron anklets, -iron being a precious metal with the Fans, - and had in her ears a pair of copper earrings two inches in diameter, and very heavy. These had so weighed down the lobes of her ears that I could have put my little finger easily into the holes through which the rings were run."

- *Du Chaillu's Equatorial Africa,* page 104.

"The men take care to put all the hardest work on their wives, who raise the crops, gather firewood, bear all kinds of burdens; and, where the bar-wood trade is carried on, as it is now by many Shekiani villages, the men only cut down the trees and split them into billets, which the women are then forced to bear on their backs through the forests and jungle down to the river- banks, as they have but rude paths, and beasts of burden are un- known in all this part of Africa. This is the most severe toil imaginable, as the loads have to be carried often six or seven miles or more."

-*Du Chaillu's Equatorial Africa,* page 197.

"It is curious what a stirring effect the sound of the tam-tam has on the African. He loses all control over himself at its sound, and the louder and more energetically the horrid drum is beaten, the wilder are the jumps of the male African, and the more disgustingly indecent the contortions of the women."

- *Du Chaillu's Equatorial Africa,* page 236.

"Many of the Hottentots wear, as ornaments, the guts of beasts, fresh and stinking, drawn two or three times, one through another, about their necks, and the like about their legs."

— *Ogilby's Africa,* page 591.

"The women are so addicted to dancing, that they cannot forbear upon the hearing of any instrument, though they be laden with one child in the belly, and another at the back, where they commonly carry them."
- *Ogilby's Africa*, page 466.

"The king of Congo eats and drinks in secrecy. If a dog enters the house while he is at meals, it is killed; and an instance is recorded of the king's son having accidentally seen his father drinking palm wine, and of his being executed on the spot."
-*Reade's Savage Africa*, page 286.

"When the aged become too weak to provide for themselves, and are a burden to those whom they brought forth and reared to manhood, they are not unfrequently abandoned by their own children, with a meal of victuals and a cruse of water, to perish in the desert; and I have seen a small circles of stakes fastened in the ground, within which were still lying the bones of a parent bleached in the sun, who had been thus abandoned."
- *Moffat's Africa*, page 97.

"When a mother dies, whose infant is not able to shift for itself, it is, without any ceremony, buried alive with the corpse of its mother."
- *Moffat's Africa*, page 48.

"They delight to besmear their bodies with the fat of animals, mingled with ochre, and sometimes with grime. They are utter strangers to cleanliness, as they never wash their bodies, but suffer the dirt to accumulate, so that it will hang a considerable length from their elbows. Their huts are formed by digging a hole in the earth about three feet deep, and then making a roof of reeds, which is however insufficient to keep off the rains. Here they lie close together like pigs in a sty. They are extremely lazy, so that nothing will rouse them to action but excessive hunger. They will continue several days together without food rather than be at the pains of procuring it. When compelled to sally forth for prey, they are dexterous at destroying the various beasts which abound in the country, and they can run almost as well as a horse. They are total strangers to domestic happiness. The men have several wives, but conjugal affection is little known. They take no great care of their children, and never correct them, except in a fit of rage, when they almost kill them by severe usage. In a quarrel between father and mother, or the several wives of a husband, the defeated party wreaks his or her vengeance on the child of the conqueror, which in general loses its life."

—Kicherer, quoted in *Moffat's Africa*, page 49.

"The women of Pongo disfigure their faces very much by making large holes in their ears, and through the cartilaginous parts of the nose. Weights are attached to make the hole large enough to pass the finger through. Pieces of fat meat are fre- quently worn in these holes, but whether for ornament or fragrance is not known. I inquired of one of them once why she did it, and received the laconic answer, 'My husband likes it.'"

—*Wilson's Africa*, page 288.

"The person of the King of Loango is sacred, and he is, in consequence, subjected to some very singular rules, especially in connection with his eating and drinking. There is one of his houses in which alone he can eat, and another where alone he can drink. When the covered dishes which contain his food are car- ried into the eating-house, a crier proclaims it, and everybody gets out of the way as quick as possible. The doors are then carefully closed and bolted, and any person that should see the king in the act of eating would be put to death. Proyart mentions the fact that a favorite dog was immediately put to death for looking up into his master's face while eating. Another is mentioned of a child that was accidentally left in the banqueting-room of the king by his father, and who awoke and accidentally saw the king eat-ing. It was spared five or six days, at the earnest request of its father, but was then put to death, and its blood sprinkled upon the king's fetich. Others might be present when the king drank, but they were bound to conceal their faces. In like manner no one is allowed to drink in the king's presence without turning their backs to him."

—*Wilson's Africa*, page 309.

"The King of Dahomi is one of the most absolute tyrants in the world; and, being regarded as a demi-god by his own subjects, his actions are never questioned. No person ever approaches him, even his favorite chiefs, without prostrating themselves at full length on the ground, and covering their faces and heads with earth. It is a grave offence to suppose that the king eats, drinks, sleeps, or performs any of the ordinary functions of nature. His meals are always taken to a secret place, and any man that has the misfortune or the temerity to cast his eyes upon him in the act is put to death. If the king drinks in public, which is done on some extraordinary occasions, his person is concealed by having a curtain held up before him, during which time the people prostrate themselves, and afterward shout and cheer at the very top of their voices."

—Wilson's Africa, page 202.

27

Huts, Hovels, and Holes (But No Houses) in Negroland

"It is impossible to look at some of their domiciles without the inquiry involuntarily rising in the mind, Are these the abodes of human beings? In a bushy country, they will form a hollow in a central position, and bring the branches together over the head. Here the man, his wife, and probably a child or two, lie huddled in a heap, on a little grass, in a hollow spot not larger than an ostrich's nest. Where bushes are scarce, they form a hollow under the edge of a rock, covering it partially with reeds or grass, and they are often to be found in fissures and caves of the mountains. When they have abundance of meat, they do nothing but gorge and sleep, dance and sing, till their stock is exhausted. But hunger, that imperious master, soon drives him to the chase. It is astonishing to what a distance they will run in pursuit of the animal which has received the fatal arrow. I have seen them, on the successful return

of a hunting party, the merriest of the merry, exhibiting bursts of enthusiastic joy; while their momentary happiness, contrasted with their real condition, produced on my mind the deepest sorrow."
- *Moffat's Africa*, page 48.

It is a curious fact that the circular form of hut is the only style of architecture adopted among all the tribes of Central Africa; and that, although these differ more or less in the form of the roof, no tribe has ever yet sufficiently advanced to construct a window."
- *Baker's Great Basin of the Nile*, page 141.

"Their sheep, goats, and poultry eat and sleep in the same hut with them, and a most intolerable stench is exhaled from all their dwellings. They do not appear to have the least affection for their offspring: a parent will sell his child for the merest trifle in the world, with no more remorse or repugnance than he would a chicken."
-*Lander's Africa*, page 348.

"These huts are erected so close to each other, and with so little regard to comfort and a free circulation of air, that there is scarcely a foot-path in the town wide enough for more than one to walk on at a time; and, not having the advantage of shady trees, the heat of the town is excessive and distressing. Its uncleanness, filth, and extreme nastiness have already been alluded to; and the odor emitted from the dirty streets is offensive and almost insupportable."
-*Lander's Travels in Africa*, Vol. II., page 45.

"Their houses somewhat resemble a beehive or ant-hill, consisting of boughs of trees stuck into the ground in a circular form, and lashed down across one another overhead so as to form a

framework, on which they spread large mats formed of reeds. These mats are also used instead of cloth, and are very effectual in resisting both sun and rain. The diameter of these dome-shaped huts varies from ten to fifteen feet."
— *Cumming's Africa*, Vol. I., page 127.

"In the construction of their dwelling-houses the Mandingoes also conform to the general practice of the African nations on this part of the continent, contenting themselves with small and incommodious hovels. A circular mud wall, about four feet high, upon which is placed a conical roof, composed of the bamboo cane, and thatched with grass, forms alike the palace of the king and the hovel of the slave. Their household furniture is equally simple. A hurdle of canes placed upon upright stakes, about two feet from the ground, upon which is spread a mat or bullock's hide, answers the purpose of a bed. A water-jar, some earthen pots for dressing their food, a few wooden bowls and calabashes, and one or two low stools, compose the rest."
— *Mungo Park's 1st Journal*, page 31.

"Houses are jotted down without any regard to the evenness or regularity of the ground on which they are erected. The higgledy-piggledy order of architecture prevails throughout; and the axiom of Bacon that a house was meant to live in,' is carried out in its most original simplicity in Old Kalabar. As I walk through the passages intended for streets, I have to scramble over eminences and down declivities in the best way I can. In a pathway between two houses opposite each other, or perhaps side by side, there may be an ascent or a descent of a dozen or score of feet; and in wet weather it is impossible to escape a foot-bath in some of the many ruts to be met with as one goes along. Heaps of dirt and all kinds of refuse are thrown indiscriminately through the town, as if to allow pasture-ground for the many turkey-buzzards, styled by Swainson, the scavengers of nature,' that congregate upon them, and have a perpetual carnival in browsing upon the festering offal."

— *Hutchinson's Western Africa*, page 116.

"Their buildings generally resemble the humbler sort of English cow-house, or an Anglo-Indian bungalow."

- *Burton's Africa*, page 90.

"Beyond the line of maritime land the dwelling-house assumes the normal African form, the circular hut described by every traveller in the interior. Dr. Livingstone appears to judge rightly that its circularity is the result of a barbarous deficiency in inventiveness."

- *Burton's Africa*, page 251.

"The inner side of the roof is polished to a shiny black with smoke, which winds its way slowly through the door. Smoke and grease are the African's coat and small clothes; they contribbute so much to his health and comfort that he is by no means anxious to get rid of them, and sooty lines depend from it like negro-stalactites."

— *Burton's Africa*, page 253.

"The settlements of the Wak'hutu are composed of a few straggling hovels of the humblest description, with doors little higher than an English pigsty, and eaves so low that a man can- not enter them except on all-fours. In shape they differ, some being simple cones, others like European haystacks, and others like our old straw beehives."

- *Burton's Africa*, page 97.

"All the accommodations of life through out this continent are simple, and limited in the greatest degree. There does not, probably, without some foreign interposition, exist in Africa a stone house, or one which rises two stories from the ground. The material of the very best habitations are merely stakes of wood plastered with earth, built in a conical form like beehives, and resembling the first rude shelter which man framed against the elements."
— *Murray's African Discoveries*, page 231.

"Except the state chairs or thrones of the great monarchs, ascended only on very solemn occasions, there is not throughout native Africa a seat to sit upon. The people squat on the ground in circles, and if the chief can place beneath him the skin of a lion or leopard, he is at the height of his pomp. For a table there is at best a wooden board, whereon is neither plate, knife, fork, nor spoon; the fingers being supposed fully adequate to the performance of every function."
— *Murray's African Discoveries*, page 233.

"Their appearance indicated wretchedness in the extreme, and they seemed to behold us with astonishment. Their dwellings were so low as to be hardly visible among the bushes till quite close to them. They were the shape of the half of a hen's egg, with the open part exposed to the weather, which must be extremely inconvenient in the rainy season, unless they are able to turn the inclosed side to the storm, which might easily be done. The inhabitants were so covered with dirt, mixed with spots of very red paint, that it appeared probable none of them had had any part of their bodies washed since they were born."
-*Campbell's Africa*, page 316.

"Throughout the whole country the huts are small, ill-constructed, and extremely filthy; the door is so low that to enter you are obliged to crawl on all-fours. The residence of each family is composed of several huts surrounded by quick hedges, planted at random and without taste. Sometimes this inclosure is formed merely of posts and rails, or a kind of palisade of straw. The streets are extremely narrow, winding, and dirty, all sorts of filth being thrown into them. Both men and women are very un- cleanly, as in all the negro villages in this country, and they rub a great quantity of butter upon their heads."

—*Caillie's Africa,* Vol. I., page 24.

"The village was a new one, and consisted mostly of a single street about eight hundred yards long, on which were built the houses. The latter were small, being only eight or ten feet long, five or six wide, and four or five in height, with slanting roofs. They were made of bark, and the roofs were of a kind of matting made of the leaves of a palm-tree. The doors run up to the eaves, about four feet high, and there were no windows. In these houses they cook, eat, sleep, and keep their store of provisions, chief of which is the smoked game and smoked human flesh, hung up to the rafters."

-*Du Chaillu's Equatorial Africa,* page 105.

"The palaver-house is an open shed, which answers the purpose of a public-house, club-room, or town-hall, to these people; they meet there daily, to smoke and gossip, hold public trials or palavers, and receive strangers."

-*Du Chaillu's Ashango-Land,* page 264.

"The best sort of Makololo huts consist of three circular walls, with small holes as doors, each similar to that in a dog-house; and it is necessary to bend down the body to get in, even when on all-fours. The roof is formed of reeds or straight sticks, in shape like a Chinaman's hat, bound firmly together with circular bands, which are lashed with the strong inner bark of the mimosa-tree. When all prepared except the thatch, it is lifted on to the circular wall, the rim resting on a circle of poles, between each of which the third wall is built. The roof is thatched with fine grass, and sewed with the same material as the lashings; and, as it projects far beyond the walls, and reaches within four feet of the ground, the shade is the best to be found in the country. These huts are very cool in the hottest day, but are close and deficient in ventilation by night."

— *Livingstone's Africa*, page 225.

"The Bosjesman has no settled residence; his whole life is passed in wandering from place to place; it even rarely happens that he passes two nights together on the same spot. One excep- tion may, however, be found to this general rule, and that is, when he has eaten till he is perfectly gorged; that is to say, when he has for several days together had as much as his almost incredible voracity can possibly eat. Such a revelry is followed by a sleep, or at least a fit of indolence, which will continue even for weeks, and which at last becomes so delightful to him, that he had rather buckle the girdle of emptiness round him, than submit to such an exertion as going to the chase, or catching insects. He is fond of taking up his abode for the night in caverns among the mountains, or clefts in the rocks; in the plain he makes himself a hole in the ground, or gets into the midst of a bush, where, bending the boughs around him, they are made to serve as a shelter against the weather, against an enemy, or against wild beasts. A bush that has served many times in this way as the retreat of a Bosjesman, and the points of whose bent boughs are beginning to grow again upwards, has perfectly the appearance

of an immense bird's nest. In this state many sorts of the pliant tarconanthus, abundance of which grows on the other side of the Great River, are often to be found; and if they have been recently inhabited, hay, leaves, and wool may be seen, forming the bottom of the nest. It is the custom which has given rise to the name by which the sav- ages in question are now known. Bosje signifying, in African Dutch, a shrub or bush; Bosjesman, consequently, a bush- man. An additional reason for giving it being derived from their often shooting at game, or at an enemy, from this retreat."
— *Lichtenstein's Africa*, Vol. II., page 46.

"The holes in the ground above mentioned, which sometimes serve these people as beds, are only a few inches deep, of a longish-round form, and even when they are to serve for a whole family, not more than five or six feet wide. It is incredible how they manage to pack together in so small a space, perhaps two grown persons and several children; each is wrapped in a single sheep- skin, in which they contrive to roll themselves up in such a manner, round like a ball, that all air is entirely kept from them. In very cold nights they heap up twigs and earth on the windward side of the whole; but against rain they have no other shelter than the sheepskin."
— *Lichtenstein's Africa*, Vol. II., page 47.

28

Gradual Decrease and Probable Extinction of the Negro Race

"I HAVE been struck with the steady decrease of the population, even during the short time I have been in Africa, on the coast and in the interior; but before I account for it, let me raise my voice in defence of the white man, who is accused as being the cause of it, Wherever he settles, the aborigines are said to disappear. I admit that such is the case; but the decrease of the population had already taken place before the white man came; the white man noticed it, but could not stop it. Populous tribes whom I saw for a second time, and who had seen no white man and his fiery water, have decreased, and this decrease took place before the terrible plague that desolated the land had made its appearance. The negroes themselves acknowledge the decrease. Clans in the life-time of old men have entirely disappeared; in others, only a few individuals remain."

-*Du Chaillu's Ashango- Land*, page 225.

"The decrease of the African population is owing to several causes the slave-trade, polygamy, barrenness of women, death among children, plagues, and witchcraft, — the latter taking away more lives than any slave-trade ever did. The negro does not seem to diminish only in the region I have visited; but in every other part of Africa, travellers, who after the lapse of a few years have returned a second time in the same country, have noticed a decrease of population. The women of the interior are prolific, and in despite of it shall we assume that the negro race has run its course, and that in due course of time it will disappear, as many races of mankind have done before him? The Southern States of America were, I believe, the only country in which the negro is known to have increased."
— *Du Chaillu's Ashango-Land*, page 435.

"The name of Hottentot will soon be forgotten, or remembered only as that of a deceased person of little note. Their numbers of late years have been rapidly on the decline. It has generally been observed that wherever Europeans have colonized, the least civilized have always dwindled away, and at length totally disappeared."
- *Barrow's Africa,* Vol. I., page 93.

"It is impossible to conceal one's fears for the ultimate existence of most of the colored races in South Africa; I mean those, in the first instance, within the colony, and those in the neighbor- hood of places where the emigrant Boers have lately settled. The lands of the native tribes become gradually encroached on; jealousies and animosities, wars and retaliations arise; the na tive tribes are driven back, lose their property, their lands, their courage; they fall back on other tribes, where they encounter more or less resistance, become

weaker and weaker, and the white man advances, and absorbs the whole."
- *Freeman's Missionary Travels in Africa*, page 68.

"At present, it appears to me that the prospects of the colored races of South Africa, taken on the broadest scale, are such as Christian philanthropy may weep over. I see no prospect of their preservation for any very lengthened period. The struggle may last for a considerable time. Missionary effort may not only save many of the souls of men, but help to defer the evil day of annihilation as to many of the aboriginal tribes. But annihilation is steadily advancing; and nothing can arrest it without an entire change in the system of government, wherever British subjects come in contact with the native tribes."
- *Freeman's Missionary Travels in Africa*, page 261.

"In our own day a disintegrating process is ever spreading among the nations of Eastern Africa, and the East Africans themselves avow that things went better with them in their fathers' time; that greater kings and chiefs existed then than now, and that a new element must be introduced among them. The descendants of Ham have outlived themselves."
- *Krapf's Africa*, page 393.

"How the negro has lived so many ages without advancing, seems marvellous, when all the countries surrounding Africa are so forward in comparison; and judging from the progressive state of the world, one is led to suppose that the African must soon either step out from his darkness, or be superseded by a being superior to himself. Could a government be formed for them like ours in India, they would be saved; but, without it, I fear there is very little chance; for at present the African neither can help himself, nor will he be helped by others, because his country is in such a constant state of turmoil he has too much anxiety on hand looking out for his food to think of anything else. As his fathers ever did, so does he. He works his wife, sells his children, enslaves all he can lay hands upon, and, unless when fighting for the property of others, contents himself with drinking, singing, and dancing like a baboon, to drive dull care away."

-*Speke's Africa*, page 24.

Rev. E. M. Wheelock, Secretary of the Board of Education of Freedmen, Department of the Gulf, formerly Chaplain of one of the New Hampshire Regiments, under date of New Orleans, Feb. 8, 1865, wrote to William Lloyd Garrison as follows: "On scores of plantations, labor was wholly suspended; and the laborers in hundreds, with their wives and little ones, had gathered around the forts and soldiers' camps. There they earned a precarious living by such uncertain and intermitted employment as they might find; the men as servants, hostlers, camp followers, and hangers-on, — their wives as cooks, washerwomen, etc. Hunger, cold, fever, and small pox were carrying off the children at a fearful rate of mortality. The morals of the men were being undermined by idleness and evil example, and the modesty of the women debauched by contact with all that is debasing in military life. From month to month their numbers visibly decreased; and it really seemed as though the Southern Negro, like the Indian, the Caffre, the Carib, and the Australian, would become extinct before the rude shock of the war, and the corrosive venom of our vices. The slave in Louisiana had become free, de facto, and in a qualified sense; but, alas! his freedom only meant the power to become idle, to become immoral, to sicken and to die."

29

Natural, Repulsive, and Irreconcilable Points of Difference, Physical, Mental, and Moral, Between the Whites and the Blacks

"So great a difference of opinion has ever existed upon the intrinsic value of the negro, that the very perplexity of the question is a proof that he is altogether a distinct variety. So long as it is generally considered that the negro and the white man are to be governed by the same laws and guided by the same management, so long will the former remain a thorn in the side of every community to which he may unhappily belong. When the horse and the ass shall be found to match in double harness, the white man and the

African black will pull together under the same regime. It is the grand error of equalizing that which is unequal that has lowered the negro character, and made the black man a reproach."
-*Baker's Great Basin of the Nile*, page 195.

"The obtuseness of the savages was such, that I never could make them understand the existence of any good principle; their one idea was power, force that could obtain all, the strong hand that could wrest from the weak. In disgust I frequently noted the feelings of the moment in my journal, memorandum from which I copy as illustrative of the time. 1863, 10th April.—I wish the black sympathizers in England could see Africa's inmost heart as I do; much of their sympathy would subside. Human nature viewed in its crude state as pictured amongst African savages is quite on a level with that of the brute, and not to be compared with the noble character of the dog. There is neither gratitude, pity, love, nor self-denial; idea of duty; no religion; but covetousness, ingratitude, selfish- ness, and cruelty. All are thieves, idle, envious, and ready to plunder and enslave their weaker neighbors.""
— *Baker's Great Basin of the Nile*, page 164.

"In childhood I believe the negro to be in advance, in intellectual quickness, of the white child of a similar age, but the mind does not expand; it promises fruit, but does not ripen; and the negro mind has grown in body, but has not advanced in intellect. The puppy of three months old is superior in intellect to a child of the same age, but the mind of the child expands, while that of the dog has arrived at its limit. The chicken of the common fowl has sufficient power and instinct to run in search of food the moment that it leaves the egg, while the young of the eagle lies helpless in its nest; but the young eagle outstrips the chicken in the course of time. The earth presents a wonderful example of variety in all classes of the human race, the animal and vegetable kingdoms. People, beasts, and plants belonging to distinct classes, exhibit special qualities and peculiarities. The existence of many hundred varieties of dogs cannot interfere with the fact that they belong to one genus, the greyhound, pug, bloodhound, pointer, poodle, mastiff, and terrier, are all as entirely different in their peculiar instincts as are the varieties of the human race. The different fruits and flowers continue the example, the wild grapes of the forest are grapes, but, although they belong to the same class, they are distinct from the luscious Muscatel; and the wild dog-rose of the hedge, although of the same class, is inferior to the moss-rose of the garden. From fruits and flowers we may turn to insect life, and watch the air teeming with varieties of the same species, the thousands of butterflies and beetles, the many members of each class varying in instincts and peculiarities. Fishes, and even shell-fish, all exhibit the same arrangement; that every group is divided into varieties, all differing from each other, and each distinguished by some peculiar excellence or defect."

-*Baker's Great Basin of the Nile*, page 195.

"The negro is a being who invents nothing, originates nothing, improves nothing; who can only cook, nurse, and fiddle; who has neither energy nor industry, save in rare cases, that prove the rule; he is the self-constituted thrall that delights in subjection to, and in imitation of, the superior races. The Aboriginal American has never been known to slave; the African, since he landed in Virginia, in 1620, has chosen nothing else; has never, until egged on, dreamed of being free."

— *Burton's Wanderings in West Africa*, Vol. I., page 175.

"Eastern and Central intertropical Africa also lacks antiquarian and historic interest; it has few traditions, no annals, and no ruins, the hoary remnants of past splendor so dear to the traveller and to the reader of travels. It contains not a single useful or ornamental work; a canal or a dam is, and has ever been, beyond the narrow bounds of its civilization."

-*Burton's Africa*, page 88.

"The African's wonderful loquacity and volubility of tongue have produced no tales, poetry, nor display of eloquence; though, like most barbarians, somewhat sententious, he will content himself with squabbling with his companions, or with repeating some meaningless word in every different tone of voice during the weary length of a day's march."

- *Burton's Africa*, page 497.

"Music is at a low ebb. Admirable tunists, and no mean tunists, the people betray their incapacity for improvement by remaining contented with the simplest and the most monotonous combinations of sounds. As in everything else, so in this art, creative talent is wanting. A higher development would have produced other results; yet it is impossible not to remark the de- light which they take in harmony. The fisherman will accompany his paddle, the porter his trudge, and the housewife her task of shelling grain, with a song; and for long hours at night the peasants will sit in a ring repeating, with a zest that never flags, the same few notes, and the same unmeaning line."

— *Burton's Africa*, page 468.

"Devotedly fond of music, the negro's love of tune has invented nothing but whistling and the whistle; his instruments are all

THE NEGROES IN NEGROLAND | 215

borrowed from the coast people. He delights in singing, yet he has no metrical songs; he contents himself with improvising a few notes without sense or rhyme, and repeats them till they When mourning, the love of music assumes a peculiar form; women weeping or sobbing, especially after chastisement, will break into a protracted threne or dirge, every period of which concludes with its own particular groan or wail. After venting a little natural distress in a natural sound, the long, loud improvisation, in the highest falsetto key, continues as before."
-*Burton's Africa*, page 497.

"The sebaceous odor of the skin among all these races is overpowering, and is emitted with the greatest effect during and after excitement, whether of mind or body."
-*Burton's Africa*, page 89.

"Up to the age of fourteen, the black children advance as fast as the white, but after that age, unless there be an admixture of white blood, it becomes, in most instances, extremely difficult to carry them forward."
-*Sir Charles Lyell's Second Visit to the United States*, Vol. I., page 105.

"A certain skill in mechanics, without the genius of invention; a great fluency of language, without energy in ideas; a correct ear for music, without a capacity for composition, - in a word, a display of imitative faculties, with an utter barrenness of creative power; there is your negro at the very best. Even these are rare, almost exceptional, cases; and to show such trained animals as fair samples of the negro is to make an exhibition of black lies. One might almost as well assert, after the sights which one sees at a country fair, that all pigs are learned; that the hare plays on a drum in its native state;

and that it is the nature of piebald horses to rotate in a circle to the sound of a brass band."

— *Reade's Savage Africa*, page 33.

"It has been proved by measurements, by microscopes, by analysis, that the typical negro is something between a child, a dotard, and a beast. I cannot struggle against these sacred facts of science."

-*Reade's Savage Africa*, page 399.

"I shall be blamed by ignorant persons when I say that, if war is waged against savages, it must be a massacre, or it is useless. Cruel as this maxim may appear, it would, if followed out, be the cause of less misery and bloodshed afterward. It must be re- membered that the minds of savages are as differently constituted from our minds, as are their bodies from our bodies. Forbearance these negroes ascribe to fear, and mercy to personal interest."

-*Reade's Savage Africa*, page 327.

"The Shangalla go all naked; they have several wives, and these very prolific. They bring forth children with the utmost ease, and never rest or confine themselves after delivery; but, washing themselves and the child with cold water, they wrap it up in a soft cloth made of the bark of trees, and hang it upon a branch, that the large ants, with which they are infested, and the serpents may not devour it. After a few days, when it has gathered strength, the mother carries it in the same cloth upon her back, and gives it suck with the breast, which she throws over her shoulder, this part being of such a length as, in some, to reach almost to their knees."

-*Bruce's Travels*, Vol. II., page 553.

"A Shangalla woman, upon bearing a child or two, at ten or eleven years old, sees her breast fall immediately down to near her knees. Her common manner of suckling her children is by carrying them upon her back, as our beggars do, and giving the infant the breast over her shoulders. They rarely are mothers after twenty-two, or begin child-bearing before they are ten; so that the time of child-bearing is but twelve years."
— *Bruce's Travels,* Vol. II., page 559.

"The women of this part of Africa are certainly singularly gifted with the Hottentot protuberance. So much de- pends on the magnitude of those attractions for which their southern sisters are so celebrated, that I have known a man, about to make a purchase of one out of three, regardless of the charms of feature, turn their faces from him, and looking at them behind, in the vicinity of the hips, make choice of her whose per- son most projected beyond that of her companions."
— *Denham's Africa*, Vol. II., page 89.

"Neither in the Desert nor in the kingdoms of Central Africa is there any march of civilization. All goes on according to a certain routine established for ages past."
-*Richardson's Africa*, Vol. I., page 305.

"There is not a tincture of letters or of writing among all the aboriginal tribes of Africa. There is not a hieroglyphic or a symbol, nothing corresponding to the painted stories of Mexico, or the knotted quipos of Peru. Oral communication forms the only channel by which thought can be transmitted from one country and one age to another. The lessons of time, the experience of ages, do not exist for the nations of this vast continent."

-*Murray's African Discoveries*, page 233.

"I found his majesty sitting upon a bullock's hide, warming himself before a large fire; for the Africans are sensible of the smallest variation in the temperature of the air, and frequently complain of cold when a European is oppressed with heat."
- *Mungo Park's First Journal*, page 41.

"They seem to have no social tenderness, very few of those amiable private virtues which would win our affection, and none of those public qualities that claim respect or command admiration. The love of country is not strong enough in their bosoms to incite them to defend it against the irregular incursions of a despicable foe; and of the active energy, noble sentiments, and contempt of danger, which distinguish the North American tribes and other savages, no traces are to be found among this slothful people. Regardless of the past as reckless of the future, the present alone influences their actions. In this respect they approach nearer to the nature of the brute than perhaps any other people on the face of the globe."
-*Lander's Travels in Africa*, Vol. I., page 176

"Clicking is a peculiarity of several South African languages. The Bushmen, Hottentots, and Kaffirs have each several clicks. The Natal Kaffirs use but three, and these not frequently, as there are few words but can be understood without the click. In the Bushmen's language, very many are used, and I have heard that a Bushman is not considered to speak his language elegantly until age has deprived him of all his teeth. These curious little men use a great deal of action during their conversation; and it is said that if a Bushman wishes to talk during a dark night, he is obliged to light a fire, to enable the listeners to see his action, and thereby fully to comprehend his meaning."

- *Drayson's Africa*, page 58.

"The Bosjesmans, indeed, are amongst the ugliest of all human beings. The flat nose, high cheek-bones, prominent chin, and concave visage, partake much of the apish character, which their keen eye, always in motion, tends not to diminish. The upper lid of this organ, as in that of the Chinese, is rounded into the lower on the side next the nose, and forms not an angle, as is the case in the eye of a European, but a circular sweep, so that the point of union between the upper and lower eyelid is not ascertainable. Their bellies are uncommonly protuberant, and their backs hollow. As a means of increasing their speed in the chase, or when pursued by an enemy, the men had adopted a custom, which was sufficiently remarkable, of pushing the testicles to the upper part of the root of the penis, where they seemed to remain as firmly fixed, and as conveniently placed, as if nature had stationed them there."

-*Barrow's Africa*, Vol. I., page 234.

"The great curvature of the spine inwards, and the remarkably extended posteriors, are characteristic of the whole Hottentot race; but, in some of the small Bosjesmans, they are carried to such an extravagant degree as to excite laughter. If the letter S be considered as one expression of the line of beauty to which degrees of approximation are admissible, some of the women of this nation are entitled to the first rank in point of form. A section of the body, from the breast to the knee, forms really the shape of the above letter. The projection of the posterior part, in one subject, measured five inches and a half from the line touching the spine. This protuberance consisted entirely of fat, and, when the woman walked,

it exhibited the most ridiculous appearance imaginable, every step being accompanied with a quivering and tremulous motion, as if two masses of jelly had been attached behind her."
- *Barrow's Africa*, Vol. I., page 237.

"The loose, long, hanging breasts, and disproportionate thickness of the hinder parts, make a Bosjesman woman, in the eyes of a European, a real object of horror."
— *Lichtenstein's Africa*, Vol. I., page 117.

"For the most part, the hordes keep at a distance from each other, since the smaller the number the easier is a supply of food procured. So trifling is the intercourse among them, that the names of even the most common objects are as various as the number of hordes. Their language is disagreeably sonorous, from the frequent clacking of the teeth, and the prevailing croaking in the throat; and it is extremely poor, no less in words than in sounds; they understand each other more by their gestures than by their speaking. No Bosjesman has a name peculiar to himself."
-*Lichtenstein's Africa*, Vol. II., page 49.

"If the ease with which a man is amused, surprised, or deluded, is a fair measure of intellectual grade, I fear that African minds will take only a very moderate rank in the scale of humanity. The task of self-civilization, which resembles the self-filtering of water, has done but little for Ethiopia in the ages that have passed simultaneously over her people and the progressive races of other lands."
— *Canot's Twenty Years of an African Slaver*, page 231.

"When two Namaquas are talking together, and one is relating a story, the listener repeats the last words of the speaker, even if he

should know as much of the matter as his informant. For instance, if a man begin his recital by saying, 'As I walked along the river, a very large rhinoceros rushed suddenly upon me.' 'Rushed suddenly upon me,' echoes the auditor. He was very fat.' 'Very fat,' the other ejaculates, and so forth.".
- *Andersson's Africa*, page 259.

"Unfortunately the people are altogether deficient of any rational or charitable feeling. Music is scarcely known, or indeed any other exertion of the mind calculated to correct or improve the natural passions."
-*Duncan's Africa*, Vol. I., page 199.

"In every part of the United States, there is a broad and impassable line of demarcation between every man who has one drop of African blood in his veins, and every other class in the community. The habits, the feelings, all the prejudices of society, -prejudices which neither refinement, nor argument, nor education, nor religion itself, can subdue, mark the people of color, whether bond or free, as the subjects of a degradation inevitable and incurable. The African in this country belongs by birth to the very lowest station in society; and from that station he can never rise, be his talents, his enterprise, his virtues what they may."
-*African Repository*, Vol. IV., page 118.

"The typical woolly-haired races have never invented a reasoned or reasonable theological system; discovered an alphabet; framed a grammatical language; nor made the least step in science or art. They have scarcely comprehended what they have learned; or retained a civilization taught them by contact with more refined nations, so soon as that contact has ceased. They have at no time formed great political states, nor commenced a self-evolving civilization."

- Hamilton Smith's Natural History of the Human Species, page 196.

"The negro is not wholly without talents, but they are limited to imitation, the learning of what has been previously known. He has neither invention nor judgment. Africans may be considered docile, but few of them are judicious, and thus in mental qualities we are disposed to see a certain analogy with the apes, whose imitative powers are proverbial."

— *Burmeister's Black Man,* page 14.

"The tune the negroes sing is very simple, entirely free from variations, and is constantly repeated in the same key. The voice is high, a sort of shrieking falsetto. The key is commonly in moll, seldom in dur, and each verse of the song terminates in a long-protracted, soft sound, in the singing of which alone can we observe anything like freedom and variety of expression. Dull and deep tones are disagreeable to the negro. He tries to raise his voice to the highest possible pitch, and even his laughter has more the sound of whistling than laughing. The shrill, drawn-out hie' they constantly emit as a mark of joyful surprise, reminded me of the harsh shrieking cries of the apes."

— *Burmeister's Black Man,* page 16.

"On several occasions, when I met with a negro with a physiognomy that pleased me, I attempted to begin a conversation with him, in order to discover his intellectual and spiritual characteristics, after having studied his body. The result, however, uni- versally satisfied me of his deficiencies in this respect, and served to confirm me in my opinion that the negro cares only for those things which belong to the very lowest grades of the human family."

- *Burmeister's Black Man*, page 12.

"There is not a single bookseller's shop in either Eastern or Western Africa."

— *Livingstone's Africa*, page 689.

"Among the negroes, no science has been developed, and few questions are ever discussed, except those which have an intimate connection with the wants of the stomach."

-*Livingstone's Africa*, page 138.

"The thermometer, placed upon a deal box in the sun, rose to 138°. It stood at 108° in the shade by day, and 96° at sunset. If my experiments were correct, the blood of a European is of a higher temperature than that of an African. The bulb, held under my tongue, stood at 100°; under that of the natives, at 98°."

- *Livingstone's Africa*, page 548.

"Among the slaves living at Aniambie, to work the king's plantations, were specimens of no less than eleven different tribes. Some old slaves from the far interior seemed very little removed from the Anthropoid apes in their shape and features, lean legs, heavy bodies, with prominent abdomen, retreating forehead, and projecting muzzles; they were more like animals than men."

- *Du Chaillu's Ashango-Land*, page 42.

"The reader who has followed me through the volume of my former exploration and the present book, will have been able to gather an idea of the general character and disposition of the negro of this part of Africa, as he now stands. I have made researches to ascertain if his race had formerly left remains, showing that he had once attained a tolerably high state of civilization; my researches have proved vain; I have found no vestige what- ever of ancient civilization. Other travellers in different parts of Africa have not been more successful than I have."

— *Du Chaillu's Ashango-Land*, page 435.

[Compiler's Note] For a fuller and more minute elucidation of the physical, mental, and moral differences which exist between white people and negroes, see the remaining portions of this work, especially the next succeeding chapter, entitled "American Writers on the Negro." The testimonies given in the present chapter are almost exclusively those of intelligent white travellers, who have seen (and who, as careful and correct observers, have always seen only with indignation and disgust) the negroes in Negroland.

30

American Writers on the Negro

THOMAS JEFFERSON, the fame of whose great intellect and commanding abilities seems to increase with the growth of time, was the first American who, having acquired a thorough knowledge of the inferior and baneful nature of the negro, wrote learnedly and truthfully about him; and who, at the same time, with the vision of an impassioned prophet, implored his countrymen to avert, by a system of emancipation and deportation, the very condition of national disgrace and ruin which has at last so nearly overtaken us. Yet such are the vagaries of certain sophists that the opinions of the renowned author of the Declaration of Independence are sometimes appealed to in support of the false positions of those who favor the recognition of the negro, upon terms of perfect equality, as a fellow-peer, a cousin-german, and a brother! The latest notable instance of this fallacy is afforded by the New York "Tribune," of April 14, 1866, in these words: -

"Mr. Jefferson is, and ought to be, held in sincere reverence by all Radicals because of his agency in basing the Declaration of Independence on the broad, comprehensive, eternal principle of Equal Human Rights. As to the fundamental base of our political system, Mr. Jefferson is and ought to be the highest authority."

Now, if we will but fairly scrutinize, and weigh well, what Mr. Jefferson really did say and write, at intervals, during the long period of the half century immediately sub- sequent to the date of the Declaration of Independence, we will find that he had, indeed, no sympathy whatever with the erroneous and unnatural views touching the negro, which are now so strenuously advocated by the "Tribune" and other oracular exponents of the Radical faith. For full proof of this, remembering that, without any specific reference or allusion to the negro, the Declaration of Independence was written in 1776, let us, in the following pages, see something of what Mr. Jefferson did pointedly and specifically write about the negro, between the date of that ever-memorable document, July 4, 1776, and the date of the death of its illustrious author, July 4, 1826: -

"DEEP-ROOTED PREJUDICES ENTERTAINED BY THE WHITES; TEN THOUSAND RECOLLECTIONS, BY THE BLACKS, OF THE IN- JURIES THEY HAVE SUSTAINED; NEW PROVOCATIONS; THE REAL DISTINCTIONS WHICH NATURE HAS MADE; AND MANY OTHER CIRCUMSTANCES, WILL DIVIDE US INTO PARTIES, AND PRODUCE CON- VULSIONS, WHICH WILL PROBABLY NEVER END BUT IN THE EX- TERMINATION OF THE ONE OR THE OTHER RACE. To these objections, which are political, may be added others, which are physical and moral. The first difference which strikes us is that of color. Whether the black of the negro resides in the reticular membrane between the skin and scarf-skin, or in the scarf-skin itself; whether it proceeds from the color of the blood, the color of the bile, or from that of some other secretion, the difference is fixed in nature, and is as real as if its seat and cause were better known to us. And is this difference of no importance? Is it not the foundation of a greater or less share of beauty in the two races? Are not the fine mixtures of red and white, the expressions of every passion by greater or less suffusions of color in the one, preferable to that eternal monotony, which reigns in the countenances, that immovable veil of black which covers the emotions of the other race? The circumstance of superior beauty is thought worthy of attention in the propagation of our horses, dogs, and other domestic animals; why not in that of man? Besides those of color, figure, and hair, there are other physical distinctions proving a difference of race. They have less hair on the face and body. They secrete less by the kidneys, and more by the glands of the skin, which gives them a very strong and disagreeable odor. This greater degree of transpiration renders them more tolerant of heat, and less so of cold than the whites. They are more ardent after their female; but love seems with them to be more an eager desire, than a tender, delicate mixture of sentiment and sensation. Their griefs are transient. Those numberless afflictions, which render it doubtful whether Heaven has given life to us in mercy or in wrath, are less felt, and sooner forgotten, with them. In general, their existence appears to participate more of sensation than re- flection. To this must be ascribed their disposition to sleep when abstracted from their diversions and unemployed in labor. An animal whose body is at rest, and who does not reflect, must be disposed to sleep, of course. Comparing them by their faculties of memory, reason, and imagination, it appears to me that in memory they are equal to the whites; in reason much inferior, as I think one could scarcely be found capable of tracing and comprehending the investigations of Euclid; and that in imagination they are dull, tasteless, and anomalous."

-*Jefferson's Works*, Vol. VIII., page 380. *Notes on Virginia*; written in 1782.

"The West Indies offer a more probable and practicable retreat for the negroes. Inhabited already by a people of their own race and color; climates congenial with their natural constitution; in- sulated from the other descriptions of men; nature seems to have formed these islands to become the receptacle of the blacks trans- planted into this hemisphere. Whether we could obtain from the European sovereigns of those islands leave to send thither the per- sons under consideration, I cannot say; but I think it more proba- ble than the former propositions, because of their being already inhabited more or less by the same race. Africa would offer a last and undoubted resort, if all others more desirable should fail."

—*Jefferson's Works*, Vol. IV., page 421. *Letter to Gov. Monroe*, Nov. 24, 1801.

"You have asked my opinion on the proposition of Mrs. Mifflin, to take measures for procuring, on the coast of Africa, an establish- ment to which the people of color of these States might, from time to time, be colonized, under the auspices of different governments. Having long ago made up my mind on this subject, I have no hesi- tation in saying that I always thought it the most desirable measure which could be adopted for gradually drawing off this part of our population most advantageously for themselves as well as for us. Going from a country possessing all the useful arts, they might be the means of transplanting them among the inhabitants of Africa, and would thus carry back to the country of their origin the seeds of civilization, which might render their sojournment and sufferings here a blessing in the end to that country."

—*Jefferson's Works*, Vol. V., page 563. *Letter to John Lynch*, January 21, 1811.

"I concur entirely in your leading principles of gradual emancipation, of establishment on the coast of Africa, and the patron- age of our nation until the emigrants shall be able to protect themselves. The subordinate details might be easily arranged. But the bare proposition of purchase by the United States gener- ally would excite infinite indignation in all the States north of Maryland. The sacrifice must fall on the States alone which hold them; and the difficult question will be how to lessen this so as to reconcile our fellow-citizens to it. Personally I am ready and desirous to make any sacrifice which shall ensure their gradual but complete retirement from the State, and effectually, at the same time, establish them elsewhere in freedom and safety. But I have not perceived the growth of this disposition in the rising generation, of which I once had sanguine hopes. No symptoms inform me that it will take place in my day. I leave it, therefore, to time, and not at all without hope that the day will come, equally desirable and welcome to us as to them."

— *Jefferson's Works*, Vol. VII., page 57. *Letter to Dr. Thomas Humphreys*, February 8, 1817.

"The bill on the subject of slaves was a mere digest of the existing laws respecting them, without any intimation of a plan for a future and general emancipation. It was thought better that this should be kept back, and attempted only by way of amendment, whenever the bill should be brought on. The principles of the amendment, however, were agreed on; that is to say, the freedom of all born after a certain day, and deportation at a proper age. But it was found that the public mind would not yet bear the proposition; nor will it bear it even at this day. Yet the day is not distant when it must bear and adopt it, or worse will follow. NOTHING IS MORE CERTAINLY WRITTEN IN THE BOOK OF FATE THAN THAT THESE PEOPLE ARE TO BE FREE; NOR IS IT LESS CERTAIN THAT THE TWO RACES, EQUALLY FREE, CANNOT LIVE IN THE SAME GOVERNMENT. Nature, habit, opinion, have drawn indelible lines of distinction between them. It is still in our power to direct the process of emancipation and deportation, peaceably, and in such slow degree, as that the evil will wear off insensibly, and their place be, pari passu, filled up by free white laborers."

— *Jefferson's Works*, Vol. I., page 48. *Autobiography*; written in 1821. --

"The article on the African colonization of the people of color, to which you invite my attention, I have read with great consideration. It is indeed a fine one, and will do much good. I learn from it more, too, than I had before known, of the degree of success and promise of that colony. In the disposition of this un- fortunate people, there are two rational objects to be distinctly kept in view. First: the establishment of a colony on the coast of Africa, which may introduce among the aborigines the arts of cultivated life, and the blessings of civilization and science. By doing this, we may make to them some retribution for the long course of injuries we have been committing on their population. The second object, and the most interesting to us, as coming home to our physical and moral characters, to our happiness and safety, is to provide an asylum to which we can, by degrees, send the whole of that population from among us, and establish them, under our patronage and protection, as a separate, free, and independent people, in some country and climate friendly to human life and happiness. I do not go into all the details of the burdens and benefits of this operation. And who could estimate its blessed effects? I leave this to those who will live to see their accomplishment, and to enjoy a beatitude forbid- den to my age. But I leave it with this admonition, to rise and be doing."

— *Jefferson's Works*, Vol. VII., page 332. *Letter to Jared Sparks*, February 4, 1824.

"The proverbs of Theognis, like those of Solomon, are observations on human nature, ordinary life, and civil society, with moral reflections on the facts. I quote him as a witness of the fact that there is as much difference in the races of men as in the breeds of sheep, and as a sharp reprover and censurer of the sordid, mercenary practice of disgracing birth by preferring gold to it. Surely no authority can be more expressly in point to prove the existence of inequalities, not of rights, but of moral, intellectual, and physical inequalities in families, descendants, and generations."

— *John Adams. Correspondence with Jefferson*, Nov. 15, 1813.

"Inequalities of mind and body are so established by God Almighty, in his constitution of human nature, that no art or policy can ever plane them down to a common level."

- *John Adams. Correspondence with Jefferson.*

"I have never read reasoning more absurd, sophistry more gross, in proof of the Athanasian creed, or Transubstantiation, than the subtle labors of Helvetius and Rousseau, to demonstrate the natural equality of mankind. The golden rule, 'Do as you would be done by,' is all the equality that can be supported or defended by reason, or reconciled to common sense."

-*John Adams. Correspondence with Jefferson.*

"It is only as immortal beings that all mankind can, in any sense, be said to be born equal; and when the Declaration of In- dependence affirms, as a self-evident truth, that all men are born equal, it is precisely the same as if the affirmation had been that all men are born with immortal souls."

- *John Quincy Adams. Letter to citizens of Bangor, Maine,* July 4, 1843.

"I would not dwell with any particular emphasis upon the sentiment, which I nevertheless entertain, with respect to the great diversity in the races of men. I do not know how far, in that respect, I might not encroach on those mysteries of Providence which, while I adore, I may not comprehend."
— *Daniel Webster*

"In my observations upon slavery as it existed in this country, and as it now exists, I have expressed no opinion of the mode of its extinguishment or melioration. I will say, however, though I have nothing to propose, because I do not deem myself so competent as other gentlemen to take any lead on this subject, that if any gentleman from the South shall propose a scheme to be carried on by this government upon a large scale, for the transportation of the colored people to any colony or any place in the world, I should be quite disposed to incur almost any degree of expense to accomplish that object."
— *Webster's Works*, Vol. V., page 364.

"It is a question of races, involving consequences which go to the destruction of one or the other. This was seen fifty years ago, and the wisdom of Virginia balked at it then. It seems to be above human reason now. But there is a wisdom above human, and to that we must look. In the mean time do not extend the evil."

- *Thomas Hart Benton.*

"Of the utility of a total separation of the two incongruous portions of our population (supposing it to be practicable) none have ever doubted. The mode of accomplishing that desirable object has alone divided public opinion. Colonization in Hayti for a time had its partisans. Without throwing any impediments in the way of executing that scheme, the American Colonization Society has steadily adhered to its own. The Haytien project has passed away. Colonization beyond the Stony Mountains has sometimes been proposed; but it would be attended with an expense and difficulties far surpassing the African project, whilst it would not unite the same animating motives."
— *Henry Clay. Speech in the House of Representatives,* 1827.

"How natural has it been to assume that the motive of those who have protested against the extension of slavery was an unnatural sympathy with the negro, instead of what it always has really been concern for the welfare of the white man."
- *William H. Seward, Speech at Detroit,* September 4, 1860.

"The great fact is now fully realized that the African race here is a foreign and feeble element, like the Indians, incapable of assimilation, and that it is a pitiful exotic unwisely and unnecessarily transplanted into our fields, and which it is unprofitable to cultivate at the cost of the desolation of the native vineyard."
- *William H. Seward. Speech at Detroit,* September 4, 1860.

"I have said that I do not understand the Declaration of Independence to mean that all men are created equal in all respects. Certainly the negro is not our equal in color, - perhaps not in many

other respects... I did not at any time say I was in favor of negro suffrage. Twice,- once substantially and once expressly, - I declared against it. ... I am not in favor of negro citizenship.
- *Abraham Lincoln, Debates with Douglas in* Illinois, 1858.

"I am not, and never have been, in favor of making voters or jurors of negroes, nor of qualifying them to hold office, nor to intermarry with whites; and I will say further, in addition to this, that there is a physical difference between the black and white races, which I believe will forever forbid the two races living together on terms of social and political equality."
— *Abraham Lincoln, Debates with Douglas in Illinois*, 1858.

"I will, to the very last, stand by the law of the State which forbids the marrying of white people with negroes."
— *Abraham Lincoln. Speech at Columbus, Ohio*, September, 1859.

"Why should not the people of your race be colonized? Why should they not leave this country? This is, perhaps, the first question for consideration. You and we are a different race. We have between us a broader difference than exists between almost any other two races. Whether it is right or wrong, I need not discuss; but this physical difference is a great disadvantage to us both, as I think your race suffers greatly, many of them by living with us, while ours suffer from your presence. In a word, we suffer on each side. If this is admitted, it shows a reason why we should be separated. You, here, are freemen, I suppose. Perhaps you have long been free, or all your lives. Your race are suffering, in my opinion, the greatest wrong inflicted on any people. But even when you cease to be slaves, you are yet far removed from being placed on an equality with the white race. You are still cut off from many of the advantages which are enjoyed by the other race. The aspiration of man is to enjoy equality with the best when free; but on this broad continent not a single man of your race is made the equal of ours. Go where you are treated the best, and the ban is still upon you. I do not propose to discuss this, but to present it as a fact with which we have to deal. I cannot alter it if I would. It is a fact about which we all think and feel alike. We look to our conditions owing to the existence of the races on this continent. I need not recount to you the effects upon white men growing out of the institution of slavery. I believe in its general evil effects upon the white race. See our present condition. The country is engaged in war. Our white men are cutting each other's throats, none knowing how far their frenzy will extend; and then consider what we know to be the truth. But for your race among us, there could not be a war, although many men engaged on either side do not care for you one way or the other. Nevertheless, I repeat, without the institution of slavery, and the colored race as a basis, the war could not have had an existence. It is better for us both, therefore, to be separated. I know that there are free men among you who, even if they could better their condition, are not as much inclined to go out of the country as those who, being slaves, could obtain their freedom on this condition. I suppose one of the principal difficulties in the way of colonization is, that the free colored man cannot see that his comfort would be advanced by it. You may believe you can live in Washington, or elsewhere in the United States, the remainder of your lives, perhaps more comfortably than you could in any foreign country. Hence you may come to the conclusion that you have nothing to do with the idea of going to a foreign country. This (I speak in no unkind sense) is an extremely selfish view of the case. But you ought to do something to help those who are not so fortunate as yourselves. For the sake of your race you should sacrifice something of your present comfort, for the purpose of being as grand in that respect

as the white people. It is a cheering thought throughout life, that some- thing can be done to ameliorate the condition of those who have been subject to the hard usages of the world. It is difficult to make a man miserable while he feels that he is worthy of himself, and claims kindred with the great God who made him! In the American revolutionary war, sacrifices were made by men engaged in it, but they were cheered by the future. General Washington himself endured greater physical hardships than if he had remained a British subject; yet he was a happy man, because he was engaged in benefiting his race, and in doing something for the children of his neighbors, having none of his own."
— Abraham Lincoln. *Address to a Deputation of Negroes*, June, 1862.

"I believe this government was made by white men, for the benefit of white men and their posterity forever; and I am in favor of confining citizenship to white men, -men of European birth and descent, instead of conferring it upon negroes, Indians, and other inferior races.".
-Stephen A. Douglas. Debates with Lincoln in Illinois, 1858.

"All the early patriots of the South-Washington, Jefferson, Madison, Monroe, Jackson, Clay, and others - were the advocates of emancipation and colonization. The patriots of the North concurred in the design. Is the faction now opposing it patriotic or philanthropic? Are they not rather, like Calhoun, working the negro question to accomplish schemes of selfish ambition, and, after his method, making a balance of power party of a phalanx of deluded fanatics, keeping the Union and the public peace perpetually in danger, and seeking power in the government through its distractions? The author of the Declaration of Independence and his associates declared equal rights impracticable in society constituted of masses of different races. De Tocqueville, the most profound writer of the Old World on American institutions, predicts the extermination of the blacks, if it is attempted to confer such rights on them in the United States. It is obvious that an election would be a mockery in a community wherein there could be no other than black and white parties. In such communities, reason and experience show that one or the other race must be the dominant race, and that democracy is impossible. This is not less obvious to the Phillips school than it is to the Calhoun school, who concur in opposing the policy of Mr. Jefferson, adopted by the president, intended to effectuate the design of our fathers to establish popular government. They concur in press- ing here the antagonism of races, and only differ in looking to different races to give them power. The result of this antagonism, so far as popular government is concerned, would be the same if either could succeed in their schemes; and you would scarcely have much preference between being governed by Jeff. Davis, as the leader of the Slave Power, and Wendell Phillips, as the leader of the enfranchised blacks. But neither can succeed. Even the Calhoun scheme, matured through so many years of intrigue by men versed in public affairs, and attended with a temporary success, is a failure as a governing contrivance, though potent still to spread ruin widely through the land, and especially to desolate the homes of his deluded followers. The Phillips scheme is the dream of visionaries wholly unskilled in government, and will be a failure from the start. He may, in turn, make victims of the negroes, as Calhoun has of their masters. But I think not. They are not ambitious of ruling white men, and will, I believe, be contented to set up for themselves, in some neighboring and congenial clime, on the plan of Jefferson and Lincoln."

-*Montgomery Blair, Speech at Concord, N. H.,* June 17, 1863.

"The problem before us is the practical one of dealing with the relations of masses of two different races in the same community. The calamities now upon us have been brought about, as I have already said, not by the grievances of the class claiming property in slaves, but by the jealousy of caste awakened by the secessionists in the non-slaveholders. In considering the means of securing the peace of the country hereafter, it is, therefore, this jealousy of race which is chiefly to be considered. Emancipation alone would not remove it. It was by proclaiming to the laboring whites, who fill the armies of rebellion, that the election of Mr. Lincoln involved emancipation, equality of the negroes with them and consequently amalgamation, that their jealousy was stimu- lated to the fighting point. Nor is this jealousy the fruit of mere ignorance and bad passion, as some suppose, or confined to the white people of the South. On the contrary, it belongs to all races, and, like all popular instincts, proceeds from the highest wisdom. It is, in fact, the instinct of self-preservation which revolts at hybridism. Nor does this instinct militate against the natural law, that all men are created equal, if another law of nature, equally obvious, is obeyed. We have but to restore the subject race to the same, or to a region similar to that from which it was brought by violence, to make it operative; and such a separation of races was the condition which the immortal author of the Declaration himself declared to be indispensable to give it practical effect. A theorist, not living in a community where diverse races are brought in contact in masses, may stifle the voice of nature in his own bosom, and, from a determination to live up to a mistaken view of the doctrine, go so far as to extend social intercourse to individuals of the subject race. But few even of such persons would pursue their theories so far as amalgamation and other legitimate consequences of their logic."

—*Montgomery Blair. Letter read at the Cooper Institute, N. Y.*, March 6, 1863.

"White men have for centuries been accustomed to vote. They have borne all the responsibilities and discharged all the duties of freemen among freemen; and it is a very different thing to take away from a freeman a privilege long exercised by him and by his ancestors, from what it is to confer one never before enjoyed upon ignorant, half-civilized Africans just released from slavery. Three generations back many of them were cannibals and savages of the lowest type of human kind The only civilization they have is that which they have received during their slavery in America. To confer this great privilege upon the more enlightened negroes might tend to elevate the mass in the end. But to confer it now upon their ignorant hordes can only degrade the ballot and the republican institutions which rest upon it. No answer to this view has ever been given, no answer can be given, by the friends of universal negro suffrage, except this: "The ignorant foreigner is allowed to vote, why not let the ignorant negro vote? Thus to compare the civilized European, accustomed to free labor, to self-support, and self-government, to all the duties and responsibilities of a freedman, and who withal, before he is allowed to vote in most of the States, must appear in open court, and, after five years' residence, prove by the testimony of two citizens a good moral character and that he is well disposed towards the government and institutions of the United States, to compare him with the poor degraded mass of Africans, plantation slaves just set free, is an atrocious libel upon our- selves, upon our ancestors, upon the results of Christian civilization, and upon that Caucasian race which for thousands of years has ruled the world. Why press this negro domination over the whites of the South? What reason can you give? The answer is, because the negroes were loyal and the whites dis- loyal. Let us examine this bold assertion. Is it true? Were the negroes loyal during the rebellion? Recall the facts. Who does not remember that at least three-fourths of all the negroes in those States during the whole war did all in their power to sustain the rebel cause? They fed their armies; they dug their trenches; they built their fortifications; they fed their women and children. There were no insurrections, no uprisings, no effort of any kind anywhere outside the lines of our armies on the part of the negroes to aid the Union cause. In whole districts, in whole States even, where all the able-bodied white men were conscripted into the rebel army, the great mass of negroes, of whose loyalty you boast, under the control of women, decrepit old men and boys, did all they were capable of to aid the rebellion.".

-James R. Doolittle. *Speech in the Senate*, January 23, 1868.

"In the name of constitutional liberty; in the name of our great ancestors who laid the foundations of this government to se- cure the liberty for themselves and for us; in the name of all who love that liberty, who are ready to struggle and if need be to die rather than allow it to be overthrown; in the name of the coming generations and that race to which we belong and which has given to the world all its civilization, I do arraign and impeach the radical policy of the present Congress of high crimes and misdemeanors. At the bar of the American people, in the presence of high Heaven and before the civilized world, I impeach it, first, as a crime against the laws of nature which God the Almighty has stamped upon the races of mankind, because it attempts to force a political and social and unnatural equality between the African and the Caucasian, between an alien, inferior, and exotic race from the tropics, with the highest type of the human race in the home of the latter in the temperate zone. Second: I impeach it as a crime against civilization, because it would by force wrench the government out of the hands of the civilized white race in ten States of this Union, to place it in the hands of the half-civilized African. Third: I impeach it as a crime against the constitution, because it tramples down the rights of the States to fix for themselves the qualifications of their own voters, a right without which a State ceases to be republican at all. Fourth: I impeach it as a crime against the constitution and against national faith, because it annuls the pardons constitutionally granted to hundreds of thousands of the most intelligent white men of the South, and in open, palpable violation of the constitution, disfranchises them. Fifth: I impeach it as a crime against the existence of ten States of the Union and the liberties of eight millions of people, because in express terms it annuls all civil government, by which alone those liberties may be secured, and places them under an absolute military despotism. Sixth: I impeach it as a crime against humanity, tending to produce a war of races, to the utter destruction of one or both, - a result which cannot be prevented except by a large standing army, which neither resources will bear nor our liabilities long survive. Seventh: I impeach it as an utter abandonment of the purpose for which the war was prosecuted, of the idea upon which we fought and mastered a rebellion."

-*James R. Doolittle. Speech at Hartford, Conn.*, March 11, 1868.

"I know it is said that the objection which is felt on the part of the white population of this country to living side by side in social and civil equality with the negro race is all a mere prejudice of caste. But its foundations are laid deeper than mere prejudice. It is an instinct of our nature. Men may theorize on the condition of the two races living together, but the thing is impossible; the instincts of both parties are against it."

— *Senator Doolittle, of Wisconsin.*

"Of all the delusions I have ever known, the idea of political equality between the black and white races seems to me the greatest. For more than four thousand years the history of this world has been written, and in all that time there is not one recorded annal of a civilized negro government; there is not one instance of political equality between the two races that has not proved injurious to both; and yet it is proposed to confer upon an inferior race the dominion over one-third of the republic, and to make it a balance of power that, nine times out of ten, would, for that reason, control the whole country. There can be but one end to this scheme, if it be much longer prosecuted. It is impossible that the race to which we belong can submit to negro domination; it is impossible that so inferior a race as the negro can compete with the white man in the business, much less the politics, of the country. The extermination of the negro, or his expulsion from this country, must be the inevitable result of the Radical policy, if persisted in. But before that happens, what untold evils may await us, what anarchy, what confusion, what impoverishment, what distress! Worse than Mexico, worse than the South American Republics, will be the condition of a large portion of this country, if that policy prevails. And here let me caution you, my friends, that the question of negro suffrage was not settled by your votes last October. It is true that you voted it down in Ohio, but it is equally true that what you refuse to permit here you are asked to impose upon others. It is equally true that what you have solemnly condemned, a Radical Congress may impose upon you in spite of your condemnation, impose upon you by an amendment to the Constitution of the United States, ratified by other States, though rejected by Ohio. If you would guard against negro suffrage, if you would guard against political equality with the negro, you must not be satisfied with sending its opponents to the Legislature of your own State, but you must keep its advocates out of the halls of Congress."

-*Senator Thurman, of Ohio. Speech at Mansfield,* Jan. 21, 1868.

"Whatever may have been the sympathies of the North on the question of freedom from slavery, you need not think they will be with the negro in this horrible contest now imminent; for when the northern man sees the mother and children escaping from the burning home that has sheltered and protected them; when he hears the screams of beauty and innocence in the flight from pursuing lust, if ever he venerated a mother, or loved a sister or wife, his heart and hand will be for the pale-faced woman and child of his own race. Whatever may have been the sympathies of the North for the negro in the claim made on his behalf for civil rights, just and generous men will turn with horror from the congressional policy that places the white race under the power and government of the negroes, and seeks to establish negro States in the Union. You have taken the robes of political power off the shoulders of white men, and you have put them upon the shoulders of negroes. Gentlemen may moralize in solemn tones, as if they came from the tomb, about the gallantry and distinguished services of the negroes in the war. I can tell you that with all the political and party ambition you have, with all the party power you have, you have not power to take the garlands from the brows of the white soldiers and put them on the heads of the negroes. You cannot do it. What is right will stand. And I can tell you that all over this land, in every neighborhood, there are the soldiers that have returned home, who will vindicate and defend their own honor against this effort to appropriate the glory of the white boys' to the negroes. There was not a battle in the war that was won by the negroes. There is not a point that was carried by them. My colleague has spoken of a column, -the column of congressional reconstruction, and has said that it is not hewn of a single stone, but is composed of many blocks.' I think he is right. Its foundation is the hard flint-stone of military rule, brought from the quarries of Austria, and upon that foundation rests the block from Africa, and it is thence carried to its topmost point with fragments of our broken institutions. That column will not stand. It will fall, and its architects will be crushed beneath its ruins. In its stead the people will uphold thirty-seven stately and beautiful columns, pure and white as Parian marble, upon which shall rest forever the grand structure of the American Union."

- *Thomas A. Hendricks. Speech in the Senate,* February, 1868.

"I lay down the propositions that the white and black races thrive best apart; that a commingling of these races is a detriment to both; that it does not elevate the black, and it only depresses the white; that the history of this continent, especially in Hispano-America, shows that stable, civil order and government are impossible with such a population. Equality is a condition which is self-protective, wanting nothing, asking nothing, able to take care of itself. It is an absurdity to say that two races, so dissimilar as black and white, of different origin, of unequal capacity, can succeed in the same society when placed in competition. There is no such example in history of the success of two separate races under such circumstances. Less than sixty years ago, Ohio had thousands of an Indian population. She has now but thirty red men in her borders. The negro, with a difference of color indelible, has been freed under every variety of circumstances; but his freedom has, in most cases, as a matter of course, been only nominal. Prejudice stronger than all principles, though not always stronger than lust, has imperatively separated the whites from the blacks. In the school-house, the church, or the

hospital, the black man must not seat himself beside the white; even in death and at the cemetery the line of distinction is drawn."
-S. S. Cox. *Eight Years in Congress*, pages 249, 250.

"Judge Douglass was right when he maintained that these commonwealths were for white men. Aside from the question of policy, there is an admitted right in each State to make or unmake its citizenship; to declare who is and who is not entitled thereto. That will not be denied. When Minnesota came here for admis- sion, that was settled. But my colleague seems to admit that political privileges, like that of suffrage, may be fixed by State laws. Indeed, the Supreme Court have decided that the State has the exclusive right so to do. If so, by what reason can a State deprive the black race of the right of suffrage, on which depend all laws, all protection, all assessment of taxes, all punishments, even the matter of life and death, and yet not have power to forbid such black race, as a dangerous element, from mingling with its population! The Constitution of Illinois, just submitted to the people, denies to the negro the right of emigrating to or having citizenship in that State. Hitherto the same prohibition has ex- isted in Illinois and Indiana, and othern western States. The right and power to exclude Africans from the States north being compatible with our system of State sovereignty and federal supremacy, I assert that it is impolitic, dangerous, degrading. and unjust to the white men of Ohio and of the North to allow such immigration."
-S. S. Cox. *Eight Years in Congress,* pages 243, 244.

"The Caucasian, or white man is five feet and between nine and ten inches high; the Esquimaux four feet and seven inches high; the Mongolian type, to which the Chinese belong, five feet and between four and five inches high. The Caucasian type weighs one hundred and fifty-six pounds; the Esquimaux ninety-seven pounds; the Mongol one hundred and thirty-two pounds. The Caucasian lives to be sixty-six years and four months old; the Mongol to be fifty-three years old; and the Esquimaux to be forty-one years old. The life-insurance companies of Europe and America all predicate their policies upon the fact that white men and women live to be sixty-six years and four months old on an average. This average is based upon observations on the duration of more than six million lives. The statistics of the British and French armies are full of evidence going to show and to prove that in height and weight no two races of men have yet been found alike. The feet and hands, the arms and legs, are un- like in measurement. The hand of the negro is one-twelfth longer and one-tenth broader than the hand of the white man; his foot is one-eighth longer and one-ninth broader than the white man's; his forearm is one-tenth shorter; and the same is true of the bones from the knee to the ankle. These last-stated measurements are given upon the authority of Sir Charles Lyell. There has not yet been found, as far as I can learn, one bone in the skeleton of the white man which does not differ both in weight and measurement from its fellow-bone which may belong to any other type of man. The skeleton is unlike in the whole in weight and measurement, and unlike in every bone of it. These average differences ought to be conclusive that they cannot and do not belong to the same type; and these unvarying dissimilarities must be produced by causes which are not accidental."

-*William Mungen. Speech in the House of Representatives,* July 10, 1867

"Some of our people who pretend to see in the Indian, the Chinaman, the Esquimaux, and especially the African, ' a man and a brother,' claim that all the wide and impassable differences which are found between the races or types of men have been produced by accidental causes, by climate, and by amalgamations. I have already, for the present at least, sufficiently answered the climatic part of this proposition, and have only to say that if it be true, as held by my Radical friends, that the negro is a man and a brother,' — that he is the offspring of Adam, that there was, in other words, but one race at first, how there could have been amalgamations' I cannot imagine. Amalgamation, in the sense in which they use it, implies a plurality of races,—just what ethnol- ogists claim; but in fact it upsets the Radical theory of the unity of races,' upon which must depend their whole argument in favor of 'equality and fraternity.' For as soon as they admit that the races are of different origins they can no longer claim that all races are equal, any more than they can claim that the horse and the ass are equal. The principle on which the argu- ment rests is identical. Miscegenation is a subject of vast importance to society, to posterity, and especially at the pres- ent time to the statesmen of our country. For it is true in his- tory and true in science that nations which allow their national stock to be adulterated, which tolerate amalgamation with other national types, will perish certainly, and perish forever. I have said that this is a question of the utmost importance to the states- men of America, of that portion of it especially which once bore deservedly the name of The United States of America;' and I say now, with all the candor possible, that if those statesmen, those gentlemen who are moulding and shaping the policy and laws and regulations for our government, fail to be guided by experience and science and history in shaping a policy to pre- vent amalgamation, misce- genation, social and political equality of the different races, white, black, red, yellow, and brown, our nation will be suffocated, as it were, by these foolish and suicidal projects, these Utopian schemes of equality of races."

—*William Mungen. Speech in the House of Representatives,* July 10, 1867.

"There are two other subjects or sciences which bear important testimony relative to the origin of types of the human races; I allude to embryology and cranioscopy. I do not profess to un- derstand either of these subjects or sciences thoroughly; but the professors of embryology assert, and they are unanimous in the assertion, that the law of life which operates to organize man in his earliest moment, that the spermatozoa and the cell formation are entirely different in each type of the human race; and that in this department of her work, as in every other, nature displays infinite variety. I repeat, then, the declaration of these learned gentlemen, that under a powerful microscope the fact that the different types of men are absolutely different creations is no longer an open question. The law which operates to organize and the being organized are different from the first and different totally. But quite the most curious, and perhaps the most impor- tant discovery which cranioscopy has made relates to the position which each type holds in the scale of civilization. It is found that the races of men whose brain measures sixty-four cubic inches or less are always barbarous and heathen people; that they have not intellectual power sufficient to frame a government nor to enact laws; in other words, to make for themselves any form of gov- ernment better than heathenism makes. The races of men whose brain measures from seventy-four to eighty-four cubic inches are the unprogressive people. They are half-civilized or half-barbar- ous; the governments they found are always despotic; the laws they enact are always peculiar, and are different from the laws enacted by any other type of people. The people of China, Japan, India, in short the greater portion of the types of man, are embraced and included between sixty-eight and eighty-four cubic inches of brain. The nationalities whose brain measures ninety-four cubic inches or upward are the only nationalities who are progressive and enlightened, who are capable of cultivating the physical sciences to practical results, and whose governments are made for the benefit of the people. Cranioscopy declares that the different types have each a different organization, in other words, a different creation; and it further declares that there are as plainly different kinds of men, having different kinds of humanities in the world as there are different kinds of beasts; that the horse and the ox are not more certainly different creations than the white man and the Indian, the Indian and the African, the African and the Chinese, the Chinaman and the Esquimaux. .. I have discussed this ques- tion of races, because it lies at the foundation of our social and polit- ical structure. All history shows that a free government, administered according to law, is impossible, unless the people who create the laws and accept them for their government are endowed with those qualities of mind and character which have never been ex- hibited by the negro race. The attempt to blend the races by the coercion of statutory enactments and military violence will be instinctively repelled by the white dominant race; and if this coercion should succeed, it would have no other result than a com- mon degradation and a common ruin."

-*William Mungen. Speech in the House of Representatives,* July 10, 1867.

"The difference is not only in the hair, but it is in the whole anatomical structure of the head, inside and outside. The negro's face projects like a muzzle, and the teeth are obliquely inserted, so that their edges meet as at projecting angles. The develop- ment of the jaw (prognathism) is in direct relation or proportion to the intellectual capacity of a people,-the prognathous being con- fined to the lowest races of men, among them the negro. Their cranial capacity is different. The volume of an American or English head is in cubic centimetres 1572-95, while that of a negro, born in Africa, is only 1371-42, and the place occupied in relation to cranial capacity and cerebral weight corresponds with the degree of intellectual capacity and civilization. The weight of the white man's brain is greater than that of the negro. The convolutions of the brain are different. The anterior and frontal lobes of the white man show a far better mental develop- ment. All these assertions are maintainable by high German, French, and English, as well as American authority; but this is not the place nor the hour for metaphysical or psychological dis- cussion. Every feature of the white man and negro differs. The nose is different. The nostrils of a Caucasian form two nearly rect- angular triangles, the hypothenuses of which are turned out- wards, whilst the septum of the nose forms a perpendicular line common to the two triangles. On taking a similar view of the negro, the nostrils present only a transverse aperture, or the figure of a hori- zontal eight united in the middle by the nasal sep- tum. The form and size of the mouth, the shape of the lips and cheeks are very different. The apish chin of the negro differs very essentially from that of the white man. The facial angle of the distinguished writer, Camper, amounts in the negro todegrees, - it may sink to 65, — whilst in the Caucasian it is rarely below 80, and frequently a few degrees higher. The negro's skull is thicker than the white man's, the cervical muscles more powerful, and, hence, the negro carries his burden on his head, and, like a ram in a fight, uses his skull. The negro's shoulder differs from the white man's. The negro's hand is larger, his fin- gers long and thin, palms flat, thumb-balls scarcely prominent. All the characters of his hand (says Carl Voght) 'decidedly ap- proach that of the Simian hand.' The leg, the calves of the leg, all differ from the white man's. 'The femoral bones, as well as the fibula, seem curved outwards, so that the knees are more apart from each other than in the white.' The pelvis is organi- cally different. The foot of the negro,' says Burmeister, 'is in everything ugly, flat, of a projecting heel, a thick, flabby cushion in the inner cavity, with wide-spreading toes. The mid- dle part of the foot does not touch the ground.' Voght, the German physiologist, calls it 'the foot of the gorilla, or, if you please, the posterior hand.' I cite these facts to show that it is not the skin alone that parts the white from the negro race, not the der-is, or epidermis, or pigment therein."

-James Brooks. Speech in the House of Representatives, December 18, 1867.

"Where, oh, tell me where, sir, has the pure-blooded negro unassisted by the white man, exhibited any of the triumphs of genius? Where have we found that race producing a Homer, a Phidias, a Praxiteles, a Socrates, a Demosthenes, a Virgil, or a Milton, or a Shakespeare? Where has it produced any great architect like Michael Angelo? Where any great poet, where any heroic soldier like Alexander, Cæsar, or Napoleon? Where any wonderful mechanic? What negro of pure blood ever started a steam-engine, or a spinning-jenny, a screw, a lever, the wheel. or the pulley? What negro has invented a telegraph, or discovered a star, a satellite, or an asteroid? What negro ever constructed a palatial edifice like this in which we are assembled, - these Corinthian columns, - these frescoed walls? Negro history makes no mark in the great world's progress. That history is all a blank, blank, blank, sir. The negro can never rise above a certain range of intelligence. The children of the negro, up to ten or fifteen years of age, may be as bright and as in- telligent as -white children. They acquire knowledge as rapidly; but after that early age the negro youth does not advance as does the white youth. While the white man is increasing in knowledge till the day of his death, the negro reaches before the age of maturity a point beyond which he cannot well advance in anything save in the arts of mere imitation."

—*James Brooks. Speech in the House of Representatives,* December 18, 1867.

"I need not cross the Atlantic to show the fatal step you are taking by this Reconstruction Bill in going into this copartnership with negroes. Our continent has been settled by two classes of Anglo-Saxon, Celt, and Teuton in the North, and the Spanish-Latin race in the South. God never made a nobler race of men than the old Hidalgos of Spain, who, under Columbus, in a little caraval of forty tons, started on the trackless Atlantic in search of the then unknown America. God never made a nobler race, I repeat, than these Hidalgos of Spain. What did they do? They ran all along the Gulf of Mexico, from Florida on the north to Cape Horn on the southern verge of South America. They settled Mexico and Venezuela, New Grenada and Chili, and Peru, and, coasting all the Northern Pacific, imprinted the holy, classic names of old Spain upon the now golden mountains and vine-covered valleys of the State of California. They climbed the snow-clad Cordilleras, and planted their banner on every hill and every valley of Mexico, Peru, and Chili. They drove Montezuma from the halls of his Aztec ancestors; and, under Cortez and Pizarro, Peruvian, Mexican, and semi-barbarian civilization fell before the mighty prowess of their arms. Their heroic deeds, their lofty chivalry, their Christian loyalty, now read more like the romances of a Froissart than, as they are, the true records of history. "Our Anglo-Saxon fathers started later from the shores of Eng- land, and landed upon the rock of Plymouth or upon the flats of Jamestown. The Puritan himself, trembling over his rock for a while, in terror of the tomahawk, ventured at last on what was then deemed gigantic heroism. He crossed the Connecticut and the Hudson, and slowly crept up the Mohawk, and halted for years and years upon Lakes Erie, Ontario, and Huron. The cavaliers of Jamestown threaded their way up the River James, stealthily wound over the passes of the Alleghanies, and looked down at last with astonishment and affright upon la belle riviere of Ohio. But all this time these heroic Hidalgos of Spain were spreading the name and fame of Castile and Arragon throughout the whole American continent, from Florida on the north to Cape Horn on the south, and from Cape Horn to California, while our Anglo-Saxon race stood shivering upon the Ohio and Lake Erie without the courage to advance further. What, sir, happened then? What has produced this difference between us and the lofty Hidalgo? Why are they fallen, these men of the Armada, so exalted among all the nations of the earth, who made our ancestors, in the days of Queen Elizabeth, tremble on the throne? Why was it that in the Mexican war one regiment of our Anglo-Saxon, Celtic, Teutonic blood, again and again put whole regiments of these once noble Hidalgos of Spain to flight at Chapultepec, the Garita, and elsewhere? I will tell you why, sir. The Latin, the Spanish race, freed from that in- stinct of ours which abhors all hybrid amalgamation, revelled in a fatally tempting admixture of blood, indulged in social and governmental copartnership with Aztecs, Indians, Negroes, one and all. The pure blood, the azure blood, of the old Hidalgos of Spain, lost and drained, dishonored and degraded, has dwindled into nothing, while the pure blood of the Anglo-Saxons, the Celts, the Teutons, abhorring all such association and amalgamation with the negro or the Indian, has leaped over Lake Erie, crossed la belle riviere, the great Father of Waters, the Mississippi, crowded the mountain passes of Colorado, Utah, Nevada, and Montana, rolled over the Rocky Mountains, and spread for hundreds of miles on the Pacific Ocean, - carrying not only there, but everywhere, triumphant, from the Arctic to the Antarctic, the glorious flag of our country, — that

emblem of a pure race, — and ever contrasting the glory and honor, the prowess of that race with the degradation of the race of these once noble Hidalgos of Spain."
-*James Brooks, Speech in the House of Representatives*, Dec. 18, 1867.

"Our four millions of negro slaves absorb the public mind, and the thoughts and the time of government, by the dangers they evoke. They have produced sectional animosity and strife where peace and good-will should reign. They have thrown the administration of the law throughout the South into lynch-law committees, and have forbidden any northern man to go there, unless he leaves his independence, and freedom of thought and speech behind him. They have destroyed all industry but their own, and made the South dependent upon foreign supplies for every article which human ingenuity has invented for the com- fort and accommodation of man. They must be sentinelled and watched, to protect society from horrors worse than war. They inspire terror during peace, and, in case of invasion, would be more fearful than the enemy. By means of their weakness they control our politics; they conquer us by abject submission; they overwhelm us by mere prolific growth; they have manacled our hands and feet with fetters of gold, and, nominally slaves, they are really the masters of our destiny."
—*Fisher's Laws of Race*, page 30.

"White men alone possess the intellectual and moral energy which creates that development of free government, industry, science, literature, and the arts, which we call civilization. Black men can neither originate, maintain, nor comprehend civilization."
- *Fisher's Laws of Race*, page 10.

"Surely no argument is necessary to prove that a nation must be happier, wiser, richer, more powerful, and more glorious, where the whole people are of the strongest, most intellectual, and most moral race of mankind, than where any portion of the people are degraded by nature, and incapable of progress or civilization. Barbarism is barbarism, whether in Africa or America; and a country inhabited by barbarians cannot be civilized. Just in pro- portion to the number of its barbarians is it wanting in the elements of civilization, and just in that proportion, too, is it weak and liable to overthrow from dangers within and without."

-*Fisher's Laws of Race*, page 33.

"Though the negro in the North is not a slave, he is made an outcast and a pariah. There is no place for him in northern so. ciety; no aspiration nor hopes to stimulate him; none of the prizes of life, wealth, power, respectability, are held out to him, to nerve his efforts and elevate his desires. He is governed and protected in all his rights wholly by the white race, without his participation. He is excluded from office, from the hustings, from the court-house, from the exchange, from every intellectual calling or pursuit, not by legal enactment, but by his own incapac- ity, and by opinion; by the feeling of caste and race, that is to say, by divine laws, which are stronger than any the legislature can make. He has no civil or political power whatever, by which to protect himself, and he may not lay a finger on one of those three wonderful boxes, the ballot-box, the jury-box, and the cartridge-box, which contain the instruments and weapons by which freemen defend their rights. They are for the white race only. A negro governor, legislator, judge, magistrate, or juryman does not exist, could not by possibility exist, in the whole North. This race is not only excluded from all political and civil place and power, but the avenues to social rank and respectability are closed against him; or rather they are too steep and difficult for him to climb. He is not a land-owner, a manufacturer, a merchant. There is no legal obstacle; but land, machinery, and ships are things he cannot manage. There are no black attorneys-at-law, physicians, authors, or capitalists in the North. The law opens to the negro these spheres of activity as widely as to the white man, but they are far beyond the negro's wildest dreams, because beyond his talents. He is thus pushed down by a superior moral and in- tellectual force, which he can neither comprehend nor resist, into those pursuits which the Saxon, and even the Celt, avoids if he can, into labors which require the least strength of mind or body, which yield the least profit, and are menial and degrading. The spirit of caste drives the negro out of churches, theatres, hotels, rail-cars, and steam-boats, or assigns to him, in them, a place apart. It drives him into the cellars, dens, and alleys of towns, into hovels in the country; and it does all this without laws, without concert or design, without unkindness or cruelty, but unconsciously, simply because it cannot help doing it, obeying this instinctive impulse, and the immutable, eternal laws by which the races of men are kept apart, and are preserved through countless ages without change. These laws are divine. They execute themselves in spite of party combinations or fanatical legislatures, or philanthropic enthusiasts, or visionary dreamers -about human perfectibility and the rights of man."

- *Fisher's Laws of Race,* pages 21–23.

"Strikingly apparent is it that the negro is a fellow of many natural defects and deformities. The wretched race to which he belongs exhibits, among its several members, more cases of lusus naturæ than any other. Seldom, indeed, is he to be seen except as a preordained embodiment of uncouth grotesqueness, malfor- mation, or ailments. Not only is he cursed with a black com- plexion, an apish aspect, and a woolly head; he is also rendered odious by an intolerable stench, a thick skull, and a booby brain. An accurate description of him calls into requisition a larger number of uncomplimentary terms than are necessary to be used in describing any other creature out of Tophet; and it is truly astonishing how many of the terms so peculiarly appropriate to him are compound works of obloquy and detraction.

"The night-born ogre stands before us; we observe his low, receding forehead, his broad, depressed nose; his stammering, stuttering speech; and his general actions, evidencing monkey- like littleness and imbecility of mind. By close attention and examination, we may also discover in the sable individual before us, if, indeed, he be not an exception to the generality of his race, numerous other prominent defects and deficiencies. Admit that he be not warp-jawed, maffle-tongued, nor tongued-tied, is he not skue-sighted, blear-eyed, or blobber-lipped? If he be not wry-necked, wen-marked, nor shoulder-shotten, is he not stiff- jointed, hump-backed, or hollow-bellied? If he be not slab- sided, knock-kneed, nor bow-legged, is he not (to say the least) spindle-shanked, cock-heeled, or flat-footed? If he be not maimed, halt, nor blind, is he not feverish with inflammations, festerings, or fungosities? If he be not afflicted with itch, blains, nor blisters, does he not squirm under the pains of boils, burns, or bruises? If he be not the child of contusions, sprains, nor dislo- cations, is he not the man of scalds, sores, or scabs? If he be not an endurer of the aches of pneumonia, pleurisy, nor rheumatism, does he not feel the fatal exacerbations of rankling wounds, tumors, or ulcers? If he be no complainer over the cramps of coughs, colics, nor constipation, doth he not decline and droop under the discomforts of dizziness, dropsy, or diarrhea? If he be no sufferer from hemorrhoids, erysipelas, nor exfoliation, is he not a victim of goitre, intumescence, or paralysis? If he expe- rience no inconvenience from gum-rash, cholera-morbus, nor moon-madness,

doth he not wince under the pangs of the hip- gout, the tape-worm, or the mulli-grubs? If he be free from idiocy, insanity, or syncope, is he not subject to fits, spasms, or convulsions?"
-*Helper's Nojoque*, pages 68-69.

"Weak in mind, frail in morals, torpid and apathetic in physique, the negro, wherever he goes, or wherever he is seen, carries upon himself, in inseparable connection with abjectness and disgrace, such glaring marks of inferiority as are no less indelible and conspicuous than the base blackness of his skin. Upon this point, all the records of the past, all the evidences of the present, all the prognostications of the future, are plain and positive. In the long catalogue of the great names of the world- which, whether they have caused nations to tremble with fear and suspense, to quiver with awe and admiration, to laugh with satisfaction and delight, or to weep with innocent sadness and love there does not appear the cognomen of a single negro! To overlook the ponderous significance of this fact, to gainsay it, to wink it or to blink it, let no unworthy attempt be made. In nothing that ennobles mankind has any negro ever distinguished himself. For none of the higher walks of life has he ever dis- played an aptitude. To deeds of true valor and patriotism he has always proved recreant. Over none of the wide domains of agriculture, commerce, nor manufactures, has any one of his race ever won honorable mention. Within the classic precincts of art, literature, and science, he is, and forever will be, utterly unknown."
-*Helper's Nojoque*, page 300.

"Shabbiness and drollery of dress, and awkwardness of gait are also notable characteristics of the negro. Faultless garments, and well-shaped hats and shoes are things that are never found upon his person. Once or twice a year he buys (or begs) a suit of second-hand clothing; but seldom does he wear any article of apparel more than two or three weeks before the outer edges of the same become ragged; then unsightly holes and shreds and patches follow in quick succession, — and yet the slovenly and slipshod tatterdemalion is as contented and mirthful as a merry-making monkey."

- *Helper's Nojoque*, page 70.

"Now come I to a subject of somewhat novel importance, subject which has occupied my attention for a great while, and one for the discussion of which, it is believed, the present is a suitable time. I allude to the presence of so many negroes in our cities and towns, - places where not one of them should ever be permitted to reside at all; and if I shall succeed, as I hope and believe I shall, in presenting such a combination of facts and arguments as will demonstrate the propriety of removing them all into the country (if far and forever beyond the limits of the United States, so much the better), I shall regard it as evidence complete that these lines have been judiciously penned. It may, I think, be safely assumed that, as a general rule, no person ought to be admitted as a resident of any city, unless he can readily command one of two things, namely, capital or talent. Of these two indispensable requisites, the negro can command neither the one nor the other; he should, therefore, never be allowed to live in any situation, or under any circumstances, within the corporate limits of any city or town.

"With few exceptions, all sane white persons have sufficient tact to render themselves useful in some manner or other, to gain an honorable livelihood, and to add something to the general stock of human achievements. If their minds can accomplish nothing in the domains of science, their hands may be rewarded in the fields of art. If they cannot invent labor-saving machines, they can make duplicates of such as have already been invented. If they cannot enrich and embellish their country, by building factories, stores, warehouses, hotels, and banks, they can always fill situations in such establishments with profit to themselves and with advantage to others. The negro can do none of these things. On the contrary, he is, indeed, a very inferior, dull, stupid, good-for-nothing sort of man. Past experience proves positively that he is not, and never has been, susceptible of a high standard of improvement. His capacities have been fully and frequently tested, and have always been found sadly deficient. To the neglect of a large and meritorious class of our own race, we have made numerous experiments in favor of the worthless negro. We have earnestly endeavored, time and again, to infuse into the brain of the benighted black a ray of intellectual light, to teach him trades and professions, and to prepare him for the discharge of higher duties than the common drudgeries of every-day life. Thus far, however, all our efforts in his behalf have proved abortive; and so will they continue to prove, so long as he remains what he always has been, and still is, a negro. Further attempts, on our part, to elevate him to a rank equal to that held by the white man, would certainly betray in us an extraordinary and unpardonable degree of folly and obtuseness. Negroes are, in truth, so far inferior to white people, that, for many reasons consequent on that inferiority, the two races should never inhabit the same community, city, nor state. The good which accrues to the black from the privileges of social contact with the white is more than counterpoised by the evils which invariably overtake the latter when brought into any manner of regular fellowship with the former.

"Whatever determination may be come to with regard to a final settlement or disposition of the negroes, — whether it be decided to colonize them in Africa, in Mexico, in Central America, in South America, or in one or more of the West India Islands, or elsewhere beyond our present limits; or whether they be permit- ted to remain (a while longer) in the United States, - it is to be sincerely hoped that there may be no important division of opinion as to the expediency of soon removing them all from the cities and towns. A city is not, by any means, a suitable place for them. They are positively unfit for the performance of in-door duties. Sunshine is both congenial and essential to their natures; and they ought not to be employed or retained in situations that could be so much more advantageously filled by white people. One good white person will, as a general rule, do from two to five times as much as a negro, and will, in addition, always do it with a great deal more care, cleanliness, and thoroughness. A negro or a negress, in or about a white man's house, no matter where, or in what capacity, is a thing monstrously improper and indecent.

"By removing all the negroes into the country, our agricultural districts would receive a large addition of laborers, and consequently, the quantity of our staple products-cotton, corn, wheat, sugar, rice, and tobacco - would be greatly increased. Crowds of enterprising white people would flock to our cities and towns, fill the vacancies occasioned by the egress of the negroes, and give a fresh and powerful impetus to commerce and manufactures. The tides of both domestic and foreign immigration, which have been moving westward for so long a period, would also soon be- gin to flow southward, and everywhere throughout the whole length and breadth of our land new avenues to various branches of profitable industry would be opened.

"Let it not be forgotten, however, that this proposition does not contemplate any permanent settlement of the negroes, even in the agricultural districts of our country. Only a temporary ac- commodation of the case is here held in view. Perhaps the best thing that we could do just now, would be to take immediate and complete possession of Mexico (we shall acquire the whole of North America, from Behring's Strait to the Isthmus of Darien, by and by), and at once push the negroes south of the Rio Grande. On no part, part of the territory of the United States, as at present organized, should any but the pure white races ever find a permanent domicile. --- - - every one of them to say the least, on no "Now comes the last, not the least, reason why I advocate the removal of the negroes from the cities and towns. I believe that the yellow fever (which is only another name for the African fever), and other epidemic diseases, those terrible scourges which have so signally retarded the growth of Southern seaports, -have, to a very great degree, been induced by the peculiarly obnoxious filth engendered by the black population. Who has ever heard of the yellow fever prevailing to an alarming extent in any city or state inhabited almost exclusively by white people? How fearfully, how frequently, does it rage in such despicable, negro-cursed communities, as Norfolk, Charleston, Savannah, Mobile, and New Orleans!

"Only from the base colored races is it, as a rule, that we are overwhelmed and prostrated by wide-spread contagions and epidemics. Even the cattle-plague, the murrain among the sheep, and other fatal distempers to which our domestic animals are subject, have almost invariably had their origin in the countries which are inhabited by the blacks and the browns, who are them- selves but the rickety-framed and leprous remnants of those unworthy races of men, who have been irrevocably doomed to destruction. It is, indeed, fully and firmly believed that the only way to get rid of yellow fever is to get rid of the negroes; and the best way to get rid of the negroes is now the particular question which, of all other questions, should most earnestly engage the undivided attention of the American people."

— *Helper's Nojoque,* pages 62–68.

"When the negro in Africa, in the year 1620, fastening anew upon both himself and his posterity the condition of perpetual bondage, allowed himself, as a guaranty of his passive and prodigious dastardy, to be brought in chains all the way across the Atlantic, it was then that, for the first time, was reached the uttermost depth of human degradation. That the negro had, and has, always been a slave, in his own country or elsewhere, according to the habitat or journeyings of his master, is well known; but it was only when, as the cringing tool of the meaner sort of white men, he came to America, that his obsequiousness and pusillanimity began to assume monstrous proportions. Of all the miscreants and outcasts who have ever brought irreparable disgrace upon mankind, the slave is at once the most despicable and the most infamous. To be a slave of the white man, yet, if possible, to be a slave exempt from the necessity of labor, has always been the ruling ambition of the negro, - not less so now than it was four thousand years ago, and not less so then than it is now."

-*Helper's Nojoque*, page 193.

"The negroes, like the poodles and the pointers, will always be the dependents and the parasites of white men, just so long as white men, unnaturally submitting to a wrongful relation, are disposed to tolerate the black men's infamously base and beggarly presence. Certain it is that we owe it to ourselves-and we ought to be able to get rid of the negroes soon; but if they are to be retained much longer in the United States (which may God, in his great mercy, forbid!) we may as well build immediately, for their relief and correction, in alternate adaptation, a row of hospitals and prisons, all the way from the Atlantic to the Pacific; and, upon the same plan, a range or series of alms-houses and penitentiaries the entire distance from Lake Superior to the Gulf of Mexico! "All the devil-begotten imps of darkness, whether black or brown, whether negroes or Indians, whether Mongols or mulattoes, should at once

be dismissed, and that forever, from the care, from the sight, and even from the thoughts, of the heaven- born whites. Wherever seen, or wherever existing, the black and bi-colored races are the very personifications of bastardy and beggary. In America, these races are the most unwieldy occasioners of dishonor and weakness; they are the ill-favored and unwelcome instruments of disservice; they are the ghastly types of effeteness and retrogression."
-*Helper's Nojoque*, pages 209-211.

"When, under the auspices of monarchical institutions; when, to pander to the cupidity of crowned heads; when, to supply the vicious necessities of courtiers and sycophants, a pack of shirtless and shiftless negroes were brought from the coast of Africa and planted in America, a pack of black and beggarly barbarians, so bestial and so base as to prefer life to liberty, — they, like all other foreign felons and outlaws, should at once have been returned to the places whence they came; or, to say the least, they should have been compelled to depart, with the greatest possible despatch, from the land which they had so foully desecrated by their odious and infamous presence. - In the political organizations of mankind, it ought to be an axiom of peculiar and universal acceptation, that he who values life above liberty is unworthy to have his existence prolonged beyond the hour when to-morrow's sun shall set. This right and truthful proposition, practically established, would leave the whole earth absolutely negroless ere the lapse of two supper-times."
- *Helper's Nojoque*, page 214.

"Under the euphemism of 'Removal,' the American government has already expelled, and rightly expelled, from time to time, more than one hundred thousand Indians from the States of the Atlantic slope, to the wild lands west of the Mississippi, - these expulsions by the government having been independently of the less systematic but (in the aggregate) much larger expulsions by unorganized communities of the white people themselves. It should also be recollected, that all the Indians thus expelled or removed,' were people of indigenous origin, antochthones, by whom the whole of America had, from time immemorial, prior to the days of Colum- bus, been held in fee-simple. Now, if we may rightfully expel the aboriginal owners of America from the old homes and possessions which they have enjoyed from a period of time so distant in the far past that it is absolutely untraceable, what may we not do with the alien and accursed negroes, who, base-minded and barbarous, and bound hand and foot with the fetters of slavery, were brought hither from the coast of Africa?"

- *Helper's Nojoque*, page 220.

"The negro should never, under any circumstances whatever, be permitted to reside in greater proximity to white people than the distance which separates Cuba from the United States; if the distance could be lengthened to the extent of one thousand miles, so much the better; if, in point of duration, rather than in point of space, the distance could be lengthened from now to the end of time (supposing such an end possible), better still.

"On the premises of no respectable white person; in the mansion of no honorable private citizen; in no lawfully convened public assembly; in no rationally moral or religious society; in no decently kept hotel; in no restaurant worthy of the patronage of white people; in no reputably established store nor shop, in no place whatever, where any occupant or visitor is of Caucasian blood, should the loathsome presence of any negro or negress ever be tolerated."

-*Helper's Nojoque*, page 219.

"To live in juxtaposition with the negro, or to tolerate his presence even in the vicinity of white men, is, to say the least, a most shameful and disgraceful proceeding, - a proceeding which, if persisted in, will, sooner or later, bring down upon all those who are guilty of it, the overwhelming vengeance of Heaven. By cringing and fawning like a cudgel-deserving dog, by passively yielding and submitting like a dumb brute, by mimicking and begging like a poll-parrot, the negro has but too generally succeeding in foisting himself, as a parasitical slave or servant, upon white men; and has thus, upon all occasions, afforded incontestable proofs of the fact that he is, and ever has been, equally with his master, a sheer accomplice in the crime of slavery."

- *Helper's Nojoque*, page 284.

"It was by no merit nor suggestion of his own, but rather by the demerits of both himself and his master, that the negro was brought to America. Not by any spirit of commendable enter- prise was he induced to immigrate hither. He came under com- pulsion; and under compulsion he must (in the event of the failure of gentler abominitions on our part) be prevailed upon to emigrate back to Africa, to Mexico, to Central America, to South America, or to the islands of the ocean. "His coming to the New World was neither voluntary nor honorable. It was not for the purpose of bettering his condition in life. He sought not an asylum from the oppressions of rank and arbitrary power. In unresistingly allowing himself to be forced from his family and from his country, without even the promise or the prospect of ever being permitted to return, and in passively submitting to be taken in chains he knew not whither, he pusillanimously yielded to the most abject and disgraceful vassalage.

"For his passage across the Atlantic he paid no money, no corn, no wine, no oil, nor any other thing whatever. He brought with himself no household property, no article of virtu (nor principle of virtue), no silver, no gold, nor precious stones. -

"He was hatless, and coatless, and trouserless, and shoeless, and shirtless; in brief, he was utterly resourceless, naked and filthy. He came as the basest of criminals, he came as a slave; for submission to slavery is a crime even more heinous than the crime of murder; more odious than the guilt of incest; more abominable than the sin of devil-worship.

"With himself he brought no knowledge of agriculture, commerce, nor manufactures; no ability for the salutary management of civil affairs; no tact for the successful manoeuvring of armies; no aptitude for the right direction of navies; no acquaintanceship with science, literature, nor art; no skill in the analysis of theories; no sentiment stimulative of noble actions; no soul for the encouragement of morality. Bringing with himself nothing but his own black and bastard body, denuded and begrimed, he came like a brute; he was a brute then; he had always been a brute; he is a brute now; and there is no more reason for believing that he will ever cease to be a brute, than there is for supposing that the hound will ever cease to be a dog, - only that the black biped, the baser of the two, will be the sooner exterminated.

"Yet this is the fatuous and filthy fellow whom, by certain degraded and very contemptible white persons, we are advised to recognize as an equal and as a brother! This is the incorrigible and grovelling ignoramus upon whom it is proposed to confer at once the privilege of voting, the right of universal suffrage! This is the loathsome and most execrable wretch (rank-smelling and hideous arch-criminal that he is), who has been mentioned as one fit to have a voice in the enactment of laws for the government of the American people. 66 Shall we confer the elective franchise on this baseborn and ill- bred blackamoor, this heathenish and skunk-scented idiot? No! Why not? Because he does not know, and cannot know, how to vote intelligently. It would therefore, to say the least, be an act of gross folly on our part, to extend to the negro the privilege of doing what the omnipotent God of nature has obviously, and for all time, denied him the power to do.

"Those of our half-witted and demagogical legislators who waste time in attempting to prove the equality of the negro, and in the drafting of absurd laws for his recognition in good faith as a citizen of the United States, might, with equal propriety, busy them- selves in the ridiculous irrationality of framing codes for allowing the gorilla and the chimpanzee to attend common schools, and for the baboon and the orang-outang to testify in courts of equity!

"No man should ever be recognized as a citizen of the United States, nor be allowed to participate in any of the rights or privileges of citizenship, who did not come hither honorably and of his own accord,— who did not immigrate to these shores, he or his ancestors, free, free from the gyves and chains of slavery. It was not of his own choosing, it was not at his own option, it was only in a state of the most abject and criminal servitude, a sort of compound felony between himself and his master, that the negro came hither from Africa. Therefore, for these and other sufficient reasons, the negro should have no voice, no part, nor lot, in any of the public affairs or private concerns of America."

- *Helper's Nojoque*, pages 215-217.

"I maintain, without reservation, the following among other opinions, that the human race has not sprung from one pair, but from a plurality of centres, that these were created ab initio in those parts of the world best adapted to their physical nature; that the epoch of creation was that undefined period of time spoken of in the first chapter of Genesis, wherein it is related that God formed man, 'male and female created he them; ' that the deluge was a

merely local phenomenon; that it affected but a small part of the then existing inhabitants of the earth; and, finally, that these views are consistent with the facts of the case, as well as with analogical evidence."
 -Samuel George Morton. *Letter to Mr. Gliddon*, May, 1846.

"After twenty years of observation and reflection, during which period I have always approached this subject with diffidence and caution; after investigating for myself the remarkable diversities of opinion to which it has given rise, and after weighing the difficulties that beset it on every side, I can find no satisfactory explanation of the diverse phenomena that characterize physical man, excepting in the doctrine of an original plurality of races."
 -Samuel George Morton. *Types of Mankind*, page 305.

"For my own part, if I could believe that the human race had its origin in incest, I should think that I had at once got the clue to all ungodliness. Two lines of catechism would explain more than all the theological discussions since the Christian era. I have put it into rhyme:

QUESTION. Whence came that curse we call primeval sin?
ANSWER. From Adam's children breeding in and in.

– Samuel George Morton. *Types of Mankind*, page 409.

"I shall conclude these remarks on this part of the inquiry, by observing, that no mean has been taken by the Caucasian races collectively, because of the very great preponderance of Hindoo, Egyptian, and Fellah skulls, over those of the Germanic, Pelasgic, and Celtic families. Nor could any just collective comparison be instituted between the Caucasian and negro groups in such a table as we have presented, unless the small-brained people of the latter division were proportionate in number to the Hindoos, Egyptians, and Fellahs of the other group. Such a comparison, were it practicable, would probably reduce the Caucasian average to about eighty-seven cubic inches, and the negro to seventy- eight at most, - perhaps even to seventy-five; and thus confirmatively establish the difference of at least nine cubic inches between the mean of the two races."

-Samuel George Morton. *Types of Mankind*, page 321.

"There are only two alternatives before us at present: "1st. Either mankind originated from a common stock, and all the different races with their peculiarities, in their present distribution, are to be ascribed to subsequent changes, an assumption for which there is no evidence whatever, and which leads at once to the admission that the diversity among animals is not an original one, nor their distribution determined by a general plan, established in the beginning of the creation, — or, - "2d. We must acknowledge that the diversity among animals is a fact determined by the will of the Creator, and their geograph- ical distribution part of the general plan which unites all organ- ized beings into one great organic conception; whence it follows that what are called human races, down to their specialization as nations, are distinct primordial forms of the type of man. "The consequences of the first alternative, which is contrary to all the modern results of science, run inevitably into the Lamarkian development theory, so well known in this country through the work entitled 'Vestiges of Creation;' though its premises are generally adopted by those who would shrink from the conclusions to which they necessarily lead."

— *Prof. Agassiz. Types of Mankind*, page 75.

"Do not the instincts of our nature, the social laws of man, all over the civilized world, and the laws of God, from Genesis to Revelation, cry aloud against incest? Does not the father shrink with horror from the idea of marrying his own child, or from seeing the bed of his daughter polluted by her brother? Do not children themselves shudder at the thought? And can it be credited that a God of infinite power, wisdom, and foresight, should have been driven to the necessity of propagating the human family from a single pair, and then have stultified his act by stamping incest as a crime? I do not believe that true religion ever intended to teach a common origin for the human race. Cain knew his wife,' whom he found in a foreign land, when he had no sister to marry; and although corruption and sin were not wanting among the patriarchs, yet nowhere in Scripture do we see, after Adam's sons and daughters, a brother marrying his sister."

-*Josiah Clark Nott. Types of Mankind*, page 408.

"Much as the success of the infant colony at Liberia is to be desired by every true philanthropist, it is with regret that, while wishing well to the negroes, we cannot divest our minds of melancholy forebodings. Dr. Morton, quoted in another chapter, has proved that the negro races possess about nine cubic inches less of brain than the Teuton; and, unless there were really some facts in history, something beyond bare hypothesis, to teach us how these deficient inches could be artificially added, it would seem that the negroes in Africa must remain substantially in that same benighted state wherein Nature has placed them, and in which they have stood, according to Egyptian monuments, for at least five thousand years."

-*Josiah Clark Nott. Types of Mankind*, page 189.

"The negro has never taken one step towards mental development, as we understand it. He has never invented an alphabet, that primal starting-point in mental cultivation, - he has never comprehended even the simplest numerals, -in short, has had no instruction except that which is verbal and imitated, which the child copies from the parents, which is limited to the existing generation; and therefore the present generation are in the same condition that their progenitors occupied thousands of years ago."

- *Van Evrie's Negroes and Negro Slavery*, page 218.

"The negro mind, in essential respects, is always that of a child, the intelligence, as observed, is more rapidly developed in the negro child, — those faculties more immediately connected with sensation, perception, and perhaps memory, are more energetic; but when they reach twelve and fifteen, they diverge; the reflective faculties in the white are now called into action, the real Caucasian character now opens, the mental forces fairly evolved, while the negro remains stationary, a perpetual child. The negro of forty or fifty has more experience or knowledge, per- haps, as the white man of that age has a more extended knowledge than the man of twenty-five, but the intellectual calibre- -the actual mental capacity-in the former case is no greater than it was at fifteen, when its utmost limits were reached."

- *Van Evrie's Negroes and Negro Slavery*, page 219.

"White husbands and wives, when one dies in early life, often remain unmarried, faithful to a memory forever; and still more frequently, perhaps, the affections that bound them together in their youth remain bright and untarnished in age and to the borders of the grave. Such a thing never happened with a negro. Not one of the countless millions that have lived upon the earth was ever kept from marrying a second time by a sentiment or a memory. With their limited moral endowment such a thing is an absolute moral impossibility. They live with each other to extreme old age, because they imitate the superior race, and because it has become a habit, perhaps; but the grand purposes of nature accomplished, there is little or nothing more, or of those blessed memories of joy and suffering, of early hopes and chastened sorrow, which so bind and blend together the white husband and wife, and often render them quite as necessary to each other's happiness as in the flush and vigor of youth."

— *Van Evrie's Negroes and Negro Slavery*, page 242.

"It may be confidently asserted that no community can be found, who, as an original proposition, are prepared to commit their industrial and economical relations into the hands of Africans. The acknowledged inferiority of the negro is a sufficient guaranty against the suicidal step. Why is it that the negro should be preferred to the white man in the occupation of our territory? There is no place, state, condition, or relation af- fecting the good of society in which the negro is not inferior to the white man. In labor, in battle, in knowledge, in council, in citizenship, in statesmanship, the white man prevails over the African. If you introduce these people into a new community, as it appears to me, for every man whose place is filled by a negro, you injure the community in that degree. If these people mingle their blood with the white race, the progeny is debased and fallen from the white status; if you hold them in slavery, they are hurtful to the progress and prosperity of the community; if you set them free, they are not desirable for citizens. There is no disguising the fact, that if you legislate to give the Africans place, position, and employment which would otherwise belong to white men, you depreciate white men, -you invidiously stigmatize their race."

- Samuel T. Glover. St. Louis, July 26, 1860.

"We have noticed, with some surprise, what we regard as a strange confusion of thought in England, in regard to the feeling here about slavery and about the negro. It seems to be taken for granted by most European, and even most British, writers upon the subject, that opposition to slavery and a liking of the negro, or at least a special good-will to him, must go together, and vice versa; and that consequently a war which was accepted rather than that the point of the exclusion of slavery from free territory should be yielded, and which was prosecuted in a great measure for the extinction of slavery where it had been already established, must have as its result the elevation of the negro to the political and social level of the dominant race, or else that its professed anti-slavery motive was a mere pretence. No supposition could be more erroneous. I tell you frankly that the mass of the people here were glad to fight against slavery, but had no intention of fighting for the negro. They felt that slavery was a great crime, a sin against human nature. They wished to purge the republic of that wickedness, but they had no particular sympathy with, though most of them much compassion for, the race against whom the wrong was committed. You in Europe seemed to be thinking about the individual negroes; we, in the mass, thought little or nothing of the individual negroes, but much of the barbarous institution of slavery."

-Richard Grant White. Letter to the London Spectator, 1865.

"In the last year of the war, a clergyman who had been a professor in the college where I studied, and who is one of those gentle, firm, wise men, with large souls, and wide sympathies, who

can control men, and particularly young men, by mere personal influence, so that when the under-graduates were unruly or had a grievance, they would give up at once to Dr. ----- for pure love, when his colleagues could do nothing, and all the terrors of college discipline were laughed to scorn, - this man went to the South on a tour of observation, and was placed in authority, as far as slavery was concerned, over a considerable reclaimed district by one of our most eminent generals. For years before the war he had been one of our strongest anti-slavery men, and had by his writings done as much as any one person in the country, who was not a professed journalist or politician, to bring about the state of pub- lic feeling that provoked secession. I met him on his return home, and had not talked with him three minutes before he said to me, 'I come back hating slavery more than ever, but loathing the negro with an unutterable loathing. What a curse to have that people on our hands!' And not long ago, one of the editors of one of the leading anti-slavery papers in the country, and one which advocates giving suffrage to the freed slaves, said to me, 'These negroes are doubt- less here by a dispensation of Providence, but,' with an earnestness which a whimsical smile could not conceal; 'oh, that the Lord had been pleased to dispense his negroes somewhere else!'"
-Richard Grant White. *Letter to the London Spectator*, 1865.

"There has never been the slightest danger of an insurrection of the slaves. The real victim of slavery is the white man. Whatever little good there is in the system, the black man has had; while most of the evil has fallen to the white man's share."
-*Parton's Gen. Butler in New Orleans*, page 99.

"The United States are young, fresh, and vigorous, abounding in wealth, exulting in strength, and eager for action. They come of a race, the Anglo-Saxon, seemingly endowed with a deathless spring and vitality, a race which crushed old Rome, when Rome oppressed the world, - which reared the stupendous structure of British enterprise, which impelled the armies of the Reformation, — which planted in the New World the hardiest of its colonists, and which now, commanding the citadel as well as the outposts of civilization, wields the destinies of all the tribes."

-*Parke Godwin. Political Essays*, page 115.

"The population in America of European extraction has grown so large, and the accessions to it by immigration are so vast, that we can begin to see that the mission of the negro here is nearly completed, and that the limits of his possible expansion may be computed. In fifty years, the white races now in the United States, and their descendants, will number more than one hun- dred millions. While it is impossible to predict exactly the march of this great multitude, or to define precisely the regions it will occupy, it is easy to see that the negro in North America must be pressed into narrow bounds. And it is in North America only that he is formidable, because it is here only that his numbers are increasing; the African race in South America and in the West Indies being either stationary or declining, except so far as it is kept up by the slave-trade, which is reduced now to a single island, restrained even there within close limits, and menaced constantly by that complete extinction which it cannot long escape."

- *Weston's Progress of Slavery*, page 158.

"The experiment of Africanizing America has had a long trial, of more than three centuries, and has failed at all points and in every particular. Of course, it was not expected to bring civilization and the arts to the New World, and it has failed even to populate it. The policy of Africanization ought now to be given up; but whether given up or not, it must soon yield to a new and better order of events."

-*Weston's Progress of Slavery*, page 161.

"Anatomy, physiology, and microscopy concur in proving that the negro is of a distinct and inferior species to the Caucasian ; and history confirms the evidence furnished by the investigation of the natural philosopher. The unvarying color of the hair, the distinctive mark of all animals incapable of civilization, - well as the peculiarity of its structure; the volume, shape, and weight of the brain, inferior to that of the dominant species, and the half-brute-like character of the physiognomy, and general formation are evidences not to be disregarded by the careful and conscientious philosopher. Neither in ancient nor modern times has the negro, even when placed under the most favorable circumstances, achieved anything of moment. The steady advance of the white species meets with no parallel in the black. The latter has proved itself, when left to itself, to be incapable of progress. Even when taught by a superior species, it soon retro- grades to hopeless barbarism. No man who values himself, who has any regard for sound morality, or who feels any desire to see intellectual progress made certain, can join in the absurd attempt to raise the negro to his own level. A movement for such ends is necessarily impotent, and can only result, at the best for the negro, in the degradation of the white."

-*Thomas Dunn English. Letter to John Campbell,* Philadelphia, 1851.

31

Mulattoes; The Offspring of Crimes Against Nature

"IN 1842, I published a short essay on Hybridity, the object of which was, to show that the white man and the negro were distinct species, illustrating my position by numerous facts from the natural history of man and that of the lower animals. The question, at that time, had not attracted the attention of Dr. Morton. Many of my facts and arguments were new, even to him; and drew from the great anatomist a private letter, leading to the commencement of a friendly correspondence, to me, at least, most agreeable and instructive, and which endured to the close of his useful career. "In the essay alluded to, and in several which followed it at short intervals, I maintained these propositions:

"1. That mulattoes are the shortest-lived of any class of the human race.

"2. That mulattoes are intermediate in intelligence between the blacks and the whites.

"3. That they are less capable of undergoing fatigue and hardship than either the blacks or whites.

"4. That the mulatto women are peculiarly delicate, and subject to a variety of chronic diseases. That they are bad breeders, bad nurses, liable to abortions, and that their children generally die young.

"5. That when mulattoes intermarry, they are less prolific than when crossed on the parent stocks.

"6. That when a negro man married a white woman, the offspring partook more largely of the negro type than when the reverse connection had effect.

"7. That mulattoes like negroes, although unacclimated, enjoy extraordinary exemption from yellow-fever, when brought to Charleston, Savannah, Mobile, or New Orleans. "Almost fifty years of residence among the white and black races spread in nearly equal proportions through South Carolina and Alabama, and twenty-five years' incessant professional intercourse with both, have satisfied me of the absolute truth of the preceding deductions."

- Dr. Josiah Clark Nott. *Types of Mankind*, page 373.

"It was not until the discovery of a new world that races of man of strikingly contrasted qualities came to intermix. In the Western world, the intermixture of nations which followed the conquests- first of the Romans, and afterwards of the northern na- tions was a union of races of equal quality; and hence it cannot be predicated that either improvement or deterioration was the result. Very different was the case in the Eastern world. There Greeks, Romans, and Goths intermingled with races greatly inferior to themselves, such as Egyptians and Syrians, and hence the deterioration to which, in a great measure, must be ascribed that decline in civilization which ended in the down. fall of the Roman power. Nature has endowed the various races of man with widely different qualities, bodily and

mental, much in the same way as it has done with several closely allied species of the lower animals. When the qualities of different races of man are equal, no detriment results from their union. The mon- grel French and English are equal to the pure breeds of Germany and Scandinavia. When, on the other hand, they are unequal, deterioration of the higher race is the inevitable result."
— John Crawfurd. Anthropological Review, Vol. I., page 405.

"Nature appears to have guarded against the alterations of species which might proceed from mixture of breeds, by influencing the various species of animals with mutual aversion from each other. Hence all the cunning and all the force that man is able to exert is necessary to accomplish such unions, even between species that have the nearest resemblances. And when the mule- breeds, that are thus produced by these forced conjunctions, hap- pen to be fruitful, which is seldom the case, this fecundity never continues beyond a few generations, and would not probably proceed so far, without a continuance of the same cares which ex- cited it at first. Thus we never see in a wild state intermediate productions between the hare and the rabbit, between the stag and the doe, or between the martin and the weasel. But the power of man changes this established order, and contrives to produce all these intermixtures of which the various species are susceptible, but which they would never produce if left to themselves."
-Cuvier. Theory of the Earth, page 118.

"In regard to the sterility of hybrids in successive generations; though Gärtner was enabled to rear some hybrids, carefully guiding them from a cross with either pure parent, for six or seven, and in one case for ten generations, yet he asserts positively that their fertility never increased, but generally greatly decreased. I do not

doubt that it is usually the case, and that the fertility often suddenly decreases in the first few generations.'
-*Darwin's Origin of Species*, page 220.

"I doubt whether any case of a perfectly fertile hybrid animal can be considered as thoroughly well authenticated."
— *Darwin's Origin of Species*, page 223.

Some one, who signs himself "Ariel," has recently published, in Cincinnati, a pamphlet, in which, with wonderful ingenuity of citation and argument, he endeavors to prove, even from the Bible itself, that the negro is a mere beast, a creature without a soul. If " Ariel's" positions be admitted as true, what terrible penalties have been incurred by the many very vile and very disreputable individuals who have violated the following law:

"If a man lie with a beast he shall surely be put to death; and ye shall slay the beast. And if a woman approach unto any beast, and lie down thereto, thou shalt kill the woman and the beast; they shall surely be put to death."
- *Leviticus XX.* 15.

"Thou shalt not let thy cattle gender with a diverse kind; thou shalt not sow thy field with mingled seed."
— *Leviticus XIX.* 19.

"Thou shalt not sow thy vineyard with divers seeds, lest the fruit of thy seed which thou hast sown and the fruit of thy vine-yard be defiled; thou shalt not plough with an ox and an ass together."
-*Deuteronomy XXII.* 9.

"The Lord spake unto Moses, saying, Speak unto Aaron, saying, Whosoever he be of thy seed in their generations that hath any blemish, let him not approach to offer the bread of his God. For whatsoever man he be that hath a blemish he shall not approach; a blind man or a lame, or he that hath a flat nose, or any- thing superfluous, or a man that is broken-footed, or broken- handed, or crook-backed, or a dwarf, or that hath a blemish in his eye, or be scurvy or scabbed, or hath his stones broken; · he hath a blemish; he shall not come nigh to offer the bread of his God.""

- *Leviticus XXI.* 16.

"You asked me, in conversation, what constituted a mulatto by our law? and I believe I told you four crossings with the whites. I looked afterwards into our law and found it to be in these words: Every person, other than a negro, of whose grand- fathers or grand- mothers, any one shall have been a negro, shall be deemed a mulatto, and so every such person who shall have one-fourth part or more of negro blood shall, in like manner, be deemed a mulatto. The case put in the first member of this paragraph of the law is exempli gratiâ. The latter contains the true canon, which is, that one-fourth of negro blood, mixed with any portion of white, constitutes the mulatto. As the issue has one-half of the blood of each parent, and the blood of each of these may be made up of a variety of fractional mixtures, the estimate of their compound, in some cases, may be intricate; it becomes a mathematical problem of the same class with those on the mixtures of different liquors or different metals; as in these, therefore, the algebraical notation is the most convenient and intelligible. Let us express the pure blood of the white in the capital letters of the printed alphabet, the pure blood of the negro in the small letters of the printed alphabet, and any given mixture of either, by way of abridgement, in MS. letters.

"Let the first crossing be of a, pure negro, and A, pure white. The unit of blood of the issue being composed of the half of that of each parent, will be $a/2 + A/2$. Call it, for abbreviation, h (half blood).

"Let the second crossing be of h and B; the blood of the issue will be $h/2 + B/2$, or substituting for $h/2$ its equivalent, it will be $a/4 + A/4 + B/2$; call it q (quarteroon), being 1/4 negro blood.

"Let the third crossing be of q and C; their offspring will be $q/2 + C/2 = a/8 + A/8 + B/4 + C/2$; call this e (eighth), who, having less than 1/4 of a pure negro blood, to wit, 1/8 only, is no longer a mulatto, so that a third cross clears the blood.

"From these elements, let us examine their compounds. For example, let h and q cohabit; their issue will be $h/2 + e/2 = a/4 + A/4 + a^3/16 + A^3/16 + B/8 + c/4 = a/16 + A/16 + B/8 + c/4$, wherein $5/16a$ makes still a mulatto.

"Let q and e cohabit; the half of the blood of each will be $q/2 + e/2 = a/8 + A/8 + B/4 + a/16 + A/16 + B/8 + C/4 = a^5/16 + A^5/16 + B^3/8 + C/4$, wherein 3/16 of a is no longer a mulatto; and thus may every compound be noted and summed, the sum of the fractions composing the blood of the issue being always equal to unit. It is understood in natural history that a fourth cross of one race of animals with another gives an issue equivalent for all sensible purposes to the original blood. Thus a Merino ram being crossed, first with a country ewe, second with his daughter, third with his grand-daughter, and fourth with his great-grand-daughter, the last issue is deemed pure Merino, having in fact but 1/10 of the country blood. Our canon considers two crosses with the pure white, and a third with any degree of mixture, however small, as clearing the issue of the negro blood."

-*Jefferson's Works*, Vol. VI., page 436. Letter to Francis C. Gray, March 4, 1815.

"Amalgamation in races is more than a revolution in government. It is an attempt to make a fundamental change in the laws of nature, and, by blending different species of the human race, create a hybrid nation. This will prove to be an impossibility. The red, white, and black races have mingled very freely on this continent, but the hybrids gradually wear out, while the old stock preserves its original type. The French, from the in- fancy of discovery on this continent, intermarried with the Indian tribes. But where is the French tribe of Indians to be found? They made the same experiment with the blacks in St. Domingo, and a mongrel race appeared, for a time, of various tints, but it is gradually vanishing. So the old Spanish blood that mixed with that of the Indians in Spanish America has almost run out, and Indians and Spaniards are as incongruous with each other as in the beginning, and the fatal result of this attempted amalgamation is shown in the degradation of both races, and in the instability of their governments. If the history of the world, and the present aspect of both hemispheres, did not make manifest the absurdity of the proposed system of mixing the black and white races in the management of a common government, and blending the two colors to make a third, or, rather, a piebald people of all colors, the repugnance of caste which has grown up in this country on the part of the white freeman to the black man, contrasted by his servile condition, from his first appearance among us, as strongly as by his ebony skin and curled hair, - certainly shows that nothing short of insanity could hope to reconcile the dominant, and, I might say, the domineering race, to such a conjunction."

- Montgomery Blair. Speech at Concord, N. H., June 17, 1863.

The following item, recently published in the newspapers, showing a determination on the part of the people of California to prevent, by law, the amalgamation of the white and black races, is, it is believed, suggestive of what ought to be done immediately by the people of that and every other State in the Union: -

"A bill introduced into the lower House of the California Legislature on the 30th of January, to prevent the amalgamation of different races of men, provides that any white person who shall be convicted of marrying or otherwise cohabiting with a negro, mulatto, Chinese, or Indian, shall be punished by fine and imprisonment, or both; and that the fact that a person beds, boards, cohabits, or intermarries with an individual of any of said races, shall be prima facie evidence that such a person is not a white citizen, and shall subject him to all constitutional disabilities imposed on persons of color."

It is said that there is not a life-insurance company in all the world that will take a risk on the life of any mulatto. Why? Because common sense and common experience alike teach that the mulatto is the offspring of a crime against nature; that he is always, even from his earliest infancy, predisposed to disease; that he seldom recovers when once overtaken by severe sickness; that he usually falls an easy victim to epidemics; and that he is (speaking briefly and to the point) a nature-abhorred and short-lived monstrosity; and yet mulattoes and negroes are the sort of creatures with whom Radical politicians would populate American States!

32

Albinos; White Negroes and Other Creatures of Supernatural Whiteness

"I WILL now add a short account of an anomaly of nature, taking place sometimes in the race of negroes brought from Africa, who, though black themselves, have, in rare instances, white children, called albinos. I have known four of these myself, and have faithful accounts of three others. The circumstances in which all the individuals agree are these: They are of a pallid cadaverous white, untinged with red, without any colored spots or seams; their hair of the same kind of white, short, coarse, and curled as is that of the negro; all of them well formed, strong, healthy, perfect in their senses, except that of sight, and born of parents who had no mixture of white blood. Three of these albinos were sisters, having two other full sisters, who were black. The youngest of the three was killed by lightning, at twelve years of age. The eldest died at about twenty-seven years of age, in child-bed, with her second child. The middle one is now alive, in health, and has issue, as the eldest had, by a black man, which issue was black. They are uncommonly shrewd, quick in their apprehensions and in reply. Their eyes are in a perpetual tremulous vibration, very weak, and much affected by the sun; but they see much better in the night than we do. They are the property of Colonel Skipwith, of Cumberland. The fourth is a negro woman, whose parents came from Guinea, and had three other children, who were of their own color. She is freckled, and her eyesight so weak that she is obliged to wear a bonnet in the summer; but it is better in the night than day. She had an albino child, by a black man. It died at the age of a few weeks. These were the property of Colonel Carter, of Albermarle. A sixth in- stance is a woman, the property of a Mr. Butler, near Petersburg. She is stout and robust, has issue a daughter, jet-black, by a black man. I am not informed as to her eyesight. The seventh in- stance is of a male belonging to a Mr. Lee, of Cumberland. His eyes are tremulous and weak. He is tall of stature, and now advanced in years. He is the only male of the albinos which have come within my information. Whatever be the cause of the dis- ease in the skin, or in the coloring matter, which produces this change, it seems more incident to the female than male sex. To these I may add the mention of a negro man within my own knowledge, born black, and of black parents; on whose chin, when a boy, a white spot appeared. This continued to increase till he became a man, by which time it had extended over his chin, lips, one cheek, the under jaw, and neck on that side. It is of the albino white, without any mixture of red, and has for several years been stationary. He is robust and healthy, and the change of color was not accompanied with any sensible disease either general or topical."

— *Jefferson's Works*, Vol. VIII., page 318.

"The name albino was originally applied by the Portuguese to the white negroes they met with on the coast of Africa. With the features of the negro and the peculiar woolly form of the hair, the color of the skin was white like pearl, and the hair resembled that of the whitest horse. The eye, instead of the jet-black hue, which seems given to the inhabitants of the tropics to enable them to bear the intense glare of the sun, was like that of the white rabbit and ferret, and like this better suited for use in the moon- light, and in places sheltered from the light of day. From this inability to bear the light, which, however, is said to be much exaggerated, Linnæus called the albinos nocturnal men. They generally lack the strength of other men; and a peculiar harsh- ness of the skin, such as is noticed in cases of leprosy, would seem to indicate that the phenomenon might result from a diseased organization. Yet the albinos suffer from no different complaints from other persons. As in their physical development, they are correspondingly deficient in their mental capacity. In the same family several children are sometimes born albinos. They are most generally of the male sex. It is not understood to what ultimate cause the phenomenon is to be attributed. It is observed in all climates, and among all races of men. Indeed, it is not limited to man; for individuals possessing the same peculiarities are found among a great variety of the warm-blooded animals, and, according to Geoffrey St. Hilaire, in fishes and some species of molluscous animals as well. Examples are not very rare among the feathered tribe, the effect being seen in the color of the plumage, as in other animals in that of the hair. The white crow and the white blackbird are albinos. Albino mice are not very uncommon. Blumenbach notices the feebleness of their eyes, and their disposition to avoid the light, by their closing their eyelids even in the twilight. The white elephants of India are venerated by the natives, who believe them to be animated with the souls of their ancient kings. In the human race, perhaps, more albinos are to be found among the negroes than among any other people; but this may be owing to the peculiarities being with them more prominent, and attracting more attention. One of the kings of the Ashantees is said to have had particular regard for these people, and collected around him about one hundred of them. According to Humboldt, albinos are more common among nations of dark skin, and inhabiting hot climates. In the copper- colored races they are more rare, and still more so among the whites."

-*New American Cyclopædia*, Vol. I., page 284.

"Albinos may be found in almost every community in Southern Guinea. Everywhere they are regarded as somewhat sacred, and their persons are considered inviolable. On no condition what- ever would a man strike one of them. Generally they are very mild; and I have never heard of their taking advantage of their acknowledged inviolability. In features they are not unlike the rest of their race, but their complexion is very nearly a pure white, their hair of the ordinary texture, but of a cream color, and their eyes are gray, and always in motion."

- *Wilson's Africa*, page 311.

"At the mouth of the Brass River, when an albino girl is sacrificed, the officiator at this ceremony is an old man named Onteroo. He has an enormous tuberosity on the back of his head; but whether his divinity is believed to exist in this or not, my informant cannot say. Several canoes accompany him and the victim, who, it seems, is quite satisfied with her fate, as she is indoctrinated with the idea that her future destiny is to be married to a white man. As soon as they reach the bar, the canoes are all turned with their heads homewards; the word is given, and the girl is thrown into the water, with a weight round her neck to prevent her floating, thus obviating the possibility of an escape."

- *Ten Years' Wanderings among the Ethiopians*, by Thomas J. Hutchinson, F. R. G. S.

"A curious superstition is connected with Parrot Island, and is observed with religious punctuality by the natives of Old Kalabar, on the occasion of need arising from its performance. Whenever a scarcity of European trading ships exists, or is apprehended, the Duketown authorities are accustomed to take an albino child of their own race, and offer it up as a sacrifice, at Parrot Island, to the God of the white man."

-*Hutchinson's Western Africa*, page 112.

33

Increasing Pre-Eminence and Predominance of the White Races

"THE Caucasian race, to which we belong, is distinguished by the beauty of the oval formed by his head, varying in complexion and the color of the hair. To this variety, the most highly civilized nations, and those which have generally held all others in subjection, are indebted for their origin. · The race from which we are descended has been called Caucasian, because tradition and the filiation of nations seem to refer its origin to that group of mountains situated between the Caspian and Black Seas, whence, as from a centre, it has been extended like the radii of a circle. Various nations in the vicinity of Caucasus, the Georgians and Circassians, are still considered the handsomest on earth."

-*Cuvier's Animal Kingdom*, page 50.

"Let us raise ourselves higher still, and pass into the province of man himself. The white race is distinguished above them all; the most perfect type of humanity; the race best endowed with the gifts of intelligence, and with the profound moral and religious sentiment that brings man near to Him of whom he is the earthly image. To this race belong, without exception, all the nations of high civilization, the truly historical nations; this still represents the highest degree of progress attained by man- kind."

- Arnold Guyot. Earth and Man, page 228.

"Let us take the head of a Caucasian. What strikes us immediately is the regularity of the features, the grace of the lines, the perfect harmony of all the figure. The head is oval; no part is too prominent beyond the others; nothing salient nor angular disturbs the softness of the lines that round it. The face is di- vided into three equal parts by the line of the eyes and that of the mouth. The eyes are large, well cut, not too near the nose nor too far from it; their axis is placed on a single straight line, at right angles with the line of the nose. The facial angle is ninety degrees. The stature is tall, lithe, well proportioned; the shoulders neither too broad nor too narrow. The length of the ex- tended arms is equal to the whole height of the body; in one word, all the proportions reveal the perfect harmony which is the essence of beauty. Such is the type of the white race, the Caucasian, as it has been agreed to call it, the most pure, the most perfect type of humanity."

-Arnold Guyot. Earth and Man, page 255.

"Asia has yielded to Europe the sceptre of civilization for two thousand years. At the present day, Europe is still unquestionably the first of the civilizing continents. Nowhere on the sur- face of our planet has the mind of man risen to a sublimer height; nowhere

has man known so well how to subdue nature, and to make her the instrument of intelligence. The nations of Europe represent not only the highest intellectual growth which the human race has attained at any epoch, but they rule already over nearly every part of the globe, and are preparing to push their conquests further still."
 -Arnold Guyot. *Earth and Man*, page 31.

"The establishment of European civilization in the New World, which has more than doubled the territorial extent of the cultivated nations, prepares an epoch of aggrandizement more rapid still. The two Americas, situated between the other four continents, seem destined to become, in their turn, a new centre of action, or a point of support for the establishment of easy and more rapid relations with all the nations of the world, and the irresistible logic of facts passing under our eyes compels us to believe that, during the epoch which is preparing, the boundaries of the domain of the civilized world can only be those of the globe itself."
— Arnold Guyot. *Earth and Man*, page 328.

"We belong to the Anglican race, which carries Anglican principles and liberty over the globe, because, wherever it moves, liberal institutions and a common law full of manly rights and instinct with the principle of an expansive life, accompany it. We belong to that race whose obvious task it is, among other proud and sacred tasks, to rear and spread civil liberty over vast regions in every part of the earth, on continent and isle. We belong to that tribe which alone has the word Self-Government."
- Francis Lieber. *Civil Liberty and Self-Government*, page 21.

"There are many nations and tribes which have already disappeared from the earth, because they did not resist the power of more powerful nations, or were unable to become powerful themselves. We do not grieve over the fall of the Celts, because we ourselves destroyed them. We look on with tranquility as the aboriginal people of America decay and pass away, while our own race is the sole cause of their destruction."

- *Burmeister's Black Man*, page 13.

"The Negro or African, with his black skin, woolly hair, and compressed, elongated skull; the Mongolian of Eastern Asia and America, with his olive complexion, broad and all but beardless face, oblique eyes, and square skull; and the Caucasian of West- ern Asia and Europe, with his fair skin and face, full brow, and rounded skull; such, as every school-boy knows, are the three great types or varieties into which naturalists have divided the in- habitants of our planet. Accepting this rough initial conception of a world peopled everywhere, more or less completely, with these three varieties of human beings or their combinations, the historian is able, in virtue of it, to announce one important fact at the very outset, to wit, that, up to the present moment, the destinies of the species appear to have been carried forward almost exclusively by its Caucasian variety."

- *North British Review*, August, 1849.

"We now come to the typical Caucasian family, which embraces the greatest cerebral development in width and depth, combined with the highest form of beauty, strength, and power of endurance, coupled with a nervous system less swayed by impulse. In this group is found the most perfect notions of the ideal beautiful, of relative proportion in art and in literature, of logic and of the mathematical sciences in general, It is here that female beauty is possessed of the highest human loveliness, grace, and delicacy; and the manly character attains the most majestic and venerable aspect."

— *Hamilton Smith's Natural History of the Human Species*, page 401.

"The Caucasian form of man combines, above the rest, strength of limb with activity of motion, enabling it to endure the greatest vicissitudes of temperature in all climates; to emigrate, colonize, and multiply in them, with the sole exception of the positive extremes. His longevity is more generally protracted, even in the midst of the enervating habits of high civilization; his solid fibre gives a reasoned self-possession and daring in vicissitudes, arising from the passions, from accident or from the elements; and his reflective powers find expedients to brave danger with self-possession and impunity. The moral and intellectual character we find to be in unison with his structure; the reasoning powers outstripping the mere process of comparing sensations, and showing, in volition, more elevated thought, more reasoning, justice, and humanity; he alone of all the races of mankind has produced examples of free and popular institutions, and his physical characteristics have maintained them in social life. By means of his logical intellect, he has arrived at ideas requisite for the acquisition of abstract truths; resorting to actual experiment, he fixed bases whereon to build demonstrable inferences, when the positive facts are not otherwise shown; he invented simple arbitrary characters to represent words and musical sounds; and a few signs, which, nevertheless, denote, in their relative positions, all the possible combinations of numbers and quantity; he has measured time and distance, making the sidereal bodies unerring guides to mark locality and give nautical direction; he has ascended to the skies, descended into the deep, and mastered the powers of lightning. By mechanical researches, the bearded man has assuaged human toil, multiplied the results of industry, and created a velocity of locomotion superior to the flight of birds; by his chemical discoveries, he has modified bodily pain, and produced numberless discoveries useful in medicine, in arts, and manufactures. He has founded a sound and connected system of the sciences in general, and acquired a critical literature; while, for more than three thousand years, he has been the principal possessor of all human knowledge and the asserter of fixed laws. He has instituted all the great religious systems in the world, and to his stock has been vouchsafed the glory and the conditions of revelation. The Caucasian type alone continues in rapid development, covering with nations every congenial latitude, and portending at no distant era to bear rule in every region, if not by physical superiority, at least by that dominion, which religion, science, and enterprise confer."

-*Hamilton Smith's Natural History of the Human Species*, page 371.

"The Saxon or Teutonic man is a lover of liberty. His is the only race that does love it, and has been able to acquire and keep it. He loves instinctively personal liberty, power over himself, freedom from the will of another. He loves also political liberty; that is to say, a share of political power, so that he may consent to any control to which he does submit, and form himself a part of the government he obeys. To such a man slavery in the abstract is revolting; but his love of liberty is, in part, love of power. He sympathizes, therefore, with the oppressed, provided he be not the oppressor, and would gladly break all chains of bondage, except those which he imposes. The characteristics of the Saxon, his practical ability and faculty for abstract thought; his passion for conquest and power, and his love of liberty, truth, and justice, whilst they make him a colonizer and a ruler, also render his rule beneficent. Churches, charities, law, order, industry, wealth, arts, and letters, follow his footsteps. The Saxon loves power; his is the conquering, colonizing race.

Wherever he goes, to India, to China, to Australia, or America, he subdues and governs the weaker and lower races."
— *Fisher's Laws of Race*, page 16.

"No delusion has so little foundation as that assumed law of climate which would confine the white races to the latitude of the free States of this Union. But when it is insisted upon in reference to our own country, where the facts which overthrow it are familiar to everybody, it is not wonderful that it is kept up in reference to countries of which we know less. When it is denied that the Southern States can be occupied by anybody but negroes, two-thirds of their inhabitants being actually whites, and the in- crease of the whites being greater than that of the blacks, what absurdities may not be maintained? "
- *Weston's Progress of Slavery*, page 159.

"Humboldt observes that the Caucasian races are distinguished by their flexibility of organization in respect to climate; and of this we have a remarkable instance in the French, who have long occupied the lower Mississippi and the most northerly of the Canadas, and without any loss of their original vigor in either of those widely separated latitudes. The descendants of that race, expelled from Acadia, suffered a dispersion equally wide, being found in the Carolinas, on the Gulf of Mexico, and on the upper St. John in the latitude of Quebec. If there are malarious regions at the South, on the coasts of the Atlantic and the Gulf of Mexico, they are of limited extent, and, as a whole, the white race exhibits as much physical vigor at the South as at the North, and, in the opinion of many observers, decidedly more."
- *Weston's Progress of Slavery*, page 160.

"I believe that the greatness or abjectness of every people is due primarily, if not solely, to one cause, race. Indeed seeing, as it appears to me, that the manifestation of the immutable qualities of race is the one great fact of history; that the annals of the world teach us that the power of race is the one master and positive force, the operation of which can be calculated upon as a certainty; that it is the primal law of humanity; that it is working as irresistibly and with action as positive and simple as it worked thousands of years ago; that at this very day it is breaking the bonds of treaties and destroying kingdoms to make nations, to deny its force, or to rate it at less than paramount importance, seems to me like calculating eclipses or building houses with like disrespect to the force and law of gravitation."

— Richard Grant White. Letter to the *London Spectator,* 1865.

"Most distinctly do I deny that this country is great only because it is spacious in the possession of dirt;' because, like Russia, it is vast, or even because, like France, it is rich and warlike. Its real greatness, I believe, with a belief having the clearness of conviction and the earnestness of faith, has its sole origin in the qualities of the race by which the land was settled and reclaimed, and by which its government and its society were framed."

-Richard Grant White. Letter to the *London Spectator,* 1865.

"It is the strictly white races that are bearing onward the flambeau of civilization, as displayed in the Germanic families alone."

-Josiah Clark Nott. *Types of Mankind,* page 405.

"History, tradition, monuments, osteological remains, every literary record and scientific induction, all show that races have occupied substantially the same zones or provinces from time immemorial. Since the discovery of the mariner's compass, mankind have been more disturbed in their primitive seats; and, with the increasing facilities of communication by land and sea, it is impossible to predict what changes coming ages may bring forth. The Caucasian races, which have always been the representatives of civilization, are those alone that have extended over and colonized all parts of the globe; and much of this is the work of the last three hundred years. The Creator has implanted in this group of races an instinct that, in spite of themselves, drives them through all difficulties to carry out their great mission of civilizing the earth. It is not reason or philanthropy which urges them on, but it is destiny. When we see great divisions of the human family increasing in numbers, spreading in all directions, encroaching by degrees upon all other races wherever they can live and prosper, and gradually supplanting inferior types, is it not reasonable to conclude that they are fulfilling a law of nature."

-Josiah Clark Nott. *Types of Mankind*, page 77.

"No two distinctly marked races can dwell together on equal terms. Some races, moreover, appear destined to live and prosper for a time, until the destroying race comes which is to exterminate and supplant them. Observe how the aborigines of America are fading away before the exotic races of Europe. Those groups of races heretofore comprehended under the generic term Caucasian, have in all ages been the rulers; and it requires no prophetic eye to see that they are destined eventually to conquer and hold every foot of the globe where climate does not interpose an impenetrable barrier. No philanthropy, no legislation, no missionary labors, can change this law; it is written in man's nature by the hand of his Creator."

-Josiah Clark Nott. *Types of Mankind*, page 79.

"When we are free from this plague-spot of slavery, -the curse to our industry, our education, our politics, and our religion, we shall increase more rapidly in number, and still more abundantly be rich. The South will be as the North, active, intelligent, Virginia rich as New York, the Carolinas as active as Massachusetts. Then by peaceful purchase, the Anglo-Saxon may acquire the rest of this North American continent. The Spaniards will make nothing of it. Nay, we may honorably go further south, and possess the Atlantic and Pacific slopes of the Northern continent, extending the area of freedom at every step. We may carry thither the Anglo-Saxon vigor and enterprise, the old love of liberty, the love also of law; the best institutions of the present age, — ecclesiastical, political, social, domestic. Then what a nation we shall one day become! America, the mother of a thousand Anglo-Saxon States, tropical and temperate, on both sides of the equator, may behold the Mississippi and the Amazon uniting their waters, the drainage of two vast continents, in the Mediterranean of the Western World; may count her children at last by hundreds of millions, — and among them all behold no tyrant and no slave!"

-Theodore Parker. Speech at New York, May 12, 1854.

"The Caucasian differs from all other races; he is humane, he is civilized, and progresses. He conquers with his head as well as with his hand. It is intellect, after all, that conquers, - not the strength of a man's arm. The Caucasian has been often master of the other races, never their slave. He has carried his religion to other races, but never taken theirs. In history all religions are of Caucasian origin. All the great limited forms of monarchies are Caucasian. Republics are Caucasian. All the great sciences are of Caucasian origin; all inventions are Cauca- sian; literature and romance come of the same stock; all the great poets are of Caucasian origin;

Moses, Luther, Jesus Christ, Zoroaster, Buddha, Pythagoras, were Caucasian. No other race can bring up to memory such celebrated names as the Caucasian race. The Chinese philosopher, Confucius, is an exception to the rule. To the Caucasian race belong the Arabian, Persian, Hebrew, Egyptian; and all the European nations are descendants of the Caucasian race.".

- Theodore Parker. Quoted in *Types of Mankind*, page 462.

"If the ancestors of the present three millions of slaves had never been brought here,- - if their descendants had never been propagated here, for the supposed value of their services, their places would have been supplied by white laborers, by men of the Caucasian race, — by freemen. Instead of the three millions slaves, of all colors, we should doubtless now have at least three million white, free-born citizens, adding to the real prosperity of the country, and to the power of the republic. If the South had not had slaves to do their work for them, they would have become ingenious and inventive, like the North, and would have enlisted the vast forces of nature in their service, wind and fire and water and steam and lightning, the mighty energies of gravitation and the subtle forces of chemistry."

- Horace Mann. House of Representatives, February 23, 1849.

"It has been said that whosoever would see the Eastern world before it turns into a Western world must make his visit soon, because steamboats and omnibuses, commerce, and all the arts of Europe, are extending themselves from Egypt to Suez, from Suez to the Indian Seas, and from the Indian Seas all over the explored regions of the still farther East. I only can see that on this continent all is to be Anglo-American from Plymouth Rock to Pacific Sea, from the North Pole to California. That is certain; and in the Eastern world, I only see that you can hardly place a finger on the map of the world and be an inch from an English settlement. If there be anything in the supremacy of races, the experiment now in progress will develop it. If there be any truth in the idea that those who issued from the great Caucasian fountain, and spread over Europe, are to react on India and on Asia, and to act on the whole Western world, it may not be for us, nor our children, nor our grandchildren to see it, but it will be for our descendants of some generation to see the extent of that progress and dominion of the favored races. For myself, I believe there is no limit fit to be assigned to it by the human mind, because I find at work everywhere, on both sides of the Atlantic, under various forms and degrees of restriction on the one hand, and under various degrees of motive and stimulus on the other hand, in these branches of a common race, the great principle of the freedom of human thought, and the respectability of individual character."

-*Webster's Works*, Vol. II., page 214.

Appendix 1: Radicalism in the South: Its Black and Blighting Sway

BY HINTON ROWAN HELPER,
Author of "The Impending Crisis of the South."
ASHEVILLE, North Carolina,
November 11, 1867.

To the Editors of the *National Intelligencer*: In the accompanying communication, addressed "To the Good People of the Old Free States," it is not at all unlikely that I have said some things to which both you and many of your readers may take exception. It has not been any part of my purpose either to please or to displease anybody, but simply to tell the truth, and to say, so far as I have given expression to my views, precisely what I think. If, in your opinion, the publication of the article would promote, even in part only, the object at which I have aimed, namely, the imparting to the public mind of the North a more accurate and adequate knowledge of the actual and prospective condition of things at the South, under the black and blighting sway of Radicalism, -you may, if you please, publish it in the columns of the "Intelligencer." Deeply impressed with the importance, at all times, of earnest and honest appeals to men's reason, rather than to their passions or their prejudices, I have purposely delayed writing what I have here written until after the partial subsidence of the general excitement and confusion which have but so recently attended the great elections in many of the whiter and (therefore) better parts of our common country.

H. R. H.

To the Good People of the Old Free States: More than ten years ago, as many of you will recollect, I, a Carolinian, made a special appeal to your enlightened and patriotic judgments in behalf of a large majority of the white people of the Southern States, the non-slaveholding whites, - who, whether they knew it or not, were greatly oppressed and impoverished by the unfortunate existence among us of negroes and negro slavery. The generous hearing which you then accorded to me inspires me with confidence that you are again prepared to listen to any protest, or complaint, or other statement from me, that has for its basis truth and justice. Thus surmising, I respectfully request that you will favor me with your attention while I explain, or while I endeavor to explain, that the great mass of the poor whites here, in whose behalf I have especially and persistently written, are still enthralled; and that, within the last few years, the condition of their thraldom has been so aggravated, that it is now in constant process of becoming worse and worse, with the further and appalling danger, under Radical misrule, of being rendered unparalleled and perpetual. Before entering directly into this subject, however, permit me to indulge in a few general but pertinent reflections. Although chiefly for the sake of the whites, yet it was not alone for their sakes that I was, and am, and always will be, hostile to slavery. I believed, many years since, as I believe now, that there is in slavery itself, and more especially in negro slavery, a moral and social guilt of no less revolting magnitude than the political blunders which are also a part of its base offspring. I believed then, and I believed rightly, I think, that the negroes ought to be freed, and then speedily colonized somewhere beyond the present limits of the United States. I do not believe, and never did believe, that the two races- the white and the black-widely and irreconcilably different as they are in their natures, ought ever to inhabit the same country. Living in close association, living together beneath the same roof, living in juxtaposition within the acknowledged limits of any hamlet, village, town, or city, or even within the boundaries of any farm or plantation, as they did live under the system of slavery, and as they still live under the condition of freedom, is, as I solemnly believe (particularly as it affects the whites), a gross shame, a shocking indecency, and a glaring crime. I believe that the whole negro race is a weak and worthless race, an effete and time-worn race, which, like the Indian race, is no longer fit, if ever fit for any useful trust or tenantcy in this world; and I believe, further, that it is the will of Heaven that all these people, and many others of similar color and character, should at once be put in position to be let alone; and that, if duly colonized, properly provided for, and then prudently and suitably let alone, Providence will soon cut them off, root and branch, and thus happily rid the earth of at least the bulk of the superannuated and inutile organisms which so unpropitiously encumber it in the current epoch.

While one of the inevitable effects of enduring any manner of association or relation between the two races is the partial elevation of the blacks, the other is only the too positive and irremediable degradation of the whites. The influence of the white on the black is always for good to the black at the expense of the white; the influence of the black on the white is always bad for the white; and the white is again, and invariably, the victim. In anything and in everything wherein the white people of the South are worse than the people of the North, and in whatever mental, moral, or material interest we of the South are less advanced than you of the North, the delinquencies or the deficiencies, as the case may be, are alone attributable to the profitless and pernicious presence of the negroes among us. In quality of population, the great difference between the North and the South is simply this: while we here are cursed with the black imps of Africa, you there are blessed with the white genii of Europe. What I would do to bring the South up to an honorable and ever-friendly equality with the North (and what must be done sooner or later, or the object thus aimed at will never be accomplished), is to prepare the way, on the one hand, for the egress of all our imps of darkness and of death, and, on the other hand, to open wide the way for the ingress of your superabundant genii of life and of light. I contend, then, that, in order to insure the true safety and success of the South, in order to maintain, in perpetuity, the integrity of our national Union, and in order to guarantee uninterrupted peace and prosperity throughout the greater and better part of this vast continent, we must, with as little delay as possible, colonize the negroes in Mexico, or elsewhere out of our own country; or, as a last but temporary method of relief from their baneful existence among us, we must remove them all, much the same as we have hitherto removed certain tribes of Indians, into one or more of the South-bordering States or Territories of the United States.

The necessity for the removal and colonization of the negroes was as plain to me ten years ago as it is to-day; but I foresaw then, and I see now, that there could be no general nor effectual demand raised for the displacement of the blacks on the one hand, and for the filling up of the South by white people from the North and from Europe on the other, until after slavery, the great nursery and stronghold of negroes, should first be abolished. Equally did I foresee then, and I perceive now, that, in a state of freedom and self-dependence, one of two fatal dilemmas would certainly befall the negro; but neither of which dilemmas was ever likely to befall him so long as he had the benefit of guides and protectors in the persons of a few unfortunate white men, his masters, who, however, as is well known, guided and protected him as an easy and questionable method of procuring their own bread and butter; and this, too, though not always wilfully, to the serious, if not irreparable, detriment of the great majority of their own white fellow-citizens. To me it was plain then, and it is plain now, that if the negro, in a condition of political equality, is left here, he will, from the fated and complicated causes of neglect and hostility on the part of the whites, gradually die out and disappear; but this not without entailing on the whites a multiplicity of long-lasting injuries and calamities meanwhile. If colonized, whether within or without the United States, and after a fair but final amount of advice and assistance, put entirely upon his own resources,—as, indeed, it is but right and proper that he should have been put long ago, -his doom, it is also plain, would be equally inevitable: it would only be, as I conscientiously believe, another use of the whites as instruments to modify, or to seemingly modify, the indestructible plan of Providence for extermi- nating the negro.

I admit, and, at the same time, insist upon it, that men, everywhere and at all times, should be exceedingly careful how they attempt to interpret any will or purpose of Heaven. Further, I will say that I do not believe that any mere man, like any one of you, or like myself, ever did, or ever will, truly interpret or explain the exact purpose of God in reference to anything whatsoever, except only and possibly through conjecture. It is true, that in years gone by the "New York Tribune" and several other gazettes of less ability and weight, seriously proclaimed me a prophet; but I deny the soft impeachment, and respectfully protest against that sort of infringement and libel on the preeminent prerogatives of the ancient Hebrews. The exercise of common sense is the only prophecy with which I have ever yet been gifted; and beyond that, in matters of seership, I never expect to be gifted. In this respect, any and every other rational white man may be, and ought to be, equally gifted; if not so gifted, it is because he is a mere idler; and if so, he is, for that reason, highly reprehensible for not improving and disciplining the mind of whatever bent or capacity which a mighty and merciful God has been pleased to create within him. "If, then, we may seek to comprehend and interpret the will of God touching any one or more of the several races of mankind, I hesitate not to say that, in my humble judgment, the efforts which the Radical and other blind and fanatical friends of the negro are now making for his retention and equality among us are directly in conflict with the Divine purpose, and are, therefore, fragrantly wrong and impiously wicked. To what end, or for what purpose, was the great Columbus and his white-faced and Heaven-guided successors in maritime discovery safely wafted to this western world but to redeem it from the fruitless occupancy and from the wild and weird desecration of the savage Indian? Why was Moses and his compatriots and kinsman, in their bloody aggressions against the Canaanites, not only permitted, but encouraged, and commanded, to leave alive none that breatheth," if it were not that Jehovah had ceased to have a use for those who had already accomplished the ends for which they had been created? If we see, or if we think we see, a purpose on the part of the Deity to cut off all the Canaanites of old, on the one hand, and all the Indian tribes of the three great Americas and their adjacent islands of modern times, on the other, it is, I contend, quite as easy for us to perceive His desire and purpose to use us, whether we be willing or not, as his swift avengers against the negroes, both in America and in Africa, first here and then there; for even before we get America filled up with the white races, we shall need. Africa as a new continent for the enterprise and habitation of the redundant populations of Europe and of other portions of the white world; and then the negroes, and all the other black and bicolored weaklings, whether in Africa or elsewhere, must stand aside, or be laid low, and give undisputed and permanent place to their white superiors. In this way, and in this way only, can this great world of ours ever be made a world given to the worship of the one only living and true God; and in no other way may we ever reasonably expect to find the mountains and the valleys, the hill-tops and the dales, the glades and the glens, auspiciously dotted over with schools and with colleges, with libraries and with churches, with galleries and with museums.

But from this cursory reference to the world at large, both as to its realities and its possibilities, let us come back for a little while to North Carolina, and to the other Southern States. And just here I want to show how, under a very criminal public policy of the past, and under a most atrocious public policy of the present, a large majority of the white people of the South have been, and are still, treated with less consideration, with less favor, and with less justice, than if they were negroes. In other words, astounding as the statement may appear, it is nevertheless true demonstrably true-that the negroes here, very many of them at least, have hitherto been afforded opportunities, for both an education and for an easy and comfortable livelihood, far superior to the opportunities which were generally enjoyed by the poorer classes of white people! A full and just understanding of this cruel and flagitious discrimination in favor of the blacks as against the whites, in favor of the incompetent as against the competent, in favor of the vile as against the virtuous, should make the blood of every decent and respectable white man, between Maine and Texas, and between Florida and Oregon, literally boil with indignation; and there should be no cessation of the quick and forcible ebullition of his vital fluid, until, to say the least, the worthy whites of the South are at last allowed a fair and equal chance with the unworthy blacks. But it is just this fair and equal chance which the slaveholders, in the time of slavery, always denied to the great majority of Southern whites; and it is precisely this fair and equal chance which is now meanly and treacherously, and with increased hardships, denied them now by those wanton and reckless demagogues who constitute a usurpatory and tyrannical majority of the present Congress.

Let me explain: As is well known, while slavery existed in the South there was no respectability of labor. Every sort of actual work with the hands, whether upon one's own account or in the way of help or assistance to others, was always looked upon as menial and degrading. Negroes, as slaves and as servants, were employed everywhere, not only out of doors, but also within doors. Indecent, disgraceful, and criminal as it was in reality, this universal rule or custom of "having negroes around" was both fashionable and aristocratic. There were never any vacancies or situations for poor white people; and yet the number of these, in the South generally, was always much greater than the number of the negroes. Just look at it! Just think of it! The mass of the white population of the South absolutely debarred from the pecuniary profits and other advantages of employment, and forced into the distant purlieus of poverty and ignorance! The base- born and incapable blacks, by the force of a vulgar public opinion, placed above the meritorious whites! Yet it was not at all because of any inherent power or good quality in the negroes that the poor whites were thus crowded away from the many desirable employments and places to which they alone should have been heartily welcomed. The fault of the thing, up to the close of the war, is traceable directly to the slaveholders themselves, who, in the short-sighted and vicious pol- icy which they pursued, made every other interest in the country, both great and small, subordinate and subservient to the negroes and negro slavery. Since the war, the blame, in a grossly aggravated and unexpected form, rests exclusively with the Radical party. The slaveholders are now beginning to see and lament the folly and blindness and bigotry of their unseemly devotion to the worthless negroes. For the sake of the country, let us sincerely hope and pray that the Radicals may soon give evidence of similar perception, and also of true sorrow for their very numerous, very black, and very grievous political sins. Never did Brahmins, Mahommedans, or Christians. sacrifice their country, their property, their friends, their family, or themselves, with more fidelity to their God, than the slaveholders here have sacrificed everything which they held dear on earth, in order to preserve alive and unscathed the negro, -the very blackest and basest wretch that ever lived. Was such black and abominable idol ever so besottedly worshipped before? Them- selves, their sons, their near and distant relatives, their neighbors, and their countrymen, all of their own kith and kin and color, the slaveholders cheerfully gave to the battle and to death; but the negro, the meanest and most degraded of mankind, was kept alive, and is still among us, a nuisance, a leper, and a plague.

Time and space both fail here of a suitable opportunity for entering into all the sad and shocking minutiæ of the cruelly unjust proscription of the Southern poor whites, who, by the common exigencies of their nature, and as the mere outskirt tenants of the rich landed proprietors, were compelled to seek such an incidental and uncertain livelihood as they could procure by hunting and fishing, and by such occasional jobs, here and there, as they could beg, too often only as a sort of special favor from one or more of their wealthier and better-hearted neighbors. Even a slight knowledge of the facts, however, and upon these facts a little sagacious reflection will enable you to perceive at once the numerous opportunities, both for education and for physical comforts, which were, as a matter of course, given to the negroes, but which, at the same time, and equally as a matter of course, were withheld from the whites. For nearly two hundred and fifty years, the negroes here, as waiters in hotels, and in the families of the most learned and refined, as barbers and as body-servants to professional men, pleasure-seekers and others, have had the constant benefit of hearing the intelligent conversation of their masters and mistresses, and also of listening to the interesting and instructive stories of well-informed visitors and cosmopolitan strangers. Retained in great numbers in the cities and towns (just where not one of them ought ever to have been, and just where not one of them ought ever to be), they always had free and undisputed admission to the public meetings in the court-houses and in the town halls, and also to the religious meetings held in the churches and elsewhere. As a class, they alone, of all the poor people in the South, had access, at all times, in the families of the rich and refined, to books, magazines, and newspapers. On the other hand, the poor whites, treated as outcasts, merely because they did not own slaves, enjoyed none of the opportunities which were thus so easily within the reach of the negroes, whether for the enlargement and cultivation of the mind, or for the health and comfort of the body; and, what is worse,-ay, what, indeed, is very much worse, the condition of things in this respect is still unchanged. Hordes of hungry, shiftless, and worthless blacks, who, relying, as of old, on their importunate and resistless art of begging, to supply themselves, among other things, with all the threadbare and bad-fitting garments of their white superiors, are everywhere offering their services for the merest nominal wages; and the old masters and employers, accustomed only to such wretched and barbarous assistance as can be got from negro slaves and negro servants, are yet under the spell of sable witch and sable wizard, and, with rare exceptions, have as yet learned little or nothing of either the advantage or the duty, the decency or the respectability, of employing and having about them none but white persons. In this way the negro, a pesterer of detestable character and color, continues to be banefully interposed between the two great white elements in the South, where, like a sluggish, yet meandering woodworm, he is all the while gnawing deeper and deeper into the vitals of first one side and then the other. Of the two classes of whites who are thus incessantly preyed upon and despoiled by the blacks, the poorer whites are invariably the greater victims; for against these are arrayed the low prejudice and the hostile influences of not only all the negroes, but (shameful and shocking to relate) of many of the wealthier whites also. This is what comes of that unnatural and execrable bond of sympathy and selfishness which has so long existed, and which still exists, between the negro owners, or those who were but lately so, and the negroes themselves; and now, to this double and distressing op- position, against which the poor whites of the South have for so long a time barely been able to offer even a feeble resistance, is added a third power, far more crafty, and far more potent for mischief than either of the others. This third power- whether it seems to be so or not, or whether it was intended to be so or not, it is so, nevertheless this third power, in alliance with the negroes and the ex-slave- holders, to utterly crush out and ruín forever the poor whites of the South, is the whole Radical party, but more especially that very unscrupulous and desperate embodiment of it now justly described and detested as the rump Congress. Under the wrongfully discriminating, negro-favoring enactments of this unconstitutional and unprincipled Congress, not only are white emigrants from the North and from Europe now coming hither in less numbers than they came under the old condition of things, but many of the whites who are already here are every day becoming more and more anxious to abandon their homes and emigrate to distant and foreign lands, rather than remain the victims of that terrible thraldom of negro supremacy, which a most mean and malignant assemblage of heartless Radicals are now fastening upon them.

Almost every day, for several months past, ever since I last returned to the State, - have I seen whole families, and sometimes two or three together, leaving North Carolina, some going in the direction of Illinois, some travelling toward Indiana, and others, of the more able and venturesome sort, bound for Brazil and elsewhere, far beyond the utmost limits of their own native soil. While thus, under the oppressive and tyrannical operations of Radical military despotisms, our own native white people are robbed of their natural freedom, and forced to flee to foreign lands, European emigrants and emigrants from the North are restrained almost entirely from coming to the South! And thus swiftly and infamously are the narrow-minded and revengeful Radicals converting all the States of the South into one vast Hayti, or Jamaica, or Mexico,- driving from the country the white people, who are, whether here or elsewhere, the only worthy and saving elements of population, and surrendering it completely to the pollution, devastation, and ruin of stupid and beast-like hordes of black barbarians.

Of the extreme poverty and distress of many of the poor whites who are now emigrating from the State, and of a still larger number who, rather than submit to the further danger and disgrace of Radical-negro and negro-Radical domination, are anxious to leave, but are destitute even of the scanty means necessary to take them away, I have scarcely the heart to speak. To enter adequately into details or particulars upon this subject in a mere newspaper article, is quite out of the question, and so I will only remark here, in a general way, but with all the emphasis of earnestness and truth, that I do not believe any people in any part of America were ever subjected to such unjust and oppressive straits, such miserable and wretched shifts, as the poorer classes of the white people of North Carolina, and of the South generally, are now having to struggle against; and all this mainly in consequence of the blundering and unconstitutional enactments, the unstatesmanlike and infamous legislation of that oligarchy of sectional demagogues known as the rump Congress.

Within the last few weeks especially, many white families have I seen leaving the State, all on foot, and barefooted at that, apparently possessed of no clothing, except the two or three soiled and tattered garments which they were wearing at the time, and carrying in a small bundle on their backs every article of property, of whatever nature or kind, of which they could claim the ownership. One family of eight persons, whom I met on the road, particularly attracted my attention; and my heart, from an involuntary feeling of commiseration, almost bled when I became a witness of their dire destitution and wretchedness. This family was composed of the father, mother, grandmother, and five children, the eldest child being not more than twelve years of age. Except the youngest child, which was in its mother's arms, all were travelling on foot, and all were barefooted, with the single exception of the father, who had on very old and rudely patched brogans. A single outer dress, of the commonest and cheapest stuff, and that much worn, and by no means clean, with a dingy-looking sun-bonnet, appeared to be the only article of clothing of which any one of the females was possessed. The head of the family had no coat; and as for the boys, uncombed, ragged, and ignorant, they had, indeed, in a truly serious and melancholy sense, almost literally "nothing to wear." Coarse straw hats, common shirts, and very common pantaloons, all badly worn, were the only things they had as shields from the weather; and these shabby vestments seemed to constitute the sum total of their personal effects. In a small cotton-cloth wallet, which was swung across the shoulders of the father, and which he evidently carried without its causing him any particular burden or inconvenience, were deposited the only movables, the only goods and chattels, the only household gods of this poor, this uneducated, this politically oppressed and unfortunate family. Nor is this an exaggerated picture. Were it but a solitary case, or but one of few, the condition of things would not be so bad; but, sad to reflect, it is only one of many, and the number is increasing. Whether fleeing from oppression (this time not so much the oppression by ex-slaveholders, as the oppression by Radicals and negroes), or whether remaining at home under the galling yoke of tyranny, the whole South is now full of just such victims as the family just mentioned. And these victims, for the most part, as poor as poor can be, and as ignorant and miserable as possible, are principally of the former class of poor whites, for the utter crushing out and destruction of whom there is now in force a most foul and formidable triple alliance of Radicals, ex-slave- holders, and negroes; but, as already intimated, the least harm that is felt from this alliance comes from the ex-slaveholders, who, for the first time in their lives, are only now beginning to accept in practice the correctness of their ancient and all-the-while preaching, that white people are better than negroes. In behalf of these long and sorely oppressed poor whites, and for the means not merely to enable them to withstand, but eventually to overcome, the threefold and iniquitous opposition thus arrayed against them, I, here and now, with all due deference and respect, appeal to God and to the good people of the North.

Scarcely anywhere can one travel in the South, at the present time, without meeting, on every hand, especially among the poor whites, and there are few now who are not poor,-numerous cases of actual want, sickness, suffering, and despair; and were it not that I fear to tax too severely your patience, I should feel it my duty to give a somewhat full and minute account of several of them. As it is, however, I will only advert to two or three cases in addition to the one already mentioned. In Marion, the county seat of McDowell county, in this State, adjoining the county in which I am now writing, and where I now reside, it was ascertained a short while since that unless the pressing necessities of a large number of the poor white people could soon be relieved, there was great danger that many of them, during the ensuing winter, would suffer intensely, if not die outright, of cold and hunger. In their behalf, an appeal was made to a few wealthy gentlemen of Baltimore, who nobly responded in the form of a liberal contribution of money. There were and are in that county, as, indeed, in every other county, district, and parish throughout the South, a great many poor widows and orphans, whose husbands and fathers were conscripted and killed during the late war, and who now, without lands, without houses, except here and there a dilapidated log-cabin, and without employment, are in a manner naked, resourceless, and starved. In view of the wretchedly ill-clad condition of these poor widows and orphans, it was thought best to spend the money, which, as already explained, had been generously contributed in Baltimore, for cotton thread, such as is used for the weaving of plain cloth, and to distribute a bunch of that, so far as it would go, to each fatherless family. Mr. Alfred Erwin, a kind- hearted and very estimable citizen of that county, a lawyer by profession, was appointed to make the distribution. As soon as it became known that Mr. Erwin had received this thread, to be given away at his discretion to the persons indicated, his office was literally besieged, until very soon there was not a single bunch left, and then it was truly touching to witness the profound disappointment and grief, amounting almost to despair, of the numerous careworn and indigent mothers who were still unprovided for, some of whom had come twelve or fifteen miles over the rough mountain roads, on foot, barefooted, and with scarcely clothes enough upon themselves to cover, in the usual way, their own persons. The sight, I say, the sight of these very poor widowed mothers having to return home empty-handed, but heavy-hearted, as I myself saw many of them returning, to rickety, cold, comfortless log cabins, in a manner destitute not only of furniture and bedding, but also of almost every other thing, except a troop of half-starved, half-clad, and helpless children, was, indeed, a spectacle too sorrowful to behold with any ordinary emotion.

During the early part of last month I was in Columbia, South Carolina. There also did I see again, as I had frequently seen before, how poor white persons are treated as the inferiors of negroes, and how to the latter are given places of in-door ease and profit, which should in all cases, without exception, be given only to the former. At different times, while walking about the city (or rather the ruins of a city, for, as is well known, it was almost entirely destroyed by fire during the brief occupation of Sherman's army, - a piece of warfare about as brave and defensible as that of Semmes, who burned unarmed merchant ships at sea), several white women and girls, who were so emaciated by a long and distressful period of hunger, little short of actual starvation, that some of them were reduced to mere skin and bone, met me in the street, and, with tears and laments, besought me for a little money to buy bread! Of one of them, who was evidently but an indifferent shadow of her former self, I asked a few questions. She was but fifteen years of age. Her father was forced into the war, and was killed. The house in which she and her mother lived, and everything in it, was burned to ashes during the great conflagration. Almost immediately afterward her mother, yielding to excess of grief and despondency, became very sick, and soon died in a paroxysm of despair and delirium; and she, the daughter, an only child, was left in the world without means, without friends, and without employment. My heart sickened under the plaintiveness, the childlike simplicity, and the obvious truth- fulness of her statement; and, regretting that I had not the ability to place in her attenuated and leather-like hands dollars instead of dimes, I returned to the Nickerson House, where I had stopped, and there I looked hither and thither through hall, parlor, dining-room, side apartments, and elsewhere, to see whether it was possible for me to obtain a glimpse of even one white servant, old or young, male or female; but I looked in vain. Again I passed into the street, and from one street into another, examining and ascertaining, as far I could perceive, whether white servants were employed in or about any of the private houses; but, alas! not one could be seen. Yet, on the right hand and on the left, as stumbling. blocks in front, and as drones and sluggards behind, I saw multitudes of sleek, stupid, foul-smelling, filthy, greasy, and grinning negroes, who, as the curse-inflicting pets, alike of infatuated and folly-governed ex-slaveholders and Radicals, were lazily occupying places which would have been infinitely better occupied by whites, and which, by the great laws that indicate the common justice and decency of things, should have been occupied by whites alone.

As is well known to many intelligent and worthy persons all over the country, this is not the first time that I have made an appeal for justice for the poor and oppressed whites of the South. Ten years ago, I made a similar appeal in my anti-slavery and anti-negro book, entitled "The Impending Crisis of the South." Four months ago I reiterated that appeal in my anti-negro and anti-slavery book, entitled "Nojoque." And yet there are certain scribblers and babblers of nonsense, mere penny-a-liners, who criticise books without reading them, who feign obliviousness of these facts, and who affect to find disagreements and antagonisms between the two publications here named. I complain of this charge simply and solely because it is not true. In such perfect accord, upon all points, are The Impending Crisis of the South" and "Nojoque," that, but for the difference in time of writing and printing, the two books might have been fitly bound together, in which case the contents of both would have formed but a single work, -two volumes in one, the whole, as a whole, and in all its parts, constituting a carefully constructed engine of literary warfare against negroes and negro slavery. The prominent and important fact that "The Impending Crisis of the South" was written in the interest of the white people of the Southern States, and was an appeal to the whites alone, and not an appeal to the negroes, to the extent of any page, paragraph, sentence, line, or word, was distinctly admitted, and elaborately dwelt upon and denounced by many of the pro-slavery politicians who, though in the wrong, were noted for their sagacity and eloquence immediately before the war; such politicians, for instance, as Pryor of Virginia, Hindman of Arkansas, and Clark of Missouri. The fact was also freely admitted, and repeatedly inveighed against with great severity by such negro-loving abolitionists (but other- wise able and excellent men) as George B. Cheever, William Goodell, and Wen- dell Phillips. Some years ago it was the boast of certain distinguished and patriotic Republicans, - Republicans who have since, Lucifer-like, fallen from the white heights of Republicanism into the black depths of Radicalism, - that no honest-minded man could calmly and attentively peruse my "Impending Crisis of the South" without learning to abhor slavery. Were it not that these same men, having ceased to be Republicans, have taken upon themselves the despicable character of Radicals, they, even they themselves, would readily perceive and acknowledge that every sane person who familiarizes himself with the contents of "Nojoque "must, by the irresistible force of the facts and logical inferences therein recorded, learn to love white people as so infinitely the superiors of negroes as to burn with a deep and unquenchable desire to save the former from any and all manner of contamination by the latter; and, therefore, to demand, with un- abating energy and firmness, as affecting the two races, an absolute, total, and eternal separation.

Because of its gross excesses, its shortcomings, and its corruptions, the first and most important thing necessary to be done, in order to remedy existing evils, is to utterly break down and destroy the whole Radical party,-a party which, in its monstrous affiliation with negroes, is bringing utter abjectness and ruin upon at least ten States of the Union, and disgracing and crippling all the others. Here, in the Southern States, the Radical influence, which is just as black and bad as it can be, coupled, not in name, but in reality, with the old slaveholding influence, keeps the negro unnaturally and dissentiously inter- larded between the two great white elements of the South, thus preventing here, among the eight millions of people who alone are good for anything, that unity of sentiment and purpose, and that harmony of plan and action, with- out which it is impossible for us ever to attain anything like permanent peace, prosperity, or greatness. Indeed, under the actual military despotisms which an unrepublican and malignant Radical Congress have foisted upon us, and under the atrocious Radical threats of un- limited confiscation and perpetual disfranchisement, leading us to fear that a still more oppressive and galling yoke is held in reserve for us, there is already an almost total suspension of all public and private works; men have no heart to do anything, their hopes and their energies have been crushed; their dwellings, their out-houses, and their fences are, in most cases, in a state of dilapidation; their institutions of learning, their churches, and their public buildings of all kinds such as were not actually burned to ashes during the war, having been greatly misused and abused are going to decay; and in many places, where at least ordinary instructors and schools are still to be found, the children, if not of necessity required to remain at home and work, are too frequently so destitute of clothing that their parents are ashamed to let them go beyond the narrow limits of their own mournfully foreboding and gloomy observation. Many of the public roads and bridges, and not a few of the fords and ferry-boats, have been so fong out of repair that they have become absolutely dangerous; and, unless, in the good Providence of God, the desolating and destructive rule of Radicalism can soon be checked and averted, those who travel here extensively, whether by steam-power or by horse-power, will do so at the imminent peril of their lives.

Especially among the negroes here crime and lawlessness of every sort are now far more rife than ever before; while, in many cases, under the vicious protection afforded them by the Radical negro bureau, before whose Dogberry agents the presence and the testimony of as good white men as ever lived are but too often treated with contempt, they (the delinquent negroes) are never punished at all; or, if punished, punished only in the mildest possible manner. I have known in- stances where white men, coming to a knowledge of crimes committed by negroes, those very whites themselves being the victims, would endure the wrong, and pass the whole matter by in silence, and without action, rather than subject them- selves to the insult, expense, and loss of time which they well knew they would be but too likely to incur by making complaint, whether at the negro bureau, or at any one of those other bureaus of military despotism, which have been so unnecessarily and so wickedly inflicted upon us by the Radical Congress. Everywhere throughout the South, the increasing demoralization of the negroes is now, indeed, sadly seen and sadly felt. Nor would it be an easy matter to make up a full and complete indictment against them of all their high crimes and misdemeanors. In every district or community of a considerable size, on the right hand and on the left, they are almost constantly committing brutal murder and high- way robbery; breaking into dwellings and warehouses; depredating on orchards, fields of grain, and granaries; appropriating to their own use other people's cattle, pigs, and poultry; stealing everything that they can lay their hands upon; outraging pure and innocent white girls; and not unfrequently, in a spirit of the most savage wantonness and revenge, setting on fire and utterly destroying the houses and other property of their white neighbors. Terrorism reigns supreme among the white females of every family, and sleep is banished.

Not far from here, I was, a few weeks ago, in a small town, where there were just eight stores, every one of which had, at different times, been broken into and robbed. Either at the actual time respectively of each robbery, or afterward, it was fully ascertained and proven, that six of these stores had been forcibly and feloniously entered by negroes, and the other two by persons unknown. All of them had been entered since the establishment of the Radical negro bureau. Prior to that time, no store in that town had ever been entered by burglars. These facts, well considered, must lead to the most solemn and profound conviction, in the breast of every right-thinking man, that the negroes, strongly fortified in the morbid and misplaced sympathy of the Radicals, are feeling themselves at comparative liberty to commit, with impunity, every species of outrage and crime.

Broken-hearted over the disastrous realities of the present, and dimly peering into the dark and uncertain future, all the white people here, of whatever condition in life, are dejected and sorrowful to an extent that I never before witnessed. Sometimes it has seemed to me that I could discern something holy, something sacred, in the deep and troubled sadness of those about me; as if, indeed, God, in his great mercy, had come to dwell in their hearts, and to protect them from further outrage. I would that this were so. Among men whose hearts are not entirely callous to every consideration of justice and humanity, there should always prevail a sentiment keenly alive to the suggestion, that there should be both a measure and a limitation of punishment. Yet, strange to say, more strange to say of white men, and still more strange to say of white men in this nineteenth century, the Radicals, as represented in the Radical Congress, seem to be actuated by no such sentiment as this. For the crimes which were committed by only a few dozen actual traitors (the more prominent and guilty of whom ought, in my opinion, to have been hanged more than two years ago), they are inflicting all manner of severe penalties and punishments on eight millions of people! They complain, and justly, of the cruel treatment and death of some thousands of Union soldiers in Libby Prison, at Salisbury, and at Andersonville; but, by laws more tyrannical and barbarous than were ever before enacted by any civilized legislature, they are deliberately crushing out the spirit and the life of millions of innocent men, women, and children! In the vain effort to exculpate themselves, they vauntingly proclaim to the world that their measures of military reconstruction were enacted in great part, if not principally, for the protection and for the benefit of Union men in the South. I tell them that the true Union men of the South (the white Union men, and except these there were none, and are none worthy of the name) detest, with a detestation unutterable, the entire batch of their disgraceful and ruinous military measures of reconstruction. With few exceptions, the white Union men of the South feel that they have been most foully and shamefully betrayed and dishonored; and we reject, with immeasurable scorn and indignation, the imputation that we have any sympathies or purposes in common with base-minded and degenerate partisans, who, like the Radicals, are abandoned to every high principle of honor and right reason. We were, and are still, Republicans; not black_Republicans, but white Republicans. Radicals we never were, nor can we be. It is, then, the Republican party, in the persons of factious and fanatical multitudes of Radical demagogues, that has left us, and not we who have left the Republican party. And I here tell these Radicals, and I tell them with emphasis and distinctness, not as a threat, but as a warning, that, in any future conflict of arms (which, however, may God and good men avert!) be- tween the friends and enemies of the Constitution, and of the Government of the United States as constitutionally organized, the better class of Union white men of the South would be precisely where they were before, they would be with the right, but not with the Radicals.

But why do I speak of a warlike contingency of this sort as being now even within the bounds of possibility? I will tell you. That the whole country, North and South, East and West, is not now in a state of general good order, peace and prosperity, is alone due to the unwise and unjust legislation of the Radical Congress. A large majority of that Congress are now evincing, or have but recently evinced, a disposition to prosecute, even to still greater lengths, if possible, their former schemes of revenge, despotism, and ruin. As a mere party measure, rank with wantonness and usurpation, they now threaten to impeach and remove a President who, though at times somewhat stubborn and imprudent, has always been rigidly faithful in the performance of his constitutional duties, inflexibly honest, thoroughly patriotic, and eminently solicitous to promote, in all proper ways, the public good. An intelligent and distinguished merchant of Boston, with whom, on a certain occasion, I dined in New York, a few months ago, remarked to me, that in his opinion the present or a future Bancroft, in detailing to posterity the true history of the administration of Andrew Johnson, would find in him the best president, Abraham Lincoln alone excepted, that we have had in America, thus far, since the days of John Quincy Adams. That was the honest opinion of a highly-educated, high-minded, and most worthy merchant of the city of Boston. Let the whole crowd of noisy radicals, who, not unlike a pack of poodles snarling and snapping at the heels of an elephant, are incessantly annoying and defaming one who is, in every good quality, vastly the superior of themselves, reflect whether the positive opinion thus expressed was not tolerably well founded. Another gentleman (and this brings me to the very gist of what I wish to say in reference to future fighting, and to beg that the radicals will give no occasion for it), a New Yorker, who occupies an important judicial position, declared to me, in June last, that in case of the attempt of the Radical Congress to remove the President in any manner, or for any cause not explicitly prescribed in the Constitution, -mind you, he did not even mention the name of Andrew Johnson, he only spoke of "the President," he, for one, would take up arms to resist the usurpation, and he believed the people would generally do the same thing. He further remarked that in such an event the war would be one merely for the preservation of republican and democratic institutions, and that it would prevail only at the North, unless the South, by her own volition, should come to be a party to it. Now, it may be that there are certain men in the South who would be more or less rejoiced at the outbreak of a war of that sort, but if so, I most sincerely hope and trust that they may never be gratified; nor will they be, unless it be through the folly and the crime of the Radical party. The white Union men of the South are not only Southerners, they are also Americans, and they wish well to the whole country; indeed, so extensive are their good will and aspirations in this regard, that they hope the day will soon come, or come some time, when the entire continent of North America, from the Atlantic to the Pacific, and from Behring's Straits to the Isthmus of Darien, shall be found to be too small to represent in full on the maps the peaceful, prosperous, and progressive superficies and boundaries of our national domain. We believe that Andrew Johnson has made, and is still making, in the person of himself, a truly able and patriotic President of these United States; and we believe further, without advocating his election or re-election, that he would make, for the ensuing Presidential term, a better President than any one of the gentlemen whose names the Radicals have yet mentioned in connection with that high office; and this simply because they have not mentioned the names of such clear-sighted and worthy Republican statesmen as Seward, Adams, Fessenden, Sherman, McCulloch, Doolittle, Browning, Welles, Raymond, and Randall; nor the names of any of those tried and trusty Democratic statesmen to whom, in magnanimous and praiseworthy coalition with the Republicans, we may yet have to look for the safe piloting of the ship of State over the many rough shoals and breakers among which the Radicals have so negligently and so culpably allowed her to drift.

We, the white Union men of the South, and all the white men here, two or three dozen arch-traitors excepted, would soon become firm and faithful friends of the Union, if they were only afforded a just and reasonable opportunity to be- come so, are very desirous that all the Southern States shall at once be prudently and properly rehabilitated; we want them to resume, without delay, their rightful status in the nation; we want them acknowledged and treated, in all respects, as free and equal States, with enlightened and republican constitutions of government, similar to those of New York, Pennsylvania, and Ohio; we want them to retain, in the amplest possible sense, both the semblance and the reality of white States, and so avoid the utter disgrace and worthlessness of becoming black States; and we insist upon it, that the infamous dogmas and teachings of the Radicals, who are so pertinaciously striving to reduce the white races of our country to the low level of negrohood, ought to be everywhere refused and rejected with the utmost disdain. We insist upon it, that the abolition of slavery among us ought to leave the negro occupying in the South precisely the same status that the abolition of slavery among you left him occupying in the North. We insist upon it, that, because of his natural inferiority, his despicable characteristics, his gross stupidity, and his brutishness, he ought not to be allowed either to vote or to hold office, nor to fill or perform any other high function which appertains, and, of right, should always appertain exclusively, to the worthy and well-qualified white citizens of our country. Speaking here only for myself, as an individual, I may say, with absolute sincerity and truth, that however much others may itch for office, there is no position of honor, trust, or profit, within the gift of any number of the American people, or any number of any other people, that I would accept, unless it came to me through white votes alone. And while this is strictly true, it is very certain, also, that, however unregenerate I may be in other respects, and it would seem that, according to the opinion of some, I am a rather sinful sort of man,- yet I feel happy in the perfect assurance that I shall never go down to the grave nor elsewhere, with the black crime resting upon my soul of having, in any contingency, or under any possible or conceivable circumstances, ever voted for a negro. We insist upon it that the enfranchisement of the negroes, and the dis- franchisement of the whites, whereby the supremacy of the negroes has already been established, or is about to be established in almost every Southern State, is a consummate outrage, an unmitigated despotism, an unparalleled infamy, and an -atrocious crime. We insist upon it that our Federal government and our State governments are, as they ought to be, republican in form, and that the military authorities ought, at all times, except only in cases of actual war, in the future as in the past, to be held subordinate to the civil authorities. We further insist upon it, that the whole drift of radical legislation, for the last eighteen months and more, has been, and still is, unstatesmanlike, unrepublican, vindictive, and despotic, - perilous to all the principles of enlightened self-government, and alarmingly de- grading and inimical to the white civilization and progress of the entire New World.

It is absurd and useless for the Radicals, while tacitly admitting the black and baneful excesses of their legislation, to tell us, in the pitiful attempt to excuse their own gross ignorance and folly, that the numerical preponderance of the whites in the South will save them from the corrupting and demoralizing influences of the negroes. As well might they tell us that a pound, or a less quantity, of strychnine would do no harm in a barrel of flour; that an ounce of arsenic would accomplish no mischief in a peck of meal: that a phial of prussic acid could effect no injury in a pitcher of water; or that one idiot, feverish and frantic with conta- gion, might not communicate the effluvium of fatal infection to a score or more of sane men. We insist upon it that it is pre-eminently our duty to be just and kind to our own race, and that the poor and distressed of the white race are those who, here, there, and everywhere, have the highest claims upon us, whether for ser- vice, for food, for clothing, for education, or for whatever other thing; and also, that if, in being but just to our own race, the negroes or others are the sufferers, that, under the inscrutable purposes of Providence, is simply their misfortune, and should always be so considered. Further, and finally, we insist upon it, that the good results which the loyal and intelligent masses of the country had a right to expect would soon follow the abolition of slavery and the suppression of the rebellion, shall neither be defeated nor indefinitely delayed; and we protest that the disingenuousness and treachery of the Radicals since the war, seriously threaten to neutralize all the wise and patriotic labors which the Republicans so heroically and so gloriously performed both before and during the war. We ask for the immediate repeal of all military laws which are antagonistic to the spirit and form of republican government, and, especially, for the speedy repeal of all such political and mercenary monstrosities as the negro bureau bill. We also ask that the expenses of the army and navy may be reduced at least one-half, and that the burdens of taxation, which now weigh so heavily upon white people, may at once be lightened.

With an eye and a purpose to these ends, we ask that every Radical Senator and Representative in Congress, and every other Radical officer in the land, whether national, State, county, or municipal, who is, or has been, an aider and abettor of that usurpatory and tyrannical oligarchy, euphemized as the American Congress, shall, one and all, at the very next elections in which their names may be brought before the people, be wholly and summarily withdrawn from official life, and that new and better men-men possessed of good common-sense- men controlled by sentiments of justice for white people, no less than by sentiments of justice for black people-men sufficiently free from sectional bias-men of enlarged and statesmanlike views-shall be elected in their stead. Let this be done, and all will be well. Let it be made manifest, and let it be proclaimed abroad, throughout the entire length and breadth of the land, that what the short-sighted and fanatical Radicals are aiming at as a mere possible good to four millions of blacks, is a positive disservice and evil to eight millions of whites. We want, and we will have, no re-establishment of slavery. It is safe to say that there are not to-day, in the whole State of North Carolina, two hundred men, of good standing or influence, who would, if they could, have slavery re-established. Indeed, I doubt whether there are five thousand white men, in all the South, who would now, or at any future time, be so unwise, so rash, and so reckless, as to undo the acts of emancipation, even if they had the power. The only persons here who, in any considerable number, would be willing to incur the odium and the infamy of voting for a return to the system of slavery, are negroes themselves, whose instincts tell them, that if really put upon their own resources in communities of white men, and in no manner propped up or sustained at the expense and degradation of a greater or less number of whites, whether by servitude, under an oligarchy of slaveholders, on the one hand, or by negro bureaus, under an oligarchy of Radicals, on the other, they will gradually fall behind in the career of life, fail to multiply the inferior race to which they belong, die out, and become fossilized. While, therefore, we are firm in the wish and purpose not to have any more slavery in the South, we are equally firm in the desire and determination to get rid of the negroes if we can, not by taking from them one drop of blood, not by hurting a single fibre of hair (or wool) upon their heads, but by colonization, in or out of Mexico; and in this effort, which will be in perfect harmony with that wisdom and patriot- ism, which, through the mighty energies and enterprises of white men, have brought imperishable greatness and glory to the North, we most earnestly and trustingly solicit your fraternal co-operation. And then, having at last imitated the good example which you have held prominently before us for more than half a century, but which, in our excessive folly and stubbornness, we have until now rejected; having filled our States, as you have filled your States, with white people, and not with such intolerable human rubbish as negroes, Indians, and mulattoes, then we mean to fight you again; not with steam-rams, cannon, muskets, bayonets, swords, nor sabres; not with any of the sanguinary and sorrowful weapons of death, but with all the pleasing and ennobling agencies of life. Then, for the first time since you wisely abolished slavery and negroes, and we foolishly retained them, will it be possible for our States of the South to begin to be equal with your States of the North. And then, as we all advance onward in the grand march of improvement, and we want tens and hundreds of thousands of you to come among us, and be with us and of us, and, at the same time, to aid us, by sound counsel and otherwise, in the varied and arduous duties and responsibilities which are now devolving upon us, we shall begin to challenge you in good earnest; not to the battle-field, but to courteous emulation and rivalry in all of the noble arts and refinements, ay, and also occasionally in some of the more innocent and manly games and sports, of peace and civilization.

Appendix 2: Identicalness of the Sentiment and Scope of "The Impending Crisis of the South," and "Nojoque." A Letter from Mr. Helper.

ASHEVILLE, North Carolina,
January 22, 1868.
To the Editors of the *National Intelligencer*:
Once more I beg leave to reiterate the fact, and, at the same time, by an appeal to the record, to offer evidences of the fact (in reply to sundry ill-founded accusations to the contrary), that my views, of however little importance they may be, touching the negro, have never undergone any change whatever. I have declared heretofore, and I now declare again, that there is, in reality, no inconsistency of statement, whether with reference to the negroes, or with reference to slavery, between my two political works, "*The Impending Crisis of the South*" and "*Nojoque*." It has been said, by many persons of loose habits of utterance, both North and South, and it is believed by some, but by no one who has ever read the book with his eyes open, that the former work, "*The Impending Crisis*," was

writ- ten in the interest of the negroes, and in a spirit of hostility to the whites. This is simply untrue. And now for the proofs of my declaration. Turn to the dedication page of" *The Impending Crisis*" (and in order that you may be enabled to do so conveniently, I herewith transmit a copy to your address), and you will there find that the book is conspicuously dedicated-to whom? Not to the negroes, mark you, nor to their masters, but "To THE NON-SLAVEHOLDING WHITES OF THE SOUTH." Does not this dedication of itself show plainly to every candid mind the Caucasian drift of the whole work?

Now, turn to the preface and see what I have said there. From the second paragraph, I quote as follows:-

"In writing this book, it has been no part of my purpose to cast unmerited opprobrium upon slaveholders, nor to display any special friendliness or sympathy for the blacks. I have considered my subject more particularly with reference to its economic aspects as regards the whites, not with reference, except in a very slight degree, to its humanitarian or religious aspects."

Without going into the body of the book, these quotations from the dedication and the preface, ought, it seems to me, to be quite sufficient; but, if you will grant me the space, I will bring forward three or four additional extracts. On page 145, I said:-

"All mankind may or may not be the descendants of Adam and Eve. In our own humble way of thinking, we are frank to confess, we do not believe in the unity of the races."

On page 85, I said:-

"Confined to the original States in which it existed, the system of enforced servitude would soon have been disposed of by legislative enactments, and long before the present day, by a gradual process that could have shocked no interest and alarmed no prejudice, we would have rid ourselves not only of African slavery, which is an abomination and a curse, but also of the negroes themselves, who, in our judgment, whether viewed in relation to their actual characteristics and condition, or through the strong antipathies of the whites, are, to say the least, an undesirable population."

On page 143, the country, at the time I wrote, having been in a comparatively wealthy and uncrippled condition, I advocated the raising of a large sum:-

"One-half of which sum would be amply sufficient to land every negro in this country on the coast of Liberia, whither, if we had the power, we would ship them all within the next six months."

Pursuing this idea of colonization, I said, on page 144:·

"Let us charter all the ocean steamers, packets, and clipper ships that can be had on liberal terms, and keep them constantly plying between the ports of America and Africa, until all the slaves who are here held in bondage shall enjoy freedom in the land of their fathers. Under a well-devised and properly conducted system of operations, only a few years would be required to redeem the United States from the monstrous curse of negro slavery."

Dozens of similar extracts might be given; but I will neither trespass on my own time by transcribing them, nor on yours by asking you to publish them. It was my intention that my " Impending Crisis" should be an earnest anti-slavery appeal to the great majority of the white people of the South, and not, in any sense, nor to any extent, an appeal to the negro; and I challenge any one to quote from the book a single page, paragraph, sentence, line, or word, that, when critically examined and fairly interpreted, will justify the assumption that I ever regarded the negro otherwise than as a very inferior and almost worthless sort of man, not to be kept in slavery, increased, and retained among us, but to be freed, colonized, justly and liberally provided for, and then put wholly upon his own resources, and left to himself.

My opposition to slavery (and, if possible, I am more opposed to it now than I was ten years ago) looked to the ultimate whitening up of all the Southern States, and not to the spreading, nor to the continuance of that foul blackness and discoloration of them which then existed, which still exists, and which the radical party are now viciously and criminally endeavoring to perpetuate. No worker in wood ever grooved a plank with more set purpose to introduce therein the tongue or the dovetail of another plank, than I wrote the "Impending Crisis" with the fixed determination, if spared, to follow the same, in due time, with "Nojoque." The abolition of slavery was only a necessary step, a sine qua non, toward the accom- plishment of a still nobler work, which, despite the formidable opposition hcoun- tered through the baseness, the treason, and the tyranny of a usurpatory Congress, is now in rapid process of consummation. A few years more, and the United States of America, if not the whole of America, will be found to be happily and prosperously and permanently peopled by vigorous and all-triumphing offshoots of the white races only.

www.ingramcontent.com/pod-product-compliance
Lightning Source LLC
Chambersburg PA
CBHW052132070526
44585CB00017B/1789